Sandy Irvine

Julie Summers' fascination with mountains developed in early childhood with skiing trips to the Alps and holidays in North Wales, spurred on by family tales of her great-uncle's exploits. She enjoys hiking, climbing and skiing with her husband and three sons. Born on the Wirral, she was educated at Bristol and London universities and worked for fifteen years as an exhibition curator for the Royal Academy of Arts and the Henry Moore Foundation.

Fearless on Everest
The Quest for Sandy Irvine

JULIE SUMMERS

PHŒNIX

A PHOENIX PAPERBACK

First published in Great Britain in 2000
by Weidenfeld & Nicolson
This paperback edition published in 2001
by Phoenix,
an imprint of Orion Books Ltd,
Orion House, 5 Upper St Martin's Lane,
London WC2H 9EA

A CIP catalogue record for this book
is available from the British Library.

ISBN 0 75381 265 7

Printed and bound in Great Britain by
The Guernsey Press Co. Ltd, Guernsey, C.I.

For Sandy

Contents

Illustrations

Unless otherwise stated the illustrations were kindly supplied by the Sandy Irvine Trust.

Brave heart at peace – youth's splendour scarce begun
Far above earth encompassed by the sky.
Thy joy to mount, the goal was all but won.
God and the stars alone could see thee die.

Thou and thy comrades scaled the untrodden steep
Where none had ever ventured yet to climb
Wrapt in heroic dreams lie both asleep
Their souls still struggling past the bounds of time

Till God's loud clarion rends the latest morn
Sleep on! We mourn not for 'tis God knows best
Then rise to greet the glad eternal dawn
Flooding with flame the peaks of Everest

F. T. Prior, 1924

FAMILY TREE

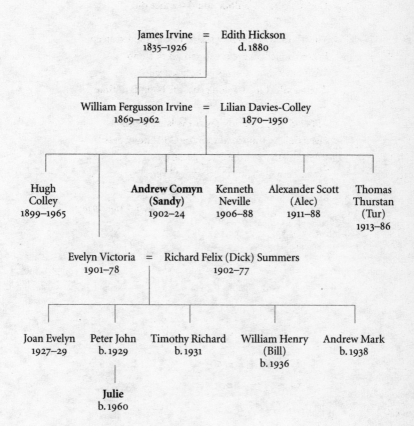

James Irvine = Edith Hickson
1835–1926   d. 1880

William Fergusson Irvine = Lilian Davies-Colley
1869–1962   1870–1950

Hugh Colley	**Andrew Comyn (Sandy)**	Kenneth Neville	Alexander Scott (Alec)	Thomas Thurstan (Tur)
1899–1965	1902–24	1906–88	1911–88	1913–86

Evelyn Victoria = Richard Felix (Dick) Summers
1901–78   1902–77

Joan Evelyn	Peter John	Timothy Richard	William Henry (Bill)	Andrew Mark
1927–29	b. 1929	b. 1931	b. 1936	b. 1938

Julie
b. 1960

Camp. I
26. Aug. 24.

Dear Mother,

As you will have read in the Times we have just suffered our second reverse. The weather has been terrible. I've been up to the North Col in a blizzard & never want to do it again – there's not much of my face left with winds of zero & below intermingled with sun temperatures of 114° carried with snow reflection.

We have now reorganised our plans & I hope to be in the 1st or 2nd party.

Geoff is considered the fittest & the next but neither being experienced climbers we can't make a single party between us. So George Mallory & Geoff, & Somervell & Norton will probably make the 1st 2 parties Odell & me to be reserve.

Afraid there's not time for more as the Post is just going & I have to go up to Camp II to make a rope ladder for them!

A touch of dysentery for the last 16 days has pulled me down a bit but I think I'm cured now. It came from eating the Rongbuk Lama's food at the Blessing!

Love to AY
in haste
Sandy.

P.S. Have no envelope so hope they get sent off at Base expalright at

Prologue

Everest Camp IV, 23,500 feet, Monday, 2 June 1924
air temperature 32° F, sun temperature 120° F

Sandy Irvine sat outside his tent, shoulders hunched, his hat pulled down over his ears, his scarf shielding his badly sunburned face. His skin had been severely blistered by the sun, and the wind on the North Col had so cracked his lips that drinking and eating had become painful and unpleasant. It was 10 a.m. and he had been up for five hours. There were no other climbers in camp. George Mallory and Geoffrey Bruce had set off two days earlier in an endeavour to climb the final 5500 feet to Everest's summit. That morning at 6 a.m. Col. Edward Felix Norton and Howard Somervell had left to make their own attempt to scale the world's highest mountain.

Sandy had cooked breakfast for them, a 'very *cold* and disagreeable job,' he had confided in his diary. 'Thank God my profession is not a cook!' He had paddled around in the snow, filling Thermos flasks with liquid, helping the climbers to check they had everything needed for two days above the North Col. He was left breathless by every exertion as he struggled to breathe in the oxygen-depleted air. As Norton and Somervell left he felt a great wave of frustration well up inside him. For six weeks he had lived with the belief that he would be making that final assault on Everest's peak, but five days earlier, after a second retreat from the mountain, the plans had had to be radically revised.

In the absence of sufficient fit porters to carry loads above the North Col, Norton, expedition leader, had announced that there would not be an attempt on the summit using oxygen. The medical officer, Richard Hingston, had examined all the men and declared Geoffrey Bruce the fittest and Sandy second, but with lack of mountaineering experience between them they could not make up a climbing party. Thus Mallory, as climbing leader, had been forced to make the decision that Sandy should be dropped in favour of Bruce, the fitter man. It was a bitter disappointment and one Sandy found hard to bear. Two days later he was fulfilling the role of support delegated to him and Noel Odell by Norton, the first time this task had been officially designated. 'Feel very fit tonight,' he had written, 'I wish I was in the first party instead of a bloody reserve.' As Norton and Somervell disappeared out of sight he saw the goal he had set himself, his own private challenge, slip from his grasp. There was no getting away from it, he was devastated.

Watching Karmi, the cook, fiddling with the primus stove, he reflected on the last few weeks when he had graduated from youngest member on the expedition, 'our experiment', as General Charles Bruce had called him, to one of the four key climbers who, it was planned, would be spared a great deal of the hard work in a bid to keep them fit for their assault on the summit. So many things had conspired against them. With a great number of the porters badly affected by the altitude, there had been problems getting the higher camps stocked, but it was principally the weather that had defeated them. They had had to contend with subzero temperatures in the camps where in the 1922 expedition climbers and porters had basked in the sun and drunk fresh water from the little streams that ran down the glacier. This year everything was frozen solid. Twice they had been forced by atrocious weather to retreat to the lower camps. Still they were undaunted but the number of fit men had drastically diminished. Now two oxygen-less attempts were being made above him. All his hard work on that infernal apparatus had gone to waste, he rued, and he was left with the feeling that, for the very first time in his life, he was facing a major personal defeat.

Looking up again, he was suddenly aware of movement above camp. Dorjay Pasang, one of Mallory's climbing party, was on his way down. Suffering badly from the altitude, he had been unable to go on beyond Camp V so Bruce had sent him back down with a note to say the others were intending to press on without him. Sandy reached for the field glasses and above Pasang he could clearly make out the figures of Mallory and Bruce. He was surprised. They were returning. He had certainly not expected to see them so soon. A hundred thoughts raced through his mind as he set two primus stoves going for the returning party. He grabbed a rope and set off to meet them above the Col.

'George was very tired after a very windy night,' he recorded in his diary that evening, 'and Geoff had strained his heart. The porters had been unable to stand the wind and even Camp V was short of what they wanted in altitude.'

As he escorted the exhausted men back into camp he wondered whether Norton and Somervell would be faring better above them. He served out quantities of hot tea and soup, helped the climbers to take off their boots and to get inside their tents. He knew that Bruce was depressed at the outcome, whereas Mallory seemed preoccupied and Sandy found it impossible to read what he was thinking, although he could sense that he was struggling to compose his thoughts.

Just before retiring, Mallory turned to him: there would be another attempt. The two of them would climb with oxygen in three days' time, providing the weather held. Sandy should go down to Camp III to prepare the oxygen apparatus and he would join him the following day after a rest. Sandy was delighted. He could scarcely believe that luck had turned again, this time in his favour. At that moment Odell, John Hazard and a small group of porters appeared from the lower camp and Sandy bounded over to Odell, his old friend and mentor, and told with evident boyish delight of the third attempt, the chance that he had little thought would now come his way. Odell recalled later that Sandy, 'though through youth without the same intensity of mountain spell that was upon Mallory, yet was every bit, if not more, obsessed to go "all out" on what was certainly to him the greatest course for "pairs" he would ever be destined to "row".'

With renewed energy and determination Sandy helped Hazard escort Geoffrey Bruce and all spare porters down to Camp III where they arrived at 4:30 p.m. He immediately set to work on two oxygen apparatus, checking that flowmeters, valves and mouthpieces were working. He cannibalised a third set to take a spare mouthpiece and found some spare valves which he carefully packed into his zip pockets 'just in case'. He was determined that it would not be the oxygen apparatus which gave out, as it had been for Geoffrey Bruce and George Ingle Finch on the 1922 expedition. He had written to his mother from the trek: 'It will be a great triumph if my impromptu ox.ap. gets to the top, I hope it does . . .' As he worked away in his tent, strewn as usual with all manner of tools, bits of frames, spare nuts and bolts, he felt a huge surge of thrill that he would, after all, have a crack at the summit as he had so desperately hoped. He was feeling fitter than he had for many days and was confident that, despite his excruciatingly burned face, he would perform well. The four days he had spent at the North Col had convinced him that he was fully acclimatized. By the time he turned in for the night he had two ox. ap. sets almost ready.

That night he got very little sleep. The sunburn that had been giving him trouble for weeks had been greatly exacerbated by the scorching sun at Camp IV. 'A most unpleasant night when everything on earth seemed to rub against my face and each time it was touched bits of burnt and dry skin came off which made me nearly scream with pain,' he wrote in his diary the following morning. Sandy knew that he would have to cope with the excruciating discomfort of taking the oxygen mask off his face which brought with it, each time, a whole new layer of skin. He could cope with pain, however, he knew that from his rowing career.

'Restful morning in camp,' Sandy wrote that day. He observed one man, a porter presumably, coming down from above the North Col into Camp IV and then a party leave the Col upwards. It was Odell and Hazard, the two scientists, going to V, Odell in search of fossils and Hazard for air and exercise. Mallory arrived in camp mid-morning and outside Sandy's tent they sat discussing their summit assault. Mallory had now been above the North Col on two occasions and knew better than anyone what to expect. At lunchtime Mallory left Sandy fiddling with the oxygen carriers and went over to Bruce who was concerned with rallying porters. Eight were willing to carry food, bedding and oxygen cylinders to Camp VI.

After an early tiffin[1] on 4 June, Mallory and Sandy set off up to Camp IV. Sandy was pleased with his performance and wrote in his diary: 'We took exactly 3 hrs going up which included about ½ hr at the dump selecting and testing oxygen cylinders. I breathed oxygen all the last half of the way and found that it slowed breathing down at least three times (using 1½ litre/min). George and I both arrived at the camp very sur-

1 A light mid-day meal, an Anglo-Indian phrase adopted by the expedition.

prisingly fresh.' At Camp IV they were greeted with the news that Odell had failed to see any trace of Norton and Somervell who were embarked upon their summit attempt. Mallory took the glasses from him and thought he could spot tracks about 700 feet below the summit. 'I hope they've got to the top,' Sandy wrote that afternoon in his diary, 'but by God I'd like to have a whack at it myself'. By evening Norton and Somervell were back in camp. They had reached a height of 28,000 feet – 1000 feet short of the summit – but had been forced to turn around as time was growing short and each was nearing the end of his physical strength. Odell and Hazard were also at IV, preparing to send Sandy and Mallory off the next morning. What a change in fortunes in two days. Now it was Sandy's opportunity. As he turned in on the night of 5 June in the tiny tent he shared with Odell he spoke again of his delight at the challenge he was about to face. Just before he went to sleep he wrote his final diary entry: 'My face is perfect agony. Have prepared 2 oxygen apparatus for our start tomorrow morning.'

The next morning after a breakfast of fried sardines, biscuits and hot chocolate, served to them in their tent by Odell and Hazard, Sandy and George Mallory left the North Col at 8:40 a.m. with eight porters.

'The party moved off in silence as we bid them adieu,' Odell wrote, 'and they were soon lost to view amidst the broken ice-masses that concealed from view the actual saddle of the North Col and the lower part of the North Ridge of the mountain.'

Sandy Irvine and George Mallory were never seen alive again.

1

A Family Legend

One cannot imagine Sandy content to float placidly in some quiet back-water, he was the sort that must struggle against the current and, if need be, go down foaming in full body over the precipice.

Jack Peterson to W. F. Irvine, 22 June 1924

I have no recollection of how old I was when my father first told me the story of Uncle Sandy. I must have been about five or six and I dimly remember wondering what he would have been like, this mysterious uncle who disappeared on the upper slopes of the world's highest mountain. I knew his brothers and sister fairly well, and to me they were all inconceivably old and immeasurably tall. They were all very kind but I was a little daunted by their dry wit and humour, which, as I was only a child, went slightly over my head. My grandmother Evelyn, Sandy's only sister, was a beautiful woman and I loved her very much. She was kind and gentle, with a lovely smile and a soft, almost musical voice. She was very fond of her grandchildren and I, as the eldest grand-daughter, felt a certain responsibility to behave like a mini-grown-up in her presence. She used to let me go into her raspberry nets and pick (and eat) as many raspberries as I wanted. They were the best raspberries I have ever tasted, pale pink and sweet. I never asked her about Uncle Sandy; she was not the kind of person a young child would quiz. I don't know whether my father had asked me not to question her, but I do remember reading the poem written in his memory which was framed and illuminated above the drinks cabinet in my grandparents' house.

When I was six we went on a camping holiday to North Wales. My father had purchased a piece of land, not six miles from Bala, from his paternal grandfather, Willie Irvine, Sandy's father, and it was called Creini. Willie had bought the land for its remoteness and beauty and when he died my father took it over because he could not bear to see it go out of the family. My mother was pregnant with my younger brother and we older three children had a marvellous time by the lake, paddling and swimming and exploring the old boat house below a rocky outcrop which we christened Mount Everest. We thought it extraordinarily high and very dangerous. We tried to climb it from the south side, but my parents knew a safer route down a grassy slope from the north side and then up to the summit, and we frequently had picnics on top, looking down onto the lake. Over the years the rock has shrunk, as childhood memories so often do. In reality it is only a fifty-foot rock and grass pitch of no particular severity (in climbing terms). But it is still Mount Everest and we still picnic on it.

Uncle Sandy was a family legend. His story has been passed down through the generations but I knew little more about him at thirty-six than I had done at six. When I myself was expecting our third son, in California, my husband Chris said it was time to find a name for the unborn child, whom we knew to be a boy. We had settled on Johnston as a middle name – it was a name from my husband's family and we thought it was suitable for a third son. The problem with the first name was solved when Chris, who was lying in the bath two days before the birth, announced that we would have to come up with a name that would suit a fair-haired boy, as we seemed to give birth predominantly to blonde, blue-eyed boys. He suggested we should call him Sandy after my great-uncle and I thought it a splendid idea. Our Sandy was born in September 1997 in Stanford, California. My father, I think, was delighted but was amused that we had assumed the name to be a shortening for Alexander whereas in Uncle Sandy's case it was a shortening for Andrew. Soon after the birth I was walking with a friend in Palo Alto when we came upon a bookshop specializing in mountaineering books. In the window was a large, glossy volume, *Everest: The History of the Himalayan Giant*. I suggested we should go into the shop to have a look and, sure enough, the book contained, amongst many other sumptuous pictures, a black and white snapshot of Uncle Sandy and George Mallory, taken by Noel Odell on 6 June 1924, leaving Camp IV on their way to the summit of Mount Everest. I bought the book. There was more information here than I had known as a child, but the basic story was the same. After that I read *The Mystery of Mallory and Irvine* by Audrey Salkeld and Tom Holzel. Here was a book with some real information about Uncle Sandy and now I was determined to find out more. I wrote to Audrey and she wrote back, almost by return, giving me what information she could and pointing out that I should talk to my cousin Julia Irvine, daughter of Sandy's younger brother Alec. He, it transpired, had written a brief history of Sandy's early life which was published in a book by Herbert Carr entitled *The Irvine Diaries*. Alec had also become the keeper of the majority of the Sandy Irvine memorabilia. A large, black deed box contained letters, photographs, newspaper cuttings, copies of the *Alpine Journal* and *British Ski Year Book* from 1924, all of which referred to Sandy. By September 1998 I was back in Britain. I told my father of my burgeoning interest in Uncle Sandy and he unearthed, quite to my surprise, a bundle of papers and photographs. That Christmas saw a further development. John Irvine, son of Kenneth, another of Sandy's brothers, sent my father twenty-five black and white photographs of Sandy dating from 1916 to 1924, including two – well-known – of him at Everest Base Camp working on the oxygen apparatus.

Winter turned to spring. On 3 May 1999 I awoke, as usual, to the seven o'clock headlines on BBC Radio 4. I was annoyed that I had forgotten to switch the alarm off, as it was a bank holiday and I had planned to have a lie-in. I listened, half asleep, to Charlotte Green reading the news. The third item brought me to life: 'Climbers on the north face of Mount Everest have found the body of the veteran climber George Leigh Mallory ...' I sat bolt upright in bed, my heart pounding. Thoughts tumbled around my head as I tried to make sense of what I had just heard.

I knew that the BBC had part-funded an expedition on Everest that spring to search for the camera that Howard Somervell, a 1924 expedition member, had lent to Mallory on his last climb towards the summit. Like the 1999 climbers, however, I had rather assumed that they would find the body of Sandy Irvine which, they believed, had been spotted by a Chinese climber at about 8200 metres in 1975. To have found Mallory, however, was of monumental significance to the climbing world, throwing new light on where the fatal accident may have happened, its timing and its possible cause.

In the days and weeks that followed the find rumours and theories abounded in equal measure. It was only when the climbers of Expedition 8000, led by the respected American guide Eric Simonson, gave their press conference in Kathmandu that the full facts about the find were revealed. There had been no camera; the further search for Sandy Irvine had not been possible for a variety of reasons, including bad weather and heroic rescue efforts of stricken climbers from other expeditions on the part of Simonson's team. The objects they had recovered from Mallory's body, letters, a knife, a pair of goggles, a watch with a broken hand, a broken altimeter, a handkerchief, were all put on display for the first time.

The media briefly buzzed, three books were written as a direct result of the expedition's findings, and yet we still knew very little more about what happened to Mallory and Sandy. Questions remained unanswered and still the climbing community could not agree on whether or not the two men were the first to stand on the summit, twenty-nine years before Hillary and Tenzing. Hillary, ever the gentleman and in a typical show of generosity, said that he would not mind if his record had been broken, but he pointed out that to conquer a summit really you have to descend successfully. On balance, the majority in the climbing world concluded that they could not have succeeded. The factors of weather, clothing, oxygen and sheer height and distance would have proven too much for the two men in the daylight available.

The discovery of Mallory's body had caught the Mallory and Irvine families almost completely unawares. It seemed sensible now to assemble and document all the material relating to Sandy Irvine under one roof as speedily as possible. The family set up a trust to take care of the memorabilia, such as it existed, and to deal with queries, questions and requests.[1] I was asked by the trustees, all grandchildren of Willie Irvine, to curate the collection of material and to set about finding out as much information as possible about their uncle. By the early autumn of 1999

---

1 At the outset it was decided that the Trust should seek charitable status in order to be able to benefit mountaineering charities from the money accrued from reproduction permissions etc.

I had collected over three hundred photographs, twenty-three original handwritten letters, articles, press cuttings and much other information besides. I wanted to share this amazing collection with all my Irvine relatives but there was no practical way to do so. Instead I decided to try and spread it more widely in the form of a book. Sandy's brief life had been filled to the brim with energy, activity, humour and kindness, and as the research progressed it became clear that there was far more to know about Sandy Irvine than anyone had hitherto guessed.

This book is a personal quest to find out more about a young man who died in the flush of youth alongside one of mountaineering's greatest legends. His name is inextricably linked with that of George Leigh Mallory, yet very little has so far been written about his short but full life. It was Audrey Salkeld who gave me the confidence and impetus to go ahead and tackle the project. 'Get inside his head, Julie, I want to know what he was thinking.' A challenge I couldn't refuse.

When I started the research I carefully sifted what we had: letters, photographs, press cuttings, Sandy's passport and a few other items of memorabilia, which over the years had been dispersed over several Irvine family members. It was wonderful material, but I felt convinced that evidence relating to the Everest expedition was missing. I asked various members of the family to check in their attics and desks, rack their brains and talk to their siblings. All of them assured me that I had what was available and that Willie Irvine would have destroyed anything else as he was so saddened by the death of his son. Rather grudgingly I accepted this version of events, and went on with my research into other areas of his life.

What was missing, presumed destroyed, was all the correspondence leading up to his leaving for Everest in February 1924 and everything to do with the expedition subsequent to that date. It niggled away at me all through the winter. In April I spent an evening with my uncle Bill Summers who told me a number of stories about visiting Willie Irvine, his grandfather, in his Welsh home outside Corwen after the Second World War. He had just passed his driving test and loved any excuse to drive, so motoring to Grandfather once a week gave him an opportunity for a good long run in his car and convivial company at the end. Like all the grandchildren, he was extremely fond of his grandfather and one of his pleasures was to fetch and carry books for the old man from his library, which was distributed in bookshelves throughout the house. He was always struck by the fact that Willie knew where every book was to be found and by the extraordinary care he took over his research. Every archaeological find he ever made was meticulously catalogued, labelled and preserved in cases in the study.

Bill recalled very clearly seeing an ice axe hanging in the gun room at Bryn Llwyn and asked Willie what it was. 'That was Sandy's,' he replied, in a voice which did not invite further questioning. 'It came back from Everest without him.' There was a similar story with Sandy's binoculars, with a boat he had made after a family holiday in 1917, and with his gun. In other words, Willie Irvine had kept a lot of memorabilia from Sandy's life and although no one was allowed to touch the objects, nor to talk to him about Sandy, they existed and were safely stored. This set me thinking again. Willie Irvine was an archaeologist and historian by leaning, although he had been a businessman all his working life. He followed these former interests with enthusiasm in his retirement and it suddenly didn't make any sense at all that he would have destroyed anything to do with Sandy.

I knew, from my research at Merton College, Oxford, home of Sandy's diaries and a few letters since Willie's death, that his sister-in-law, Agnes Davies-Colley, had been involved after Sandy's death in fielding some of the correspondence. The story had always been explained to me that Sandy's mother, Lilian, was so distraught by the loss of her son that she could not face the letters of condolence or contact with the other members of the 1924 expedition. Agnes, or Aunt Ankie as she was known to the family, had lived her last years at Bryn Llwyn with Willie and Lilian and had died in the house at the end of the Second World War. A meticulous hoarder, she left precise instructions as to how her worldly goods should be distributed at her death. Would she have thrown the material away? Possibly. But my hunch was not.

As I got more involved in the story I was able to make a fairly accurate list of what I believed would have existed immediately after Sandy's death. I was so certain that if the material existed it would all be found in one place that I began to nag members of the family about it. My cousin at the Davies-Colley home, Newbold, turned over the attics,

making huge bonfires of mouldy mattresses and general rubbish accu-
mulated over several generations. But there was nothing on Sandy
Irvine. Finally, I persuaded another of my cousins to go through the
attic at Bryn Llwyn, and locate any likely boxes which we could go
through to be absolutely sure. Jenny and Julia Irvine, who have been so
supportive throughout this whole research period, agreed to have a final
trawl. On one of her visits up north at the beginning of May 2000 Julia
collected three trunks that had belonged to Sandy's elder brother Hugh
and which had been at Bryn Llwyn since the death of his son in the
1970s. Once the boxes were in her London house she set about going
through them. In the first two trunks was a mountain of material
referring to Hugh's life but little else. We spoke at the beginning of the
second week in May when she found a very poignant letter from Lilian
Irvine in June 1926 (two years after Sandy's death) describing how she
had put red roses below the Mallory and Irvine Memorial Window in
the cloisters of Chester Cathedral.

Then, on Saturday 13 May she telephoned again. She had found
everything in the third trunk. 'What do you mean, everything?' I asked,
flabbergasted. 'Well, everything you said would be there is there.' We
talked for about twenty minutes and it became abundantly clear that
not only had she found what I believed would exist, but more material
besides.

I soon saw that Willie and Lilian had kept all the letters Sandy had
written to them from the boat, the trek and the mountain – eleven long
letters in total. Then there were the most fascinating photographs from
the trek, which he had sent back to his sister Evelyn. These snapshots,
albeit very high quality snapshots taken on a plate camera, had been
developed for him by Benthley Beetham, another expedition member
and keen photographer, and Sandy had carefully wrapped each photograph and negative in paper on which he had written a description. I
knew exactly what these were as he had mentioned the fact that he
had sent them to Evelyn in his diary entry of 11 May 1924, but it was
nevertheless a tremendous surprise to find them in amongst the papers.
Then there was a roll with a piece of paper wrapped round it and on it, in
blue crayon, were the words 'Plans for Oxygen Apparatus ACI [Andrew
Comyn Irvine] 1923'. I honestly held my breath as I unwrapped this

13

bundle, and with good reason. Here was the most professional set of diagrams in perfect condition, indicating Sandy's suggestions for modifications to the 1922 oxygen apparatus. These were sent to the manufacturers Siebe Gorman in the autumn of 1923 with long notes showing in the greatest detail, his modifications for the valves, flow-meters, cylinders, carriers, everything. But they were totally ignored. I am no scientist, but I could appreciate from the meticulous notes and exquisite drawings that Sandy had clearly spent the whole of his last term at Oxford working on the oxygen apparatus, to the considerable detriment, I suspect, of his own studies.

The trunk contained other treasures too. An address book, two wallets with press cuttings about his rowing career and his brief but exciting motorbike stunts in North Wales, a leather patch from his Everest ruck-sack. And on the expedition, newspaper clippings galore. Willie Irvine not only had kept everything, but had actively added to the archive by getting a press agency to make a collection of every cutting they could find about Sandy. The great value in this collection is that it comprises over two dozen articles from the local Birkenhead, Liverpool and Man-chester papers that I had never seen.

Last but not least I found the letters of condolence. Over seventy of them had been kept out of the 500 written to the family after Sandy's death. Every letter was marked 'answ' in blue pencil and an accom-panying list confirmed that Willie, Aunt Ankie or Evelyn had replied to every letter they had received.

Never in my wildest dreams had I ever considered that such a priceless collection of memorabilia would exist. I had been writing the book for six months and now I suddenly had the material to write the story of Sandy Irvine's Mount Everest expedition experience from his completely fresh, valid and, most importantly, personal standpoint.

2

No Soap in the Bath

I am busy turning up the cuffs of a new suit for Sandy. At last he has finished out your old garden suit. He has not done badly at all in clothes though he is such a smut.

Lilian Irvine to Hugh, 2 December 1914

Sandy Irvine was born to be brave. From early childhood he stood out as a boy without fear, who would dare almost anything and, for the most part, got away with pranks that others might have been roundly punished for. Trees and ladders were there to be climbed and bicycles to be ridden as fast as possible with brakes used only at the very last minute. A strong rebellious streak and a lust for adventure were curbed only by extraordinary self-discipline, imbued in him at an early age. His early years were dominated by the strict regime in which the children were brought up, rules substituted for overt love and affection.

Both parents had been brought up in deeply religious families, an ethos they sought to pass on to their children from the outset. They instilled in them a respect for discipline, a strong sense of duty and a feeling that childhood was at times to be endured rather than enjoyed. If some tribulation befell them, it was considered character forming.

Sandy was born on 8 April 1902 at 56 Park Road South, Birkenhead, the third child of Willie and Lilian Irvine, and was christened Andrew Comyn after an Irvine relative who could trace his ancestry to the time of Robert the Bruce. His elder brother Hugh was born in 1899 and his sister Evelyn in 1901. Then in 1906 Kenneth was born, followed in 1911 by Alec and in 1913 by Thurstan, who was always known as Tur. Until he went away to school, Sandy's social life revolved almost exclusively around the family, with most holidays taken in North Wales or the Lakes, in the company of uncles, aunts and cousins from both sides of the family. Often there would be upwards of twenty children and thirty adults.

Sandy's father, William Fergusson Irvine, was my great-grandfather. He was known to his friends and family all his life as Willie. Physically he was splendid. At five feet eleven and a half inches he was appreciably taller than his father James. He always remained slim and his bearing, like his manner, was upright and dignified. In old age he had a ring of bright white hair around his bald head and a white moustache which lay thick on his deep upper lip. As a young man he had waxed the ends of his moustache into points but it never looked as kempt as some of the splendid specimens sported by his peers.

All his life Willie preferred one-to-one company, but for all that he was sociable and the home in Birkenhead and later at Corwen, in North Wales, was frequently full of visitors, usually extended family and friends of the children. Eight or ten at the dinner table was very much the norm. His digestion gave him trouble throughout his life, a problem that Sandy inherited, and once he found a formula which kept him fit and well, he stuck to it rigorously until the day he died. To the end of his life he ate stewed apple and baked egg custard for pudding at lunch and dinner, and had beside him at his place at the head of the table a whisky decanter and a soda syphon. He poured a good measure of whisky into a tall tumbler and filled it to the brim with soda water. This he drank during the meal, both at lunch and dinner. As far as anyone can remember it was the only alcohol he ever drank. After lunch and dinner he would smoke an oval Egyptian cigarette with his coffee. My cousin recalled recently that early in the Second World War his daughter Evelyn bought for him 15,000 of these cigarettes in vacuum-sealed tins. At least two of these tins still survive, so he had a lifetime's supply from the early 1940s. His routine was never varied and it clearly suited his delicate digestive system as he lived until he was ninety-three. He finally gave up changing for dinner during his eighty-eighth year.

Willie Irvine was the second son of James Irvine and Edith Hickson. He was born in 1869 in Claughton, Birkenhead. Two sisters followed in 1870 and 1871, and a third son in 1873. Edith died in 1880 and James remarried in 1884. Two further children were born. In keeping with the Scottish Presbyterian household where religious observance was dominant, Willie was brought up never to show his feelings and always to put duty before pleasure. When his mother was dying he sought permission from his father to go to her bedside and read aloud to her the twenty-third Psalm. He was eleven years old. He was a deeply sensitive person but he had been brought up to suppress his feelings at all costs, something which he passed on to his children: giving in to emotions was, he believed, a sign of weakness. He was careful, dutiful and logical, always anxious to keep to the rules yet he was in many ways a man ahead of his time. His sense of duty was coupled with a strong belief that his children should be allowed to follow their desires and inclinations as they grew older.

Willie was educated at Birkenhead School until sixteen when he went into business with his father. He was at heart an academic, contemplative rather than competitive, and although he worked in business until he was fifty-five, he followed his academic interests and ultimately career until he was over ninety. On his retirement from business he bought a house called Bryn Llwyn near Corwen in North Wales. His love of the countryside was coupled with his interest in the archaeological sites he discovered on land near Bala which he purchased in 1934. He told people he had been influenced in his decision to move to North Wales by his sons' love of the mountains and their desire to be close to the excellent climbing in Snowdonia.

Sandy's mother – Lilian Davies-Colley – was the third of six children of a Manchester solicitor, Thomas Charles Davies-Colley. She was the only one of the four daughters to marry and her sister, Agnes, remained very close to her all her life and was a regular visitor at the Irvine family home in Birkenhead.

When my father and I were going through Willie's diaries, tiny notebooks with a code of initials which took us some time to decipher, we discovered that he had proposed to Lilian on a stile on Thurstaston Common on Ash Wednesday, 19 February 1894. This date struck a chord with my father who recalled taking my mother to meet Grandfather soon after the two of them had become engaged. It was Ash Wednesday 1958 and Willie said to them, 'I proposed to Grannie the last time Ash Wednesday fell on this date.' We checked, and he was right: it was exactly sixty-four years to the day.

Lilian was described by her fourth son as 'slightly formidable but wholly lovable' and this trait manifested itself early on in the manner of the acceptance she gave Willie, she would marry him but only after she had extracted a promise from him that he would remain in business rather than following the academic career he wished to pursue. She told him she hoped to have a large family and to keep and educate them in comfort. This, she knew, she could not do if he were earning an academic salary.

She was an extremely determined woman who knew how to get her own way, usually without confrontation. Her instinct led her to mould her children rather than to mother them. If one or other of them took a tumble she would reach for the cotton wool and iodine, rather than for the child to comfort him. She believed that 'Little children should be seen and not heard' and she would often use the saying as a rebuke. If they ever asked her the question 'Why?' she would respond, 'Because Y is a crooked letter'. Lilian's doctrine was that you couldn't expect life to be fun all the time and being brought up correctly was a serious business. Her youngest son, Tur, once said to my father by way of explanation, 'We Irvines were conditioned never to show any emotion at all. To do so was unmanly and showed lack of self-control.'

Lilian was an excellent organizer. She busied herself with preserving fruit and eggs, making jam and saw to it that the gardener kept her well supplied with vegetables and fruit. She also kept chickens and bees and the sight of her in her beekeeper's hat and black muslin veil was pretty awe inspiring. One of her nieces remembers being very impressed by her ideas for dish-washing machines and gymnastic apparatus in the nursery. Perhaps it was from Lilian that Sandy inherited his love of practical problem-solving. It was a full-time job looking after such a large and hungry family, even with domestic help. Nevertheless, she was always happy to have nieces and nephews to stay during the holidays and the house was frequently full to bursting with children. Some of those who came were unused to the strict regime of 56 Park Road South: they found Uncle Willie and Aunt Lilian rather severe and did not like the way they made fun of children. Lilian was particularly tough on the Irvine nieces and nephews, one of whom – Lyn – wrote later, 'we were sensitive and did not like the way they made fun of the children'.

Lilian's matronly manner was complemented by her poise. She was relatively tall and she always walked with her back straight, as if she had a book on her head. She had worn her very fine long brown hair in a bun for as long as anyone could remember. Indeed she was already wearing the bun when she was photographed aged seventeen. She favoured dresses with high collars, always with the small gold container pinned to them that held the fine gold spring-loaded chain attached to her pince-nez. She seldom went outside without a hat and she always wore sensible shoes. A handsome rather than beautiful woman, she inspired respect rather than affection. My cousin Anne remembers being made by Lilian to lie at the age of six on a Victorian backboard after Sunday lunch for quarter of an hour, half for posture, half for digestion. She also used to insist that the older children learn a psalm by heart before they were allowed outside into the garden to play. This tradition continued into the early 1940s when my own father remembers weeping as a little boy because he could not commit to memory a long psalm and was desperate to go out into the garden to join his brothers and cousins.

Agnes, or Aunt Ankie as she was known to Lilian's children, has become something of a family legend. She is remembered for being eminently shockable and somewhat prim. She was a nurse all her life and her last post was as matron at the Mile End hospital in London. Following her retirement she spent the last years of her life at Bryn Llwyn. Aunt Ankie was extremely pious and her nephews, with the exception of Sandy's youngest brother Tur, spent a great deal of time trying to, and succeeding in, shocking her. They had a passion for ruthless rhymes which they would recite within her hearing. One my grandmother Evelyn distinctly recalled Sandy reciting in front of Aunt Ankie went:

> Tell me, Mama, what is that mess,
> That looks like strawberry jam?
> Hush! Hush! My child, 'tis dear Papa
> Run over by a tram.

For all that she was very fond of the children and they of her. When she was due to go into hospital for an operation in 1920 Sandy wrote her a cheerful letter enclosing some photographs which he hoped she would enjoy when she was able to sit up and look at them. But he just couldn't resist a shocking opening to the letter and wrote, 'Dear Aunt Ankie, I am most awfully sorry to hear that you are going to be cut to pieces tomorrow.'

Sandy was the first of the Irvine children to be born in Birkenhead. Willie and Lilian had bought a house in Liverpool when they married but it soon became apparent that a larger home was required for their expanding family. They decided to move back across the River Mersey to Birkenhead, the burgeoning new town at the head of the Wirral peninsula.

Number 56 Park Road South had plenty of room for the growing family and the children had a large nursery on the third floor where they had their meals and spent the majority of their time when not outside. Lilian would visit the children in the nursery or school room as and when it suited her but visits from their father were so infrequent as to be events of considerable note and worthy of comment. As a father Willie was a benevolent authoritarian and found parenting easier as the children grew up and he could establish more adult relationships with them. When they were younger he preferred to see them in contexts he could readily understand, such as at church, although when he was on holiday he seemed to relax and enjoyed spending time with them, teaching them to fish or cycle. It was almost as if he could not permit the home regime to be disturbed either for himself or for them. He felt it his duty to instil in them the same values that he had learned as a child. In the mornings the children rose at seven o'clock but were not allowed to speak to each other under any circumstance until family prayers were said before breakfast at quarter to eight. Sunday worship, matins and evensong, was a normal part of family life, with the children attending all services with their parents. This was as much the case when they were away on holiday as it was at home.

Sandy's place in the family had a good deal to do with the way his character developed. The first three children were all born within three years of each other, there being only fourteen months between Sandy and Evelyn. He was a determined little boy and could be very demanding when he didn't get his way. Being the youngest of the three he had to fight for attention and was often jealous when Evelyn or Hugh stole the limelight. The focus of his love was his mother whom as a boy he adored above all else. Even into adulthood he communicated with her rather than Willie, as the others tended to do. Although she was frequently frustrated by his mood swings and his oversensitive reaction to her teasing, she understood his insecurities and seems to have found a way to inspire his confidence. For all that she was very tough on him and maintained her physical and emotional distance from him, as she did from the others. When separated from Lilian, Sandy missed her and wrote to her regularly with news updates from school and home, but always first enquiring after her health and well-being.

The social life of the children revolved around the family and Sandy was always popular with the twenty or so cousins, although it was probably as much for his reputation as a dare-devil as for his camaraderie that they admired him. He came to believe that if he were special then others would take notice of him, and the way this manifested itself was by doing unusual or daring things. In this he miscalculated Lilian and she often despaired of his pranks. Of all of them he was the one she had to watch out for, even in mundane matters. She told Hugh once that she had been reading an article from the newspaper at tea 'keeping an eye on Sandy and the cake round the edge of the paper!' Sandy felt that to be ordinary meant being boring, a nobody, and although this is not a particularly unusual trait in a little boy, it certainly proved to be a powerful motivating force later in his life.

His older brother Hugh was tough on Sandy and Evelyn, taking it as his role as eldest son. He could be authoritative and felt a responsibility for keeping the younger ones in check, while himself remaining a little aloof. This left Evelyn and Sandy to team up as a formidable pair. Once Sandy was old enough to play sensibly with Evelyn, who was herself very mature and composed, he began to learn that positive attention-seeking was the better way to draw attention to himself. She encouraged him to do daring deeds and would often as not join in. For example, the two of them, having discovered that Hugh did not have a head for heights, would shin up the nearest ladder and challenge him to join them.

Sandy encouraged Evelyn to climb trees and cycle with him, earning her in the process the reputation of being something of a tomboy, which she relished. With five brothers she was constantly having to prove to herself that she was at least as good as they were. She surprised her parents by learning to ride a bike before Hugh and said later that this was out of sheer determination not to be labelled a typical little girl. Anyone who ever came into contact with my grandmother would never have dared to even harbour such a thought, let alone express it. Sandy and Evelyn were extremely close from early childhood onwards and Evelyn's influence on him was a very positive one. She provided the warmth and attention lacking from their mother and she treated him as an equal rather than as the irritating younger brother he felt Hugh found him. She adored his pranks and would regale her friends with tales of his latest exploits but she was also a steadying influence on him and succeeded, I think to some extent, in saving him from undertaking anything too wild or dangerous.

Evelyn was arguably the most academic of all the children. She went from Birkenhead High at fourteen to Wycombe Abbey where she was later deputy head girl, playing lacrosse and tennis for the school. From there she went to Oxford, a rare achievement for a girl in those days, where she read Inorganic Chemistry, graduating in 1924 with what today would have been a First Class Honours degree. While at Oxford she gained a Blue for lacrosse, practised Jujitsu and learned to fly Avro 504s, getting her wings in 1923. Her warmth and generosity made her loved by everyone and she had the ability to make anyone feel special. She was a match for her brothers both emotionally and physically, and shared their love of adventure. Her mother described her as being rather forgetful and her father despaired at her untidiness. She told her son Bill that once Willie had walked past her bedroom, which was in a terrible mess, and made as if to throw up. She swore after that she would become more organized and tidy. Sandy was equally untidy and was constantly tearing his clothes and wearing out his shoes, causing Lilian endless mending work about which she complained bitterly. 'Sandy's uniform is rotten,' she lamented in a letter to Hugh, 'he gave an extra spring to save himself on a slide today and it is cracked right across his knee. I shall have a terrible business to make it look decent'. Unlike Evelyn, Sandy never learned to be tidy, although he was later credited with being a good organizer. There is a running theme of chaos surrounding his immediate affairs and his letters home from school when he was well into his teens were full of instructions to send something here or there, collect this trunk or that suitcase. Even at 26,500 feet on Everest in 1924 Odell could not resist a wry smile at the untidy state of his tent.

There were various schools in Birkenhead that were patronized by the middle-class families and one of these was Birkenhead Preparatory, which Sandy attended from the age of seven, following Hugh in autumn 1911 to Birkenhead School. He was not particularly academic and did not shine, but he was aware that his parents wished him to gain good marks. This led to him being insecure and sometimes worried that he was not good enough and he made a point of writing to his mother, when his place in the form order was announced, hoping that she was pleased with his performance. The headmistress of the Preparatory, Miss Cox, was a formidable woman who took the view that children needed licking into shape and she was tough on them. Sandy disliked being criticized and could be rebellious and difficult, which did not endear him to Miss Cox in the slightest. An event of real significance during these school years was relayed by Sandy in a letter to Lilian during the winter of 1909. The headmaster of the Senior School, Mr Griffin, had been delivering a stern lecture to the children about the dangers of the ice on the school pond and promptly demonstrated the danger by falling through himself. 'Most of the ice has thawed and all the place is horrid slush, it was such a funny thing Mr Griffin was telling us to be so careful on the ice on Tuesday and he fell in himself.' The delight of the prep school boys on that occasion was quashed instantly by the eagle eye of Miss Cox. Sandy wrote to Lilian the following day: 'Miss Cox is quite well, Mr Griffin is none the worse for falling through the ice.' I note that Miss Cox is mentioned first. She clearly made an impact on him, however much he disliked her.

The majority of the family holidays before the First World War were spent either on the North Wales coast or in the Lake District. Willie and Lilian would rent a cottage or house, Lilian spending three or four weeks there with the children and maids while Willie visited them for perhaps a fortnight. It was a major undertaking to organise these holidays for the family still had no motorcar. They would all travel by train from Birkenhead and be met by a coach and horse at the other end. The amount of luggage was astonishing and in one photograph from the summer of 1902 Sandy's huge black pram is strapped to the top of the coach, which is already piled high with trunks, suitcases and hat boxes. All the children wore hats with huge brims to keep the sun off their fair skin and Lilian clothed them all in dresses until they were four or five, when the boys graduated to shorts and sailor tops.

Willie enjoyed spending time with the children on their family holidays and it was always he who introduced them to new activities. In 1907 he taught Hugh, Evelyn and Sandy to fish in the river at Capel Curig and photographs show him explaining patiently to Sandy the ins and outs of using a home-made fishing rod. At that age, Sandy was stocky, very blonde and had a solemn, thoughtful air about him. In the photographs of him from the pre-War period he is always looking preoccupied and even slightly whimsical. I rather suspect he and Evelyn cultivated this air for the benefit of their mother who was the chief photographer. Frivolity and high spirits were not acceptable. If Lilian were going to give the children a treat, such as a biscuit, she would make them all line up in front of her with one hand behind their backs and the other outstretched, clean palms upwards, like a little row of supplicants. She was a great believer in the benefit of long walks and from a very early age they were taken either by a nanny or Lilian herself into the hills. These walks were not to be taken lightly, they were to be appreciated. When one Irvine cousin spent part of a walk around the southern shores of Ullswater telling Evelyn a story about some historical romance she had been reading, Lilian rounded on the poor child, accusing her of being a proper little Philistine by chattering away a lot of nonsense and distracting Evelyn's attention from some of the most beautiful scenery in England.

As soon as the children learned to ride bicycles they were accorded a greater degree of freedom and were allowed to go off into the hills and the villages on their own. At nine Sandy was a very keen cyclist and proud of the fact that he had a cyclometer on his bike which Evelyn did not. They explored around Capel Curig and chased down the narrow lanes, each daring the other to ride ever faster and not to use their brakes until the very last minute. Evelyn also loved cycling and wrote of one of their rides at this time: 'In the afternoon we went for a bicycle ride; it did not seem a bit long but Sandy told us by his cyclometer that we had gone almost 11 miles, just 10⅞ miles. There were some lovely spins down the hills which were very steep and I went down them without any brakes on.' It was at about this age that Sandy's love of adventure began to grow and he relished the freedom that his bike gave him. He was an enthusiastic cyclist but throughout his life he suffered a series of calamities through riding them too hard. By the autumn of 1923 he had solved the problem of bicycles – he switched to a tricycle.

In 1912 the three older children spent Easter without their parents in Ross-on-Wye with relatives and it was from this holiday that I chanced upon two diaries, one written by Evelyn, then eleven, and one by Sandy, aged ten. Sandy's diary is brief and factual. The first entry reads 'Arrived 5.25 p.m. No soap in bath, did without.' The following day, the entry reads 'That night had soap in bath.' Phew, order restored! Such an oversight never would have occurred at Park Road South. On the third day he wrote that he had been made to sit down to write his journal. I am not sure that this was ever his favourite occupation, but some of the entries are funny and they clearly had a very enjoyable holiday, punctuated, as it was, by many church services, sometimes as many as three in one day. Sandy always struggled with writing, even into adulthood. His spelling was poor and his grasp of grammar meagre but he had a wonderfully expressive way of conveying excitement, especially in the form of letters. His best letters tended to be written when he was bubbling over with enthusiasm or anger, whereas his later diary entries are generally somewhat more considered and have led people to conclude that he was wooden and inarticulate. Nothing could be further from the truth.

Hugh was very much the grown-up boy on this holiday and he saw to it that the two younger children did what they were told and behaved in a seemly manner. Frequently he was allowed to ride with Aunt Edith into Ross-on-Wye while Evelyn and Sandy were obliged to stay at the house and play in the garden with the other cousins. This never bothered them. On the contrary, it meant they were left to their own games, with Evelyn joining in all the more 'boyish' activities. She was rather scornful of her girl cousins and their lack of knowledge of boys' sports, complaining that in a football match between the boys (Cambridge) and the girls (Oxford) 'of course the boys won because most of the girls knew nothing about football hardly'. She was always keen to be involved in everything the boys did and once prevented from joining the boys – when Hugh was riding in the donkey cart and Sandy pedalling beside them – she remained up a tree and sulked.

Three extra children was a burden for Aunt Edith, especially as the Irvine children appeared to have boundless energy. Clearly at a loss one afternoon as to what to do with them, she invited them to collect dandelion heads for her, offering them one penny (about 50 pence in today's money allowing for inflation) for every 100 dandelions. After Sandy and Evelyn had both earned 3d she put the rate up to 1d for every 500 dandelions. Evelyn collected dandelions all afternoon and Sandy noted, with some awe, that she had collected 20,000 heads! Evelyn put it at a rather more conservative figure of 2300.

The hero of the holiday for Sandy was cousin Jack who, at about fifteen, was considered to be very grown-up and experienced. He allowed Sandy to use his powerful telescope and explained to him what was happening during an eclipse that they witnessed during their stay. He treated Sandy with a degree of respect that he was not used to and Sandy responded well, showing genuine interest and enthusiasm for everything he was shown – from dead rats to hatching chickens. Jack also played the organ and one day while he was practising in the church he allowed Sandy and Evelyn to sit either side of him and operate the stops, pulling them out and pushing them in as instructed. I imagine that the workings of the organ were of far more interest to Sandy than the music Jack was playing.

The following summer Willie decided to take the whole family to stay in Peel on the Isle of Man. It was a great success and they had planned a further visit to Peel in 1914 but were unable to go because of the outbreak of the First World War. The highlight of the holiday for Sandy were the trips they made on a racing yacht called the *Genista*. He was so impressed by this boat that on his return to Birkenhead he made a scale model of it, enlisting the help of one of the maid's friends. This was carvel-built, the stakes being the wooden slats from old-fashioned venetian blinds, with riggings and sails. It was an accurate copy and he gave it the same name as the yacht. The model *Genista* outlived Sandy by many years. It was kept in the study at Bryn Llwyn and no one was allowed to play with it. Years later Alec observed one of my cousins looking at it and said, 'It's not bad for a boy of eleven I suppose, but what that boat really deserves is a Viking funeral.' I am sure Sandy would have heartily approved of the sentiment. He would never have liked to think that the family had put him or anything he made on a pedestal. In the recent find the model was discovered, somewhat altered but essentially in good condition, although without its rigging. Alec was right – it wasn't bad for a boy of eleven.

Sandy had persuaded Willie to let him have a workshop in the back yard at Park Road South and it was here that he made his models and carried out his scientific experiments. Willie was not particularly practical but he could see that Sandy had a real flair for engineering and science. Sandy guarded this room fiercely and possessively, not allowing anyone to enter it without his permission. He wrote anxiously to his mother on one occasion, 'tell Mrs Killen not to let anyone into my room because she knows where the key is'.

He used the workshop all his life, designing bits for the family cars, fixing household tools and making models. When he sailed for Everest in February 1924, he left behind him a disassembled 1922 oxygen apparatus on which he had been working avidly at Oxford and then at home for nearly four months. When Willie returned it to the Royal Geographical Society in 1924, he wrote to the Secretary, Arthur Hinks, that Sandy had been working on it right up until the day he sailed for India. He added that he wasn't sure all the bits were there, so completely had Sandy dismantled it.

In July 1914, the house was full of Irvine cousins from Aberdeen who had come to share a holiday at Peel. During dinner – always a very formal occasion – Willie returned from the telephone, in those days a new and awesome invention. Still clutching his spotless napkin, he went slowly upstairs to the schoolroom where the assembled children were playing after supper. Such a visit was almost unprecedented. He looked grim: 'We shan't be going to the Isle of Man, children,' he said. 'England is at war with Germany.'

The five older children, Hugh, Evelyn, Sandy and their two cousins Edward and Lyn, were dispatched to stay at the Davies-Colley family home, Newbold, outside Chester. The house was owned by Lilian's bachelor brother Tom who had inherited it from his uncle, and it was supposed to be haunted. The house is a large brick mansion with a turreted tower at the front and a further, slightly lower octagonal tower at the back overlooking the gardens.

When the children arrived at Newbold they found that Uncle Tom was away all week in Manchester, returning only at the weekends. They were given a free rein to roam in the extensive grounds, being looked after mainly by the housekeeper and the groom. The housekeeper they never saw but the groom took full charge and planned many outings in the trap. Hugh had a shotgun and they all had fishing rods, so their days were filled with outdoor activities and there was never a moment to be bored. Hugh and Sandy climbed up to the top of the tower and threw home-made spears into the gardens and filled Uncle Tom's salute cannon with black powder and gravel which they fired hopefully at the rabbits that cropped the short grass between the formal yew hedges. They discovered to their joy that nobody very much cared when they went to bed so after supper they played steps on the lawn until it was too dark to see. Such freedom was new to Evelyn and Sandy and they greatly relished it.

There were no newspapers at the house and all of them apart from Hugh were completely oblivious of the war until Uncle Tom took them to Beeston Castle, a medieval fort perched high on a hill some ten miles from Newbold. On the way they saw cars with flags on them and heard talk of fierce battles being fought in France. It seemed a world away from their own idyllic existence and none of them, with the exception of Hugh and possibly Edward, had really any idea what it all meant. Within four years two of them would have fought in France, one dead and one wounded.

Newbold held great attraction for the children but there were frightening things about the house which deeply impressed them. Half-way up the stairs was a large painted cut-out of a woman peeling apples into a bowl, two-dimensional but highly coloured. Newbold had no electricity, being lit by oil lamps, so when it was time for the children to go upstairs they had to collect a candle. These were lined up on a table at the bottom of the stairs with a candlestick for each child and a box of matches. Evelyn said she remembered that she and Sandy always dashed breathlessly up the stairs because as they passed the Apple Woman with their flickering candles the light danced on the image and it gave the impression that she was moving.

The greatest attraction for Sandy at Newbold was the room containing all Uncle Jack's Crimean uniforms including his sword, his folding candle lantern, and his tent. Sandy had a photograph of the room in his album and it was a place where he loved to spend time alone. In addition to the war regalia, there were also telescopes and microscopes, gyroscopes and all sorts of other unidentifiable things with wires, wheels and whirring parts. This room he found irresistible and there was no one at Newbold to tell him to keep out. Whenever the other children noticed he was missing they would be certain to find him there, studying the workings of this or that machine, poring over diagrams in the dusty books which lined the walls. The hours he spent in the room reinforced his already great interest in adventure and invention.

Towards the end of the first summer of the war, Evelyn and Sandy spent two weeks in Glasgow with their McNair cousins, Willie's sister Helen having married a Dr McNair in the 1890s. The McNairs were an adventurous bunch and they had an exciting time which Sandy relayed in a rather breathless and hurriedly written letter to his mother, a style that became his own whenever he had some great experience to describe: 'I am having a splended time one day we went fore an eight hour voyage down the Clyde and round Bute we saw on the Clyde about 90 Cruisers and 15 Torpedo Destroyers being built and a Light Cruisers seemed to be garding the mouth; Bute was awfuly nice.' The spelling and lack of punctuation probably contribute to the breathless impression, but the experience on the Clyde was a great one for him and he drew on the letter four exquisite and perfectly observed sketches of a naval destroyer that they had seen. He told his mother that everyone up in Glasgow was talking about the Russians and he was very excited by the whole atmosphere, wishing madly that he could be on a destroyer 'like Uncle Leonard'. It was on this holiday that the McNair cousins christened him Sandy, on account of his fair hair and his name Andrew. 'Sandy Andy'

29

is what he became on the holiday and he liked Sandy so much that he decided to change his name. It was typical of him, even at that age, to seize upon something that appealed to him, to take it seriously and ensure that everyone around him recognized its importance to him. Up until this date he had used his full name, Andrew, but on his return from Glasgow he announced solemnly to the family that from now onward he wished to be known by everyone as Sandy. They abided by his wish and only rarely after that did anyone ever refer to him as Andrew.

When Willie Irvine came to choose a school for his sons he elected to send them away rather than to have them educated in Birkenhead as he had been. He chose Shrewsbury School for several practical reasons. First and foremost it was on the excellent train line from Birkenhead and Chester but, secondly, it served as the public school for the North Wales, Midlands and Liverpool areas. Since 1913 there have been over twenty Irvine and Davies-Colley sons, nephews and grandsons educated at Shrewsbury but none of them has had as spectacular a career at the school as Sandy.

He went up in the autumn of 1916 and from the very outset he thrived. Released from the formal and rigorous upbringing to which Lilian had subjected all her children, he flourished in the congenial public school atmosphere. He found that he was able to give vent to the energy that had been building up and the means of expression he found was in sport. His life at Shrewsbury was a truly happy one and he gave back to the school as much as he got out of it, winning the admiration of the boys and masters alike.

In the nineteenth century Shrewsbury had had an excellent academic reputation in the Classics. At the beginning of the twentieth century Moss, who had been Headmaster for forty-two years, retired and was replaced by the Revd C. A. Alington, who, unlike Moss and many of his predecessors, was an Oxford rather than a Cambridge man. He was thirty-five and had spent his time since Oxford as a Master at Eton. He was described by one historian as a breath of bracing and invigorating air, and certainly the changes he introduced at the school affected every possible aspect of life there. The masters, both old and new, responded to Alington's challenges to introduce a wider culture and vivify teaching methods, so that by the time Sandy arrived in 1916 the school was a stimulating, challenging and, above all, exciting place. He found himself in a world that was never dull and full of changes. From the outset he was completely enthused by the whole experience.

One of the outstanding aspects of Shrewsbury for Sandy was the potential for athletics. It quickly became apparent that he was an exceptionally gifted sportsman and to his delight this was encouraged and highly valued. He represented the school in cross-country running, athletics and, most significantly and with the most conspicuous success, rowing. Sandy's rowing career was by any measure a glorious one. His passion for a sport in which passions run high anyway was absolute, and he was as committed to rowing as it was possible to be. He was extremely fortunate that his time at Shrewsbury coincided with the true flowering of the English orthodox style of rowing and the school's meteoric rise to fame at Henley that resulted from it.

One of Alington's sincerest desires during his tenure as Headmaster was to raise the standard of rowing at Shrewsbury and to see them beat his old school, Eton. To this end he succeeded in appointing two strong rowing coaches straight from Oxford, Evelyn Southwell and Arthur Everard Kitchin. Southwell was killed in the First World War but Kitchin, or 'Kitch' as he was known to his colleagues,[1] remained at Shrewsbury for the whole of his working life. He was the premier exponent of the English style of rowing, a brilliant coach and his success with the Shrewsbury crews was partly down to his meticulous dedication to style.[2] He more than fulfilled Alington's ambition over the years and in 1912 Shrewsbury School was racing at Henley for the first time in its history.

Social contact prior to Shrewsbury had been mainly with his own large family; here Sandy met for the first time boys from different backgrounds and cultures and he formed over the years many friendships. His loyalty to his friends was absolute and he valued this more highly than anything else. The closest and most enduring friendship he

---

1 He was Ev to his friends, Kitch to his colleagues, the boys nicknamed him 'The Bull'.
2 'The characteristic of the style is a long arc of continuous boat moving power for a given fore and aft travel, a hard but precise catch, ergonomic use of legs, body and slide together, and a held-out stroke with clean blade extraction.' Richard Owen in *Arthur Everard Kitchin*, 1997.

established was with Richard Felix (Dick) Summers, whom he met on the fives[3] court in their first week of term. Dick was small, dark haired, anxious and very shy, completely the opposite to Sandy, but they hit it off immediately. Over the years they shared many pleasures, a great deal of fun and some anxious times. 'We had very much in common', Dick wrote years later, 'both being mechanically minded and interested in cars, and both having the same sort of ideas and ideals. He was undoubtedly the best of the family, although like all of us he had his faults.'

Dick was the youngest son of Harry Summers, a steel magnate from Flintshire who ran the family works, John Summers & Sons, on the banks of the River Dee. In May 1889 'HS', as he was known all his life, married Minnie Brattan, the daughter of a Birkenhead architect. They had four children, three boys and a girl, of whom Dick was the youngest, and enjoyed an affluent and happy life. Then came a blow from which the family only ever partially recovered. Minnie was nursing HS, who had contracted viral pneumonia, when she contracted septic pneumonia and died a few days later. Dick grew up essentially an orphan. After Minnie's death HS devoted himself more wholeheartedly than ever to the steel works and when he wasn't there or in London on business he would be in the workshop at his house, Cornist Hall in Flint, making grandfather clocks, his other great passion. Dick was brought up at Cornist, alone with Nanny Blanche Barton. She did the very best she could for him, but was far more indulgent of him than his own mother would have been and he reached adulthood claiming that he never ate anything that flew, swam or crawled.

Dick had no recollection of why HS sent him to Shrewsbury when his brothers had both been to Uppingham, but it was in many ways a lucky break for him. Dick was an able sportsman, he had a gentle, dry sense of humour and he knew and understood about cars. This last helped to form part of the enduring bond between Dick and Sandy, and the Irvine and Summers families became closely linked from that time on, producing two deep friendships, a passionate love affair and a long and happy marriage.

3 Fives is a game in which a leather ball is struck by the hand against the wall of a prepared court. It originated at Eton where it was played against the Chapel wall.

Shrewsbury School was divided into a number of houses and over the next decade all the Irvine boys joined No. 6, or Moore's House, under C. J. Baker, a chemistry master with a distinctly enlightened outlook. Baker was also something of an inventor and he succeeded in capturing Sandy's imagination and encouraged him to follow his engineering interests at the school, often at the expense of his other academic work. Sandy's interest in matters academic was sporadic and he concentrated on those areas that were of real interest to him. He was easily influenced by the enthusiasm of his teachers in the scientific subjects, but Latin, Greek and Literature were of neither interest nor use. What he really enjoyed was working on an engineering problem in the school laboratories and workshops. The First World War presented him with just such an opportunity.

The impact of the war had a dislocating effect on the school in that boys left at odd times to join up and the casualty lists marked the end of many promising lives. For Sandy the reality of the war came home when Hugh was enlisted in 1917. He joined the Royal Artillery and spent three months training near Exeter before he went out to fight in France. In 1918 a German high explosive shell landed in a gas dump close to where he was standing. The shells didn't explode but they burst and he and a lot of other soldiers were splattered with liquid mustard gas. The gas got on the collar of his uniform and as it soaked through the cloth burning the skin on the back of his neck very badly. He had an open wound all down his back which never really healed and he was troubled by it for the rest of his life. My father once told me that Hugh had to have the wound dressed twice a day by a nurse until he died. A few weeks after Hugh was injured, Sandy's cousin Edward was killed in France and the whole family mourned the loss of this quiet, gentle young man.

Sandy himself was too young to enlist but an engineering problem occupied him for the greater part of the autumn of 1917. His interest in war machinery was probably sparked in part by Baker who, assisted by Higgins, the school laboratory steward, is credited with inventing a very early form of delayed-action bomb – an invention intended to spare lives but to damage property. At any rate, Baker did not discourage

Sandy although the hours he spent in the labs must have been to the detriment of his schoolwork.

Shrewsbury School had acquired a German machine gun which had been captured by the British. History does not relate how it was that the gun came to be at the school, but it became the focus of Sandy's attention for a matter of many weeks. He had heard that the equivalent British weapon had suffered some considerable numbers of very awkward stoppages. Guns would jam and the result was that as much as half the machine gun force could be out of commission at any one time. Sandy was given permission, presumably by Baker, to strip the gun down and study its mechanics. He dismantled it entirely in the school workshops and spent endless hours making minute observations about the mechanisms. It is an example of his extraordinary ability to focus on a problem and worry at it like a terrier with a rat until he found an explanation or came up with a solution. What he in fact established and what he suggested was that the different manufacturers of the ammunition were making their ammunition to a slightly different size. This was not necessarily because they intended to but because in making 10 million rounds or 100 million rounds the dies that made the bullet cases would distend. If the case for the bullet was too big it became a tight fit in the gun and the result would be a stoppage. Whether or not this find was ever passed on to the War Office is not known but it encouraged him to go on and find solutions to other problems concerned with the machinery of war.

Following his work on the German machine gun, Sandy turned his attention to aeroplanes, having heard from Hugh of some of the problems experienced by the air corps. He invented, apparently from scratch, an interrupter gear which would permit a machine gun to fire through the propeller[4] without making holes in it. A logical and simple solution to a real problem. He also designed a gyroscopic stabilizer for aircraft and caused a small stir by sending off beautifully worked up designs for these two inventions to the War Office in London. The War Office had been sent many proposals during the course of the war but it was most

4 The correct nomenclature is 'airscrew', but it has always been referred to as 'propeller' within the family.

unusual for such an accomplished design to be submitted by a fifteen-year-old school boy. Unfortunately both had been anticipated in essence by Hiram Maxim[5] but Sandy received most warm congratulations from the authorities and instructions to go on trying. His ability to find solutions to problems was so wholly accepted within the family that no one considered his achievements as particularly remarkable. When later a lot of fuss was made about his redesigning an oxygen system for the 1924 Mount Everest expedition no one was surprised that he advocated a complete rebuild of a system which had itself been designed by some of the most respected brains in the RAF.

Despite the war family life continued in very much the same way as it had done prior to 1914. Willie, at forty-five, did not enlist but he became an officer in the Birkenhead volunteer force and was awarded the rank of captain in recognition of his contribution. In their usual generous and hospitable spirit, the Irvine family invited Dick Summers to join them on their family holiday in Summer 1917. Thereafter he became a regular visitor and spent holidays with them every year until 1923. The family was very kind to him and he was regarded quite quickly as simply another son or brother. He joined in all activities with pleasure and had the added attraction of having access to a motor car which he would bring along, thus giving them all even greater freedom than they found on their bicycles.

During the first summer term that Sandy was at Shrewsbury, 1917, in keeping with tradition, new boys were divided between the two sports of rowing and cricket. To qualify for membership of the Boat Club Sandy had to swim four lengths of the baths in rowing kit. Those who elected to try their hand at rowing and had passed the swimming test, as Sandy did, would then be put into a tub with a boy of roughly matching size. A tub pair is a sort of aristocratic rowing boat, but with two single oars only, one for each boy seated one behind the other, and a seat at the stern with elaborate curly metalwork and, sometimes, a cushion, on which would be seated an older boy who would steer, coach and assess the potential and merits of the new recruits. As Sandy looked to have good potential, he was quickly picked up by the Captain of Boats

5 Sir Hiram Maxim (1840–1916) British inventor.

and his rowing career was underway. As well as tubbing Sandy was soon rowing in a single seat sculling boat, a narrow racing boat with a pair of sculls (oars) and a balance problem. Soon he was rowing two hours a day, five days a week. On Thursday afternoons there was Officer Training Corps activity, which interfered with his rowing schedule, and on Sunday the Lord's Day was strictly observed, with two services at Chapel and a Divinity lesson in the afternoon.

From the tub Sandy rapidly graduated to the house IV, a rowing boat with four fixed seats and four single oars. The main event for the house IV was the Bumpers or Bumps as it is now more commonly known. This was a fiercely contested inter-house event which was rowed towards the end of the summer term. By the summer of 1918 Sandy had come to Kitch's attention and he was rowing in the Second VIII. In February 1919 he once again took part in the Challenge Oars, the main house race run on a knock-out basis. It was rowed over a distance of 1 mile and 50 yards from Greyfriars Bridge to the Priory Wall on the River Severn below the school. The event gave Kitch a key opportunity to have a good look at the boys' performance and from that he could work out a rough cut for the First VIII. Sandy impressed him and he was selected amongst the other probable candidates for the First VIII. The training for the eights began in March and continued in earnest after the Easter holidays. It needed to, for at Henley they were up against fierce competition, not only from other schools but also from the Oxford and Cambridge Colleges. The school boys were rowing against men at least two and a half years their senior and considerably heavier and stronger.

Henley Royal Regatta was established in 1839 after the town fathers observed that races had been held on the river attracting a lively interest. They felt that an annual regatta 'under judicious and respectable management' would be of wide appeal. It is still held annually at the beginning of July and forms an essential part of the British summer calendar alongside Ascot and Wimbledon. By the early twentieth century the character of the Regatta was well established. Henley's atmosphere is undoubtedly unique and an early twentieth century description of 'blue skies, pink champagne, the razzle-dazzle of the parasol' is as accurate today as it was in Edwardian England. There were bands playing, oarsmen young and old in their brightly coloured blazers displaying their club loyalty, laughing, talking, debating, and reminiscing. Henley is a veritable pageant but for a provincial school whose only experience of competitive rowing was on the upper Severn in front of other boys and a few proud parents, it must have seemed extraordinarily exotic and daunting in equal measure.

The regatta had been cancelled during the First World War and in 1919 it was decided that the first post-war regatta should be dedicated to those who lost their lives in the fighting. It was thus known as the Peace Regatta and marked a new and optimistic beginning in the history of Henley.

The Shrewsbury First VIII was entered for the Elsenham Cup, that year's equivalent of the Ladies' Plate and open as usual to both schools and Oxbridge colleges. Sandy was rowing at 4, in the 'engine room' of the boat, the power house for the stronger boys. Of the other crew members exceptional boys who went on to compete in university and college boats sometimes against Sandy, were M. H. (Bunjy) Ellis at stroke, W. F. Smith at bow and W. F. Godden at 7.

Seasoned rowers tell me that the pressure of rowing at Henley can never be overestimated. Sitting in the boat at the starting line waiting for the start (which to this day is by verbal command) can be a daunting experience. From the water the scene is two lines of white piles marching into the distance marking the course; on either side of these spectators, boats and trees, the valley sides seeming to close in on the river and then, so close, the opposing crew. 'What you never do at the start,' Richard Owen[6] told me, 'is to turn round and look up the course!'

Kitch knew exactly what to expect from Henley and had explained, lectured, briefed the boys on what they would encounter. His hard work paid dividends and the crew was confident and performed magnificently. In their first race, the sixth heat of the Elsenham Cup, Shrewsbury defeated Pembroke College, Cambridge; in the eighth they rowed against and beat Magdalen College, Oxford 'in one of the finest races of the Regatta'. Shrewsbury led at the start and were half a length up at the quarter-mile but Magdalen drew inexorably up until they were neck

6 Richard Owen was a member of the 1960 and 1961 Shrewsbury First VIIIs which won the Princess Elizabeth Challenge Cup at Henley two years in succession.

and neck at the mile post. But Kitch's coaching told and his crew proved strong finishers and they ran out here by three-quarters of a length. It was a particularly sweet victory for Sandy as his brother Hugh was rowing at 7 in the Magdalen boat. Shrewsbury's semi-final heat was against Lady Margaret Boat Club and they won that with style by one and a half lengths. The other semi-final was also rowed between a school and university crew, Bedford against New College Oxford, Bedford winning by three lengths. The final was held on the Saturday and in a magnificent race Shrewsbury defeated their old rivals Bedford by one and a quarter lengths in 7 minutes and 21 seconds.

Sandy's account of the race was written in a typically breathless letter to his mother the following day. On their return from Henley they had been welcomed as heroes by the whole school and he had had almost no sleep at all.

It was the most awful race I have ever rowed, because Bedford were such a colossally strong crew, though they had an ugly style but weight was all on their side. They are all (with the exception of their captain) the most dirty looking loathly crew I have ever known & so we were determined that it would be too disgraceful a thing to let them win. At the start we drew away as usual, but only by a canvas[7] this time as they were very fast off the mark. They soon picked this up & were a canvas ahead at the ¼ mile. At the ½ mile they had ½ a length lead & at the ¾ mile they had a good ¾ lengths to spare & most of the crowd had given up all hope but as soon as we passed the ¾ mile signal post, stroke knew it was the moment to start work, until then we had been rowing a much slower stroke than they & so had plenty of reserve energy, & from just after the ¾ mile post stroke started to bring her in properly; we gave her 4 tens running & by the mile post were a good ½ length up on them (I've never worked so hard in all my life). When the mile telegraph went up, 1 went up before 2 & a colossal shout of Shrewsbury went up. We brought it in for the last ½ mile harder than I ever thought we could. We went up splendidly right to the end & Bedford crocked up altogether.'

It was a jolly good race for the spectators but not for us as we were all absolutely rowed out. We soon forgot our troubles in the congratulating crowd of Old Salopians & in getting the cup. We all get a topping little Victory Regatta Silver

7 i.e. by a small margin of ten feet, the 'canvas' being a racing boat's covered prow.

Medal (about the size of 5/- piece & twice as thick). The best of the lot is that we get our oars with the VIII & its victories printed on it.

We got home at 5.30 this morning (Sunday) & found every body up & at the station & got a terrible reception. (The school bell was broken in the effort) it was nearly as bad as Armistice Day.

This was Sandy's first taste of victory and he loved it. For him sport was all about winning and this time he and the other eight men had done it spectacularly. He concludes the letter in a typically tongue-in-cheek way, 'I've not had a wink of sleep since Friday night except a few minutes during the Sermon today, so I feel like bed.' Sleeping during Chapel was considered a punishable offence and Lilian would have been aware of that as well as being shocked herself that he could have admitted to such a thing. But Sandy challenged her views and beliefs constantly and really she could not criticise her son in the light of his achievements.

For the school it was a triumph of the first order. The Elsenham Cup was proudly displayed at the school for the next forty-five years, until it was placed on permanent loan to the National Schools Regatta in 1964. Kitch was privately ecstatic and was showered with compliments for his coaching brilliance. The crew was loudly commended, both in the press, and by the staff and boys. W. Bridgeman, Chairman of the Governing Body of Shrewsbury School, wrote Kitch a letter on House of Commons notepaper in which he congratulated the Boat Club on 'their conspicuous success at Henley' and Kitch on his 'admirable skill' with which he 'showed them the way to Victory'. Barely able to conceal his intense satisfaction, Bridgeman went on: 'I beg you will convey our high sense of pride in the boys' triumph to the members of the Boat Club and our satisfaction, at the laudatory comments which were so freely poured upon the style and spirit of the crew.'

The success of 1919 led Kitch to believe that the Ladies' Plate, the most coveted Cup at Henley for the public schools and colleges, was within their grasp. In the summer of 1920 he put together an even stronger crew than in 1919 which, once again, included Sandy who now rowed at 6. The promotion from 4 to 6 was a natural one, for as a rower becomes more experienced he generally moves towards the stern of the boat. In

1921 he was at 7 and so on bow side.[8] Unsurprisingly Sandy got on well with Kitch. He had absolute faith in his coaching and his dearest wish was to help him fulfil his ambitions for the First VIII. The respect was mutual and Kitch later described Sandy as a 'pillar of strength … cheerful, resourceful and indefatigable'. Kitch's great talent was that he could bring out the best in a rower and Sandy responded to that. He knew, from his own experience, what it felt like to get it right: and he had the ability to convey this to his crews. He and Sandy had similar physiques and were both notably fair-haired, but they also shared the understanding of the difference between rowing hard and rowing flat out. Sandy had the confidence to do the latter, giving 110 per cent of himself in the full knowledge that he would not crack up. Such a boy is a great asset to a rowing crew.

Henley 1920 was disappointing for Sandy after the success of 1919. Winning was the only acceptable outcome of a race for him.

We were a better boat slightly than last year but to be put up against a heavy crew of men, fresh, when we had rowed a race 5 hours before against a wind that you couldn't bicycle against, to draw the worst station (supposed to be 1 to 1½ lengths slower) & then lead to half way & row a losing race the last half way, & row them to ½ length in the best time of the day over the course & considering that a fortnight before two of us had been in the Sanny & before that the boat had been broken up for 3 weeks with individual attacks of flu! I could lay any money that we could have beaten Christ's College given either station if we were fresh, but bad luck is bad luck & you cant fight it.

As so often in his correspondence with her, arrangements occupy the first part of the letter, with instructions and explanations for Lilian. This was as much so later in his life and even when he was sailing for Everest he was still asking her to pick up the pieces he had left behind. At this point he was concerned with the forthcoming summer holidays.

I will send my trunk & suitcase by advance passenger on Tuesday 26th probably. My bicycle will have to be left here as the back peddling brake did break & coming

---

8 This means that he was ambidextrous and could row on either side of the boat, a gift not given to all, and confirming him as a natural.

adrift got mixed up in the 3 speed hub & locked the back wheel throwing me off &
smashing all the gears. It will take a couple of months to repair probably. I will
want dirty whites (Tennis things) & shirts & socks washing & Pyjamas & New blue
suit & dress cloths taking up to the Lakes, but those I could chose for myself on
Thursday 5th & bring up with me on Friday 6th in the (Hudson or YOUR Standard
if either is left) or on a Bean chassis & bring Dick with me or by train as far as I
can (or on the Clyno?!!!) If you could leave me a small trunk I could chose all my
things & bring them which would save you a lot of packing & looking out of
clothes.

Poor Lilian! She despaired of his untidiness and chaos in his personal
affairs but there was little she could do at this stage to change him.

In amongst all these organisational arrangements he suddenly has a
random thought about cars and instructs her: 'Never get Dunlop tyres
for your Standard get Goodyear or Firestone.' Only after this does he
get around to inviting her and Willie down to Shrewsbury for the
Bumpers Races. Taking place after Henley as they did, the Bumpers
Races were not always popular with the boys who had performed at
Henley but Sandy, obsessed by rowing and, moreover, by his loyalty to
his house, had been busy preparing for them with his usual gusto. As
he had succeeded in crippling his own bike he was forced to borrow
another in order to be able to race up and down the tow path coaching
his house IVs. But this too was not without complications. 'Since Henley
I have had nothing but bad luck (& I haven't broken a mirror),' he
admitted.

I had quite intended to live on the 4 ½ shillings I have left till you come down at
the bumpers but while coaching a boat 2 days ago on Mr Kendall's bicycle I had
the misfortune to nearly run over a child on the tow path & in my attempt to stop
smashed the back brake. It must have been in a very fickle condition but the fact
remains I broke it & it was up to me to get it repaired at once. It was a beastly
bowden coir brake & without a workshop I could not do it myself. I got it done &
they charged 4/6. I argued them for about 10 minutes but could make no impression
(it ought have cost 1/6 at the outside). The net result was that I had to borrow
4/0 & was left with ½ which won't even pay for this letter to be posted.

The letter goes on in extraordinary detail about his financial commitments for the few weeks before he saw Lilian again. He needed money to tip the Shrewsbury boatmen, anxious to be on the right side of them as he was to be Captain of Boats in 1921, he owed Kitch money from Henley and required journey and pocket money for the camp he was going on immediately after the end of term. 'I expect you will be absolutely fogged by this letter', he concluded. 'I am pretty fogged with all these arrangements & preparations for the Bumpers, tubbing 3 boats & doing the "Higher Certificate" at the same time. If I have not brainfever already I will have soon.' This is vintage Sandy. His energy and enthusiasm for everything he does just bursts out of the letter. But there is also, tucked away amongst the humour and chaos of his thoughts, a genuine kindness and generosity towards others. He is concerned to acknowledge the very hard work that the boatmen have done for the VIII throughout the summer, both in preparation for Henley and also on the house boats. He also takes the trouble to tip the House John. Then there are the little digs at his mother which he cannot resist: 'Talking of Henley I have my accounts to give of it & will leave it to your judgement what you think ought to come out of my pocket.' He goes on to list in great detail the expenditure he had incurred at Henley, including repair of a broken canoe paddle. He explains this as well. 'The last named Broken canoe paddle was a most unfortunate accident and came from trying to race another canoe on Sunday afternoon before the races. As you see after paying Kitch & the Mission boats I had £2 one for July & one for Henley & also you will see that those went on unfortunate accident & 2 prs white socks & a very little frivolity which is quite natural after 6 weeks of strict training & hard work.' A little frivolity! Lilian knew all about Sandy's little frivolities and probably disapproved of them but there was nothing she could do now to rein him in. Henley is physically draining for the oarsman but there is plenty of opportunity to let off steam after the racing and I strongly suspect that Sandy was a leading light in the post-race frivolities.

Sandy, through his friendship with Dick, came into contact with wealth on a scale he had not hitherto encountered. Although his family was 'comfortably off', there was no room for extravagance on Willie's income with six children to feed and educate. The Summers family, by comparison, was extremely wealthy and had ostentatious properties and big fast cars. Sandy always respected Dick for being totally unspoiled by his money; it had not bought the family happiness. 'There are few people in the world it hasn't spoiled', he wrote to Dick in 1923, 'and I think quite candidly that you and Geoffrey are the only two people that it hasn't affected in the least. I don't often say nice things about people but I generally tell the truth!'

Soon after Sandy had begun at Shrewsbury he was invited to spend time during the holidays at the Summers family home at Cornist Hall in North Wales with Dick. Cornist Hall is not one of North Wales's most beautiful houses but what it lacks in architectural merit it makes up for in size and position. It was not a modest house. At Cornist there was a tennis court, a swimming pool, a beautiful walled rose garden (which still exists) and extensive grounds leading down towards Flint with views over the Dee estuary.

What Cornist also boasted were garages with gleaming cars, tenderly cared for by the chauffeur, Dick and HS. Cars have been an inevitable cause of friction, delight and disaster in our family ever since they were invented. HS had been an early owner of a motorcar and in 1907 had been spoken to firmly by a Chester magistrate for driving down Bridge Street without due care and attention. He had accidentally put his foot on the accelerator rather than the brake pedal, ploughing into a flock of sheep and killing several of them. He was advised thereafter to leave the driving to his chauffeur. Dick's elder brother Geoffrey was also a keen motorist and a great deal more accomplished than his father. He had taught Dick to drive at the age of seven. It was at Cornist that Sandy learned to drive a car and under Geoffrey and Dick's supervision became a very able driver.

Dick's interest in cars extended way beyond those he drove himself and he fed Sandy endless information about the merits or otherwise of certain models that the Irvine family was considering acquiring. The family did not own a car until 1916 when they took delivery of a second-hand chocolate-coloured 1914 Briton which was immediately nick-named the Choccy Bus. When Hugh joined the RAF in 1917, the duty of chief motor mechanic fell to Sandy, Willie being entirely impractical in matters mechanical. The Choccy Bus was desperately unreliable and by 1919 (the frequent breakdowns and near-disasters, such as the steering habitually sticking at full left lock, ceased to be accepted as either funny or inevitable.). Sandy was deputed to scour the motoring journals for a newer and more reliable marque. This he did with his usual dedication and Dick was more than helpful in supplying the literature. They pored over every publication they could find, checking prices and delivery times, comparing performance and the availability of spare parts. Sandy wrote long and confusing letters home to his parents, blinding them with science and enthusing about the relative attributes of different makes. He wrote to his father in November 1919, 'I have just heard that Padmore has just got his new Austin, which was ordered as far as I can gather a few weeks before ours. If there is no chance of getting one for years how would it be to try & get a Varley-Woods at £660 or an Angus-Sanderson at £450?' He had convinced himself, nevertheless, that the Austin was the vehicle for them and ultimately advised his father that 'the Austin will be well worth waiting for if there is any chance of getting it before the summer holidays'.

As it happened the Austin never materialised and Willie purchased an Essex in addition to the Standard that he had bought for Lilian. The family were now the proud owners of two cars and were about to acquire a third. This elicited further correspondence from Sandy on the subject of motoring. To his mother he wrote: 'I'm glad you like your Standard & I'm sure you will like the Swift much more when it comes. It's much comfier on bad roads & will last for ever as is shown by Geoffrey Summers's which is 6 years old & as good as new, perfectly silent & wonderfully easy to control.'

Dick had introduced Sandy to Harry Ham, chief car mechanic in the Summers' passenger car garage at the Works, in about 1918 and Sandy became a regular visitor to his workshop, asking him endless questions and tinkering with anything Harry would let him get his hands on. Such was the respect that the mechanic had for Sandy's practical skills that when the Essex needed, in Sandy's opinion at least, substantial work doing on it to cure the rattles and bangs, he helped Sandy rebuild the car almost completely in the summer of 1920. The pistons were replaced, the bearings scraped – a job requiring considerable skill – and together they cut out the rivets and bolted the chassis with a view to curing the 'rock'. When the bolting was finished, Sandy picked up one end of the car and shook it vigorously to see that he had eliminated the rattles. Not the action of a weakling. He said that the engine was so improved that when some road-hog in a bull-nosed Morris cut in on him near Queensferry, Sandy chased him in reverse, overtook him and delivered a long lecture on selfish driving. After that the Essex continued to give good service to the family, ending up in a Welsh scrapyard in 1926. It apparently did not occur to Sandy to send through notice of his modifications to the manufacturers as to how he and Mr Ham had solved the squeaks and bumps in the car. This was in contrast to Dick who was constantly haranguing car makers with his ideas and suggestions, mostly on the subject of petrol consumption about which he was decidedly fanatical.

Another attraction for Sandy at Cornist was HS's second wife, Marjory. After his wife had died in 1906 HS had immersed himself in business but in his private life he was lonely. In 1916, on a visit to London a doctor friend told him over a nightcap in the Liberal Club of a pretty young girl who was a patient of his, currently recovering from an appendix operation. Her name was Marjory Agnes Standish Thomson, a chorus girl with a small part in a revival of the musical *Charley's Aunt*. He suggested HS pay her a visit and from the moment he saw her he was completely captivated. She was very pretty, with dark hair, bright blue eyes and a charming, sunny personality. After only three visits he proposed to her and she agreed to marry him. When she told her friend and fellow chorus girl, Elsa Trepess[9] about HS, Marjory enthused, 'He's very rich, I'll marry him, yes, I'll marry him and we'll have a marvellous time. But don't tell the nurses!' Harry Summers was middle-aged, squat and balding and could not have been her ideal choice, but he was rich and kind and Marjory envisaged a marvellous life of pleasure and luxury. They were married in January 1917, shortly after his fifty-second birth-

9 By an extraordinary coincidence my father, Peter, came to meet Elsa Trepess or Elsa Bottomley as she had become. He was being interviewed for BBC television and the sound recordist who had been busy below the interview table popped his head out at the end of the session and said 'My grandmother knew your grandmother!' After a brief conversation my father was able to establish that he was referring to Marjory. A meeting was set up between my father and Mrs Bottomley in 1978 and his subsequent notes give me this detailed background.

day, and at nineteen she became mistress of Cornist Hall. The marriage was doomed from the start: Marjory was far closer in age to HS's children, Dick being only five years her junior. 'So far as I was concerned,' he wrote later, 'I was always very good friends with Marjory, and as I grew up I found her quite amusing, but of course she had no idea of looking after a person of my age.'

Initially Marjory rather enjoyed her new life. She entered Cornist like a whirlwind, startling the staff right, left and centre with her extravagant ways and her sometimes impulsive and impatient manner. HS tolerated her independence since her vivacious nature brought the light and laughter into his life that had been lacking. But before long, life at Cornist began to pall and Marjory was bored. She turned her attentions to the young officers at the nearby army camp at Kinmel and RAF Sealand, close to the steel works. She used to invite them to dine and party at Cornist, entertaining on a flamboyant scale and making serious inroads into the wine cellar. Marjory took immense pleasure in teaching her guests to dance to the latest tunes and many a young man learned to foxtrot at Cornist. She also liked the blues and introduced Dick's friends, as well as the officers, to the delights of dancing the blues with her, but her *pièce de résistance* was the twirl. Cornist was alive with the sounds of dancing and laughter late into the night – such a dramatic contrast to the house when HS was at home.

For Sandy, Marjory added an exotic sparkle to his visits to Cornist. She introduced him to the kind of entertainment that would have been frowned upon by his parents. She took him and Dick to the theatre in Liverpool and London, they drove out in the Rolls Royce for extravagant picnics, and of course she taught him to dance. Dick was always glad to have Sandy to accompany him when Marjory was entertaining and Sandy was always quick to admit how much his friendship with Dick had enriched his own life: 'I never in my life will be able to repay you for all your kindness & the good times you have given me.' He wrote later, 'Just think for one moment what I would be like if I had never met you – probably never seen Town at all, certainly no Theatre – no workshop – no fun with cars – no Brooklands – no priceless holidays in the Lakes.' And no Marjory.

This was all far from the reality of life in Park Road South where

Sandy and Evelyn, on return from their respective boarding schools, found their younger brothers growing up rapidly. They were tolerated by Evelyn and Sandy but if they stepped out of line and interfered with the older pair there could be trouble. All three younger brothers recalled being made by Sandy to stand on a pile of sticks or a plank over bricks while Sandy ignited home-made gunpowder that he had placed beneath. He told them they were taking part in a scientific experiment in which he would establish whether gunpowder exploded upwards or sideways. They were always eager to be involved with Sandy's tests so readily agreed to participate. There would be a blinding flash and whichever brother was in for the treatment would be fired off the pile. The 'experiment', as he and Evelyn called it, could be construed as a kind of initiation. The youngest, Tur, actually sustained a perforated ear-drum as a result.

Sandy rowed again at Henley in 1921 where the school VIII achieved a great but masked achievement. They became only the second school ever to break the seven-minute barrier, the first having been Eton in 1911, and this rowing as the losing crew against Pembroke College, Cambridge in the semi-final of the Ladies' Plate. Pembroke had already set a very fast time the day before against Trinity College, Oxford, winning by the tiny margin of six feet and had set a new course record for the Ladies' of 6 minutes 55 seconds. They matched this time in their race against Shrewsbury which they won by three-quarters of a length, which means that Shrewsbury would have crossed the finishing line in 6.57 or 6.58 minutes. A stupendous effort and an extraordinary achievement. 'Think for a moment what it must have felt like at the Mile', Richard Owen wrote to me, 'rowing 40, just down, boys against men, and everything to go for and nothing to lose against the crew that had already broken the course record the day before!' There was another hidden consolation for Sandy: his crew had again showed itself faster than his brother's Magdalen crew, which ultimately won the Grand that year, when they returned a time of 7.15 half an hour earlier. Kitch, who always kept coaching notes, recorded that Sandy and Smith had 'out-rowed' the other oarsmen: as stern pair they had put up a rhythm and a pace that the others could not match. Both Sandy and Smith had the experience of knowing that they could push themselves beyond the limit and come through, as they had proven in 1919 and went on to prove in 1923 as adversaries.

Sandy's last year at Shrewsbury was a very busy one. As head of Moore's House and Captain of Boats he had his work cut out for him. In addition to this he was meant to be studying for his Higher Certificate, the rough equivalent of A levels, which he had to pass in order to earn a place at Oxford. The tenor of his term as Head of House was unusual in the context of the public school traditions of the time. Rather than pushing the new boys around and issuing punishments, he preferred to encourage them and not only if they were good at sport. Of one of his quieter contemporaries who had not excelled in any field at the school he wrote in the House fasti, or record book: 'Quiet and persevering, he knew his own mind and made a good monitor.' Of his friend Ian Bruce, who took over responsibility for the house rowing after Sandy had left, he wrote: 'Captaincy passes to I. R. Bruce who we feel sure will leave no stone unturned or water unchurned in his efforts to put Moores at the Head of the River' (a reference to the fiercely contested inter-house boat races which took place each summer).

Sandy had great patience with the boys in the years below him and showed them acts of kindness and generosity which one does not always associate with a nineteen-year-old schoolboy. When I was going through the seventy-plus letters of condolence I found one from a woman called Muriel Roberts whose son had been a first year at Shrewsbury when Sandy was Head of House. Hesketh, the boy, had been dangerously ill in a nursing home in Shrewsbury and Sandy had made the effort to call and enquire about him daily.

When Hesketh was to have visitors Sandy used to come & sit with him, & cheer him up, & really helped him get better. Then sweetest of all, Sandy found out that Hesketh had no appetite, & little parcels kept arriving anonymously. – it was Sandy. Said he thought Hesketh might be tempted to eat. His sweetness used often to bring tear to my eyes. Then it was so lovely as Sandy was a preposter & school idol, and my boy a new nonentity! He told me the many little yarns in which you & your husband figured, & Evelyn appeared to be the apple of his eye. He brought her to Criccieth to see us. Sandy was everything that a young man should be, & if my boys grow up to be half as fine a character as he was – & is – I shall not have brought them up in vain.

Sandy's friendly and generous nature, which this letter shows, was a key part of his character. He had inherited his father's warm and unselfish attitude to people but he was never a do-gooder and he loved daring escapades. A famous or, rather, infamous story stems from this period. The Alington Hall at the school was used as a gymnasium. There was a very narrow ledge below a beam, about eighty feet up in the gables of the hall. On the beam was inscribed 'Thou shalt not be found out – 11th commandment'. Sandy succeeded, with the assistance of an accomplice, in climbing up into the roof, tip-toeing, while bent double, along the joists until he was able to get onto the tiny ledge and standing on it, precariously balanced, wrote on the wall 'A C Irvine Capt. March 29th 1921, W F Smith Sec'. At that time Sandy was Captain of Boats at the school and Smith was the Secretary. The difficult bit, a current master at Shrewsbury told me, would have been getting up to the joist in the first place. 'There is a metal fire escape now but then there would have been an internal ladder and to get onto this would have involved the leg up', presumably from Smith. The story acquired a legendary status and over the years a few other bold boys added their names to Sandy's and Smith's. When Hugh Irvine visited the school in the late 1920s he was shown the signature by Edward Oliver, the School Engineer, who was evidently both proud and impressed.

Sandy left Shrewsbury with a wonderful reputation as a sportsman and as a role model for the younger boys. One master, Freddie Prior, wrote this remarkable tribute in the house fasti in 1921: 'He had a remarkable capability for leadership and unusual determination. He had a genius for organization and any arrangements to be made could be left in his hands. Above all things a practical person, resourceful in an emergency, always rising to the occasion with some ingenious device for avoiding or overcoming every obstacle.'

3

Into the Blue

It sometimes happens when one is endeavouring to select a man for a particular job that the very kind of man one has been seeking turns up.

Noel Odell, November 1924

In the summer of 1919 the family rented Gladys Cottage in Llan-fairfechan, a coastal town situated opposite Angelsey, about six miles west of Colwyn Bay, and a popular holiday resort for the Cheshire middle classes in the early twentieth century. Llanfairfechan is dwarfed by the mighty Penmaenmawr quarry which produced most of the stones for the cobbled streets of Lancashire in the nineteenth century. In the early twentieth century the quarry was in full swing and the miners, used to the seasonal work the quarry offered, built houses that they inhabited in the winter and let out to guests in the summer. The railway from Chester was diverted via Llanfairfechan in 1868 and the resort took on its present character from that time. It is still essentially a Victorian village with a very pretty front onto the sea, and the village backs onto the hills behind that lead, eventually, to the Carneddau, Wales's northernmost range of mountains.

Sandy had minutely organized the travel arrangements to Llan-fairfechan. The family arrived by car, train and he by motorbike com-plete with sidecar, to Alec and Tur's delight. The holiday was spent walking, scrambling and biking in the hills. Kenneth was now old enough to join in with Sandy and Evelyn. Four years younger than Sandy and five years older than Alec, he was what he as an adult described as a 'staircase child'. He was strong, athletic and fearless with a great sense of humour and this endeared him to their friends. Sandy even let him ride his precious motorbike.

The two youngest boys looked up to the three eldest with more than

Lilian Irvine,
aged 17

Right Willie Irvine
with Sandy, Evelyn
and Hugh, January
1905

Below Willie Irvine
teaching Sandy to
fish at Capel Curig,
August 1907

Sandy rowing at no. 6 for Shrewsbury (far boat) against Christ's College, Cambridge, Henley Royal Regatta, 1920. Christ's won by half a length

Oxford Boat Race Crew, Putney, March 1923.
Sandy at no. 3. Milling (at 7) was replaced by Gully Nickalls

Captioned by Sandy: 'Clyno on Foil Fras 3,091 ft' 17 August 1919

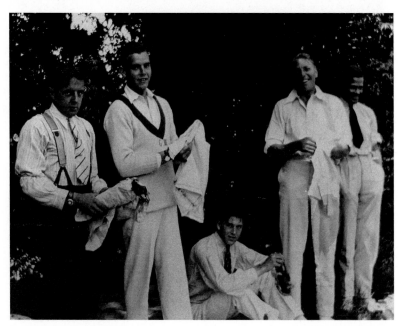

Summer 1922 in Oxford.
L–R: Dick Summers, Geoffrey Milling, another, Sandy, A. T. Wilder

Sandy and Marjory in the rose garden at Cornist, Summer 1923

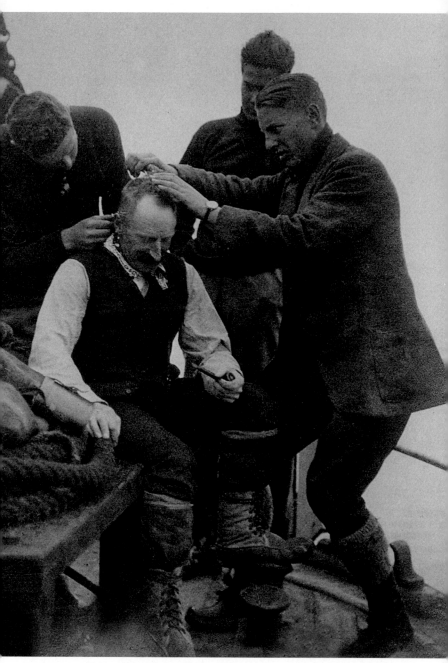

Tom Longstaff aboard the SS *Terningen* having his hair cut by Sandy
and another, A. T. Wilder watching

Above Lomme Bay
Glacier, Spitsbergen

Boots hanging out
to dry at Camp IV
on the sledging party
across Spitsbergen,
August 1923

At the top of a climb in Norway, L–R: R. A. Frazer, Geoffrey Milling, Sandy

Photographed by Sandy on the final day of the trek: Odell standing, Milling and Frazer on sledge no. 2

Notes for Future

Pipe cleaners.
Climbing boots
Sacks that don't shrink
Pockets in cloths
Felt under sleeping bag
Short light ice axe long pick + weight
well in the head

Notes for Future. This list was made in the front of Sandy's Spitsbergen note-book

a touch of awe. Hugh was, after all, twelve years older than Alec and fourteen years older than Tur. Evelyn they adored as an older sister, but Sandy was really special to them. More than either of the other two he was fun. Alec recalled the utter thrill he felt when Sandy put him in the sidecar of his motorbike and took off up into the hills above Gladys cottage. He couldn't see out very well but the occasion made a deep impression on him, one which in later life, when thinking about Sandy's motorbike, he recalled with great glee.

It was with the sidecar attached that my own happy memories are concerned. Llanfairfechan was, in those days, the centre of a number of small bridle-ways just big enough for a motor-bicycle combination. My younger brother and I were often pressed (to our great delight) in to 'hold the sidecar down'. My recollection is looking over the side of the sidecar down onto the top of fir trees, and of bracken flashing by at our nose level. But I have never been back again to make the great mistake of refurbishing those early memories.

The motorbike, a Clyno, had been acquired by Sandy two years earlier and he was very proud of it. His parents despaired of his adventures on the bike and tried, in vain, to stop him from undertaking some of his more hair-raising exploits. One day during the holiday Sandy had the bright idea that he should attempt to ride the Clyno over the Carneddau and back to Llanfairfechan, something no one had apparently attempted before. He went against the express wishes of Lilian and Willie but when he set his mind on proving something to himself he was not easily deterred. There was no mountain track up to the ridge and the way was entirely pioneered by him. On the summit of Foel Grach, the third highest of the Carneddau, he encountered a couple who were walking across the range. Unsure of his exact bearings he enquired politely whether he was heading in the right direction for Llanfairfechan. The man replied that he was and Sandy thanked them and went on his way. The couple, Noel and Mona Odell, who were on a walking and climbing holiday in North Wales, were very struck by what Odell later described as the intrepid young motorcyclist. Sandy's feat attracted great attention locally and at least three newspapers carried the story of the young man who had been brave enough to take a motorcycle into the mountains.

One of the local papers reported: 'Mr Andrew Irvine, son of Mr Fergusson Irvine, of Liverpool, who is staying at Gladys Cottage, Llanfairfechan, has ridden a motor-cycle to the top of Foel Grach, which is 3000 ft high. There is hardly any track up the mountain which is very steep.' Sandy, who shied away from bragging, nevertheless carried this press cutting in his wallet, which was returned from Everest by Odell after his death, so there must have been a certain amount of quiet personal pride in his achievement. I discovered the wallet among Sandy's possessions in May 2000 and the press cutting was still there, neatly folded behind his university timetable.

When Odell met Sandy on top of the Carneddau he was twenty-nine and at the peak of his strength and fitness. He had been a member of the Alpine Club since 1916 and was considered to be a climber of some note, having made difficult ascents in the Alps, including the Aiguille du Tour in the Mont Blanc range in 1908 at the age of eighteen. Like many climbers Odell had begun his career in the back garden. As a very young boy he started climbing elm trees with his sisters and soon graduated to illicit roof climbing at the family house in Brighton in his early teens. On a family holiday in the Lake District when Odell was fourteen he made a secret and unauthorized ascent of Causey Pike, a fell near the western shore of Derwent Water, which he thereafter termed his 'nursery slope'. Even this modest 2000 ft hill provided a slight challenge: it was a very hot day and he became thirsty, so he took a drink from a mountain beck only to discover a few feet higher up a dead sheep lying in the water. Needless to say, on his return to the family he was considerably unwell.

Eventually his family was forced to acknowledge his love of climbing and in 1910, at the age of twenty, he was introduced by his father to the brothers Ashley and George Abraham of Keswick. George was a gifted and respected photographer, but he was also an able climber. Before the First World War the Abraham brothers had published a book on rock climbs in Wales that at the time had provoked something of an ideological debate. Some argued that climbers should seek routes for themselves rather than relying on publications to guide them, others were less discreet and were plainly annoyed that their territory had been invaded by 'outsiders', climbers from the Lake District. George arranged for Odell to be given climbing instruction by George Woodhouse, a teacher from Sedburgh School. Together they climbed many of the famous Lakeland crags including Raven Crag and Bowfell Buttress.

With climbing skills more finely honed, Odell returned to the Alps, where he did twelve seasons in the company of some of the best known Alpinists of the day. It was on one of these trips that he climbed with R. A. Frazer, with whom he later made two trips to Spitsbergen, one of the Norwegian islands inside the Arctic circle. Odell was not only admired by his fellow climbers, he was loved by them. As a man he was genial, easy-going and loyal. He never forgot his friends and was, for the whole of his life, a great letter writer.

In the summer of 1920 Sandy again encountered Odell in North Wales. This time he was with Evelyn. According to Odell they shared a car with a mutual friend who was driving them to climb Tryfan. Strangely neither party made themselves known to the other although they both record the fact that the 'meeting' took place. Evelyn at that stage was wearing her hair in a bob and was often dressed in shorts and was on more than one occasion taken for a boy, something she rather relished. They ran up Tryfan in plimsolls, passing Odell and his climbing partner who were better equipped with hobnailed boots and proper climbing gear. Evelyn used to love telling the story of this escapade when the two of them were seriously frowned upon by the 'real' climbers who were overheard to say 'bloody young fools!' as she and Sandy ran past them.

The following year the family borrowed a house from a business associate of Willie's called Crow How, a beautiful Lakeland stone house about half a mile outside Ambleside. It had ten bedrooms and extensive gardens so there was plenty of room for guests. That year they were joined by four of Evelyn's friends from school, including Audrey Pim who turned out to be a talented amateur photographer. She captured much of the atmosphere of the holiday in her photograph album, recording meticulously all the places they visited, the excursions they made and the sports they played. Apart from tennis and golf, at which Sandy and Audrey teamed up and won convincingly, they also made their way into the hills to indulge in fell walking. Typically, where Sandy was involved, these frequently turned into outings with an interesting added dimension. On one occasion, Sandy, Evelyn and Kenneth, accompanied by John Bromfield and Audrey, climbed Helvellyn via Striding Edge. The trek is a good four hours from Glenridding, on the shores of Lake Ullswater, and the exciting bit of the climb comes close to the end via the spectacularly precipitous Striding Edge, a rocky arête or ridge, which drops away on one side some 600 feet to Red Tarn and on the other side some 1000 feet into the valley of Patterdale. Even under the most perfect and windless conditions it is a strenuous pull uphill from Glenridding and then a very alarming few hundred feet along the ridge, which is not for the faint-hearted nor those with no head for heights. Audrey snapped a beautiful shot of Striding Edge from below just as the sun was disappearing over the summit horizon. It must have been pitch dark by the time they reached the summit. Sandy had elected to climb the arête at sunset, which added a certain drama and excitement and meant that as they ran down the back side of the mountain towards Thirlmere they were descending in the dark.

On leaving Shrewsbury in 1921, Sandy applied to study chemistry at Magdalen College, Oxford. He had been preceded to Oxford by Hugh, who was reading History at Magdalen, and Evelyn, who was reading Inorganic Chemistry under the auspices of the Recognized Society of Women Students, which later became St Anne's College.

Sandy's academic record was found wanting, although he had succeeded in passing his Higher Certificate in Physics, Chemistry and Mathematics. Even in the days when academic qualifications were not the only requirement for securing a place at the university, the Master, Sir Herbert Warren, felt unable to offer him a place. Sir Herbert later deeply regretted the decision but at the time Sandy was left wondering which college might accept him. He knew full well that his rowing record would count greatly in his favour and he turned to his friend and former housemaster, C. J. Baker who himself had been at Merton College at the end of the nineteenth century. Baker knew and liked Merton's Warden, T. E. Dowman, and put in a good word for Sandy. It was agreed that he would be offered a place at the college subject to his attending a crammer for the Michaelmas term of 1921 and passing Responsions, the examination formally required to qualify for entry as an undergraduate at Oxford University.

The crammer was run by A. Theodosius, another friend of Dowman, and was located in Merton Street, a mere stone's throw from Sandy's prospective college. Once there Sandy made a great effort to get to grips with Latin, Greek and modern languages, but it was a struggle. At the time when he was sweating away at the crammer the selection process for the university boat crew was underway, starting with the 'Varsity Fours' – in which each college enters its very best crew, including Blues,[1] then followed by the Trial VIIIs held at Wallingford in early December. One of his overriding reasons for wishing to get to Oxford was to continue his rowing career and in December 1921 it must have looked to him as if he would have to bide his time for a whole year before taking part in trials for the Boat Race. This would have been an irritation to him, because, as usual, he had his sights set high on a place in the university boat.

But his work at the crammer paid off and by the end of December 1921 Willie Irvine had received two letters. One was from Theodosius and the other from Dowman. Theodosius had grown to like Sandy over the term and was prepared to recommend him to Merton although he could not help mentioning to Willie the 'meagre knowledge of Latin and French he brought with him ... His French prose had some serious howlers.' He concluded the letter: 'The Boy is a bit overworked just now but I hope he will quickly pick up. I have liked having him – he is persona grata with us all and I have found him reliable in every way.' Dowman was prepared to look leniently on Sandy's application, presumably in view of what Theodosius had said about him but also because he was doubtless keen to have someone of Sandy's athletic brilliance, which would bring benefit to the college. He wrote to Willie: 'We are willing to admit your son into residence next term in spite of his not having passed the whole of Responsions.' With some relief Willie relayed this good news to Sandy who took up his rooms in college on 20 January 1922, although he was made to re-sit his Responsions three times until he finally passed them all in the Autumn of 1922.

Merton College, despite its peaceful appearance, had a reputation for gaiety which extended back to the Civil War and for many years it was reputed to have the best kitchen in Oxford. By the 1920s the college was in the capable, if at times controversial hands of H. W. Garrod, a tutor

1 Men who had previously rowed in the Boat Race against Cambridge.

in Literature and Classics. Although Sandy had little to do with Garrod academically, he knew him well from the bowls games on the college lawns, a regular fixture that along with chess, allowed Garrod regular contact with the undergraduates. Merton admitted about twenty new students each year, so that the total number of people in the college including the fellows and dons, numbered about 120. Sandy was given an attic room overlooking one of the courtyards. He shared a staircase and a 'scout' with an American called Alatan Tamchiboulac Wilder, known as 'AT', a fellow sportsman and subsequent close friend. The scouts were menservants who attended to the needs of the under-graduates, lighting fires in their rooms and making them breakfast each morning. The scouts were more than just mere servants and took great pride in their men and the antics they got involved in. Sandy quickly established a good relationship with his scout, Owen Brown, and soon trusted him to look after his goods and affairs on his behalf. Brown later described Sandy as a 'kind friend' to him. Sandy's closest friend at Oxford, though, was a man called Geoffrey Milling, who had come up to Merton the previous year from Radley. Milling came from the Isle of Wight and shared with Sandy a distinguished school rowing career. They met in their first week when Sandy was offered a place in the Oxford Boat and Milling was rowing at 7. They had a lot in common, apart from their passion for rowing, and Milling was instrumental in ensuring that Sandy was quickly immersed in College life.

Much has been made of the hedonistic atmosphere that pervaded Oxford in the 1920s and the image of the cultivated, fun-loving student from an upper-class background for whom university was nothing but a 'sort of passionate party all the time'. Louis MacNeice, a contemporary of Sandy's at Merton, wrote in his autobiography: 'I had not gone to Oxford to study; that was what grammar-school boys did. We products of the English public schools went to Oxford either for sport and beer-drinking, in which case we filled in time deriding the intellectuals, or for the aesthetic life and cocktails, in which case we filled in time deriding the athletes.' That is not however the whole picture and Sandy, anyway, did not belong to the group of aesthetes on whom this rather idyllic image is based. During the 1920s there was a growing number of students who came from middle class families, often of the first generation to attend university. These young men were pursuing a university degree with a view to beginning a career after three years of study.

For Sandy the change from public school to Merton appeared never to be a problem. First, the regime at Shrewsbury had been somewhat more enlightened and relaxed than in other public schools and, secondly, there can be no doubt that coming into Merton with an outstanding rowing career behind him, he was quickly included in the elite of the college. He became something of an instantaneous celebrity when he was offered, in his first week, a place in the university boat – a singular honour and distinction for a freshman and a mark of his strength as an oarsman. The decision taken by 1922 President of the Oxford University Boat Club (OUBC), D. T. Raikes, to include Sandy in his crew was a bold one. What led to its being taken is not recorded but he clearly felt confident in requisitioning the untried freshman, who had missed the Trial VIIIs in December by not yet being a member of the university. By all accounts he was not disappointed. Sandy was singled out by the local press who, whilst observing the training in February, deemed him to be a decided acquisition.

Training for the Boat Race was neither as scientific nor as arduous then as it is now, nevertheless it was a punishing schedule and the crew had only two and a half months to prepare before they were to race Cambridge on 1 April. During that time the crew were relieved of their studies – much to Sandy's delight – and trained first in Oxford and then Henley, moving down to the tideway at Putney at the beginning of March for the final days of training.

The Oxford and Cambridge Boat Race predates the Henley Royal Regatta by ten years. It has been rowed on the tidal Thames in London since 1830 and from Putney to Mortlake, a distance of 4 miles 374 yards in a time of about 20 minutes, since 1845. In the nature of all such events, the Boat Race is a private challenge match between the two universities concerned and as such has only its own rules. The formal challenge is made annually and the conditions of the race do not change except by mutual agreement. The popularity of the Boat Race was ascribed by Gully Nickalls[2] to the Englishman's innate respect and affection for

2 President of the OUBC, 1923.

routine, at any rate as regards his sporting fixtures. The fact that it is rowed in March, a month when the country can expect anything from bright sunshine to a blizzard, may too have something to do with its popularity. 'The sight of sixteen young men rowing up the river in the minimum of clothing', Nickalls wrote, 'is a hopeful and encouraging sign; a harbinger of the warm days of summer which, ever optimistic, we believe are waiting for us in a few weeks' time.' From the point of view of the oarsmen, past and present, it was and is a singular honour to be asked to take part in the Race and to be a member of a winning crew is a matter of lifetime pride. This was very much the case in the 1920s, when Sandy was rowing, all the more so because Oxford had not won the Race since 1913[3] and it was becoming something of a concern to the OUBC that they were consistently outperformed by their rivals.

The OUBC in 1922 was able to draw on the expertise of three immensely experienced coaches, Dr Gilbert Bourne, E. D. Horsfall and Harcourt Gold, who worked hard and uniformly together. They succeeded in impressing the rowing journalists who reckoned the 1922 crew were almost up to the standard of the 1912 crew, the last but one to beat Cambridge. In the Race Oxford did not live up to their early promise and were beaten by Cambridge in a fast time by four and a half lengths. The critics held that the Oxford crew lacked experience and that the younger men would have to be worked hard if their form was to improve. Of Sandy, one testy correspondent wrote: 'Irvine is quite promising, and he will finish more firmly when he has more experience.'

Back at Oxford after the Easter holidays Sandy got on with the real business of being at university. He had chosen to study chemistry although his natural bent was towards engineering, not an Oxford subject at the time. His tutor, Bertram Lambert was intrigued and exasperated by him in equal measure. While he showed real passion for laboratory work and a fascination for experiments, much of Sandy's work at Oxford had little to do with the set curriculum. He was too busy chasing ideas that appealed to his inventive side and would pursue them at the expense of his degree subjects. They came to an amicable

3 The Race was interrupted by the First World War and Cambridge won all 3 rowed in 1914, 1919 and 1921.

agreement on his academic studies and he passed Parts I and II of his chemistry exams and, eventually, Responsions. The science subjects had a fuller timetable than the humanities and Sandy had to attend ten lectures and tutorials a week, including three on Fridays and one on Saturday morning. With this, his rowing and the inevitable socializing that went on in college, his time at Oxford was filled to overflowing. As in everything else he did, he put his heart into university life.

Evelyn was embarked upon her own university career and living in North Oxford, in a boarding house on the Woodstock Road. She and Sandy were often seen together. He was useful as a chaperone to theatres, to the occasional dance and to the Merton Commemoration Ball two years running. At entertainments, such as dinner parties, women were very much in the minority. She was a great asset: not only was she very beautiful, but she was also intelligent and independent, able to keep up a conversation with anyone. Sandy thought the world of her and regaled her with all his latest exploits which she would then in turn relate to the girls in the boarding house. They were always delighted to hear what he had been up to and thought Evelyn immensely sophisticated as she had an entrée into the world of the university whereas they, as one of her friends wrote to me, 'practically needed written permission to talk to a man'. In the end Sandy's friends, who admired Evelyn a great deal, were able to help her after his death by protecting her from the newspapers in a most extraordinary and dashing way.

Each college had a dining club to which had a distinctive character of its own. The Myrmidon Club at Merton attracted the 'hearties' who 'were wealthy and well connected, but also dissolute and daring, in the habit of breaking college windows and college rules'. This description refers to one episode after which a letter was received by the club's President reminding him of the curfew hour for guests and pointing out that he was sure that members of the club had no intention of breaking either rules or windows. It is hardly surprising that the club had a reputation for scarcely contained revelry. One of the key members of the Myrmidon Club was George Binney, a year or two older than Sandy and a very active undergraduate. He was the chief organizer of the Oxford University Arctic expeditions to Spitsbergen in 1921 and 1923. Milling was also a member of the Myrmidon Club and he invited Sandy to join them at one of their dinners. Sandy fitted the bill and was elected a member in June 1922. They met twice a term in college and dined out at least once, usually at the Gridiron Club, returning to one or other of their rooms for dessert, drinks and a game of chance. College rules dictated that all guests must depart by 11 p.m. but there were several occasions when guests stayed beyond this hour and had to be sur-reptitiously 'removed' in cloak and dagger operations. An episode recorded in the club minutes referred to 'one guest [who] remained in college until well after twelve and had to be let out by devious ways under the supervision of the President and Mr Irvine.' In 1924 Sandy was elected, in absentia, Honorary Secretary of the Myrmidon Club but unfortunately never returned to take up the post.[4]

Dick Hodges, an old Salopian and member of the Myrmidon Club in the early 1920s, recalled on his honeymoon an episode concerning Sandy. He and his new wife were dining at the Lygon Arms Hotel, in Broadway gazing into the magnificent Jacobean fireplace when Dick suddenly said, 'Whenever I'm in this room I'm reminded of Sandy Irvine!' 'Oh yes,' replied his wife with some trepidation. 'We'd come over for dinner,' Dick explained, 'and Sandy disappeared. We had given up search-ing and were about to return to Oxford when Sandy shouted at us from the rooftops. He'd climbed that chimney.' This is so typical of Sandy. He didn't climb the chimney as a dare, he didn't even tell anyone he was going to do it, he just set himself a private challenge and got on with it.

Sandy's exploits were never malicious and he was not given to boast-ing; they were just the result of his uncontainable high spirits and his constant need to push himself. He despised pretension and was extremely impatient with anyone who was prone to boasting. Once, when a friend of Hugh's turned up to see them at home in a new car, Sandy became infuriated by the endless bragging of the car's owner, and determined to teach him a lesson. He disappeared from the room and when it came time for the young man to leave he discovered that his precious car had been put up on blocks by Sandy, upon the pedestal he

4 The minute book records: 'Mr Irvine, proposed by the President, & seconded by the Secretary, elected the Hon. Sec. to the Club in succession to the latter, but before the end of the same week the terrible news had been received in this country that that gentleman had most tragically yet most gloriously lost his life in this year's expedition to ascend Mt. Everest.'

had metaphorically placed the car himself. The man was big-headed and needed taking down a peg or two in Sandy's opinion.

When Sandy returned to Oxford for the Michaelmas term in 1922 his mind was once again focused on rowing. This year he was able to go through the proper procedure, as he saw it, first rowing in the 'Varsity Fours' for Merton and then the University Trial VIIIs. He wrote to Dick Summers:

I'm so sorry I didn't write to let you know about altering the date of our visit to Town, but I have been for the last week in a Nursing Home with rather bad blood poisoning. I only came out yesterday. It was darn bad luck getting it. It started three days before the 1st round of the Varsity IVs. So I didn't dare to see a doctor as I knew he would stop me. I felt like death when we had to row & we lost to B.N.C [Brasenose College] by ⅕ sec. No average person could judge a timed race with signals to ⅕ sec. Still it was just as well. B.N.C. had a walk over the rest of the time & won easily. Blast it.

The ability to perform well even when he was clearly below par was something he proved on several occasions during his life, most significantly and repeatedly on the Everest expedition in 1924.

At the end of the letter he congratulates Dick on winning a motor race but cautions him with a tale which is very telling of his attitude to life. 'A man at New College has just had both eyes taken out (one was left on the road) & his whole face smashed in. And never lost consciousness, poor fellow, I should rather be killed than live like that.'

Unsurprisingly Sandy was again selected to row in the university boat and this year the president was his friend Gully Nickalls. Coaching followed the same procedure as the previous year, with the initial training taking place on the home waters in Oxford under the supervision of Dr Bourne who had also made some improvements to the 1923 boat. After six weeks there the crew moved to Henley, where they stayed in the Leander Club and were coached by Horsfall. During the period at Henley Gully Nickalls developed jaundice and his place at 7 had to be taken pro tem by Geoffrey Milling. The press followed the boat and assessed its progress in long columns in the *Times* on a twice-weekly basis. The paper's special rowing correspondent, although very critical of individual oarsmen and once again of their personal faults as he saw them, was nevertheless impressed by the crew and claimed it to be the best Oxford boat crew since 1911. They must have been improving! In 1922 they were compared only with the 1912 crew.

By the time the crew arrived at Putney on 6 March Nickalls was sufficiently recovered to row half-days with Milling acting as spare during the afternoon sessions. From the middle of March onwards there was real interest in the two crews on the tideway. The press sensed that this might be the year that Oxford fought back and regained the lead from Cambridge who had won the last four races. The coaching of the Oxford boat was handed over to Harcourt Gold who was to put the finishing touches to the crew and was renowned for his ability to do so. Old Blues were out in force to study the Dark Blues' form, piling onto the coaches' launch when they could while other followers braved the cold winds and grey skies to watch the progress of the training from the banks of the river. One lady I heard from, who was then a girl of fourteen, remembers watching Oxford in 1923 as they came off the water and carried their boat to the boat house. She was rather overwhelmed by the sight of these splendid specimens in their rowing shorts and sweaters. 'They were almost like gods,' she said, 'we just stood and stared in awe and admiration. And there was Sandy, one of *them*, smiling at *me*.'

As Sandy was busy training for the Boat Race his friend George Binney was fully occupied with trying to put together the second Oxford University expedition to Spitsbergen. He had organized the first trip in 1921 which had been a qualified success as they had had much trouble getting through the pack ice. This time, with the benefit of experience, he had put together a much stronger team and his plans, stores and equipment were both better thought-out and more up to date. Using the good contacts he had made in the Alpine Club in 1921 he was again fortunate to recruit Noel Odell as geologist, R. A. Frazer as surveyor and, at the last minute, Dr Tom Longstaff as medical officer and naturalist to the team. He set about selecting other, younger, men from the university to make up the sledging and exploration teams. As President of the Myrmidon Club, Binney had had the opportunity to get to know several very strong, athletic types whom he considered to be serious contenders. He suggested to Odell that it might be worth taking Geoffrey Milling and Sandy as two of the strongest for his sledging party.

The remaining members of the expedition were A. T. Wilder and Basil Clutterbuck from Merton and from other Oxford colleges, Elton, T. C. Gundry, and E. Relf. Geoffrey Summers, Dick's elder brother, who had been granted leave from the steel works to accompany the expedition, was to be in charge of the cine filming. There was still one space to be filled. Sandy immediately suggested that Binney recruit his friend, Ian Bruce, who was studying at Cambridge, but who was equally strong and athletic and had a taste for adventure. Binney agreed and asked Sandy to approach him. Bruce was delighted to be asked but somewhat anxious about the arrangements. His mother had had endless questions for him when he put the proposition to her and in a letter to Sandy he asked for reassurance on several points: 'Re our Poling expedition! I wrote to my mater as soon as I got your letter and the first thing she said to me was "Is there going to be a doctor with you?" just like her to ask. By the way, if we do go to the North Pole I hope I'm not the only Tab [Cambridge man].' Sandy reassured Bruce in his anxieties and was eventually able to send him the good news that they would be accompanied on the expedition by Dr. Tom Longstaff, who had returned the previous autumn from the 1922 Everest expedition. This evidently calmed Mrs Bruce who gave her permission for her son to go. Bruce concluded his letter to Sandy, 'I'm coming up for the Boat Race, so I may see you then. I suppose you're hard at it now, I wish you personally beaucoup de luck, but may your split-arse[5] boat sink during the race.'

On the Wednesday before the Race Odell met Milling and Sandy at the Norman Hotel, Putney where the Oxford crew were having a champagne dinner. Binney had suggested the two of them as likely candidates for his sledging party and Odell came to Putney with the express purpose of checking them out. He knew that they were splendidly fit but he wanted to assure himself of their suitability for inclusion in what would be surely the toughest aspect of the trip, a thirty day trek on foot across snow and ice. He sat between the two of them and had a very amusing evening by all accounts. Both men were enthused about the Spitsbergen expedition and delighted at the prospect of being

5 'Split-arse' means 'very fast' in 1920s slang.

included in the sledging party. Odell later recalled this first meeting when he asked them to join and referred particularly to Sandy's alacrity: 'He seemed at once to typify all that I was looking for and all that is so essential in the make-up of one that is to be not merely a useful, but also a genial, companion under the trying conditions of the Arctic. Adventurer by nature that he was, he jumped at the idea though I must admit I abundantly emphasized the labour and hardships of sledging, and spoke little of the delights of skiing over virgin glaciers, and exploring unknown peaks.' Odell also suggested that Sandy might join him for a climbing weekend in North Wales over Easter. Geoffrey Summers, who was to be in the climbing party, had already mentioned this possibility to Sandy who had again responded with his usual eagerness, and Odell left Putney that evening with five tickets for the Boat Race and two recruits to his sledging party.

The Boat Race was held on Saturday 24 March 1923. The *Times* rowing correspondent assessed the two crews and came down slightly in favour of Oxford believing them to be the better crew by a small margin. He was much taken by the new design of their boat, which was held to be an excellent craft, sixty feet long, 24 ¾ inches at its widest point, and 9 ⅝ inches at the greatest depth.

It was a perfect spring day on the Saturday; a relief after the weeks of cold and rain, and the spectators turned out in their tens of thousands along the banks of the Thames. The Irvine and Summers families had teamed up for the race and were standing on the roof of Willie's younger brother Leonard's ice factory in Beaver Lane, Hammersmith where they had an excellent view of the middle part of the course. Odell and his guests were also watching from the factory roof, which was so crowded that he never actually met up with the families.

Oxford won the toss and chose Surrey, the more southerly station, with Cambridge on Middlesex. This gave Oxford the advantage of the big long bend after Hammersmith Bridge, but Cambridge had the best of the water off the start and then again over the punishing last section from Barnes Bridge to Mortlake. Cambridge rated slightly higher off the start but come the mile, Oxford had staved them off and had actually taken a lead of a few feet. When the crews reached Hammersmith and the cheering family crowd, Oxford were half a length in the lead, although Odell thought it was closer to a length and a quarter, from his perspective at least. At Chiswick, Oxford had increased their lead to two lengths, and there looked to be a chance they might even have the race well in hand. But Cambridge, magnificently stroked by W. F. Smith, Shrewsbury's strokeman and Sandy's Vice Captain from the 1921 Henley epic, put on a tremendous spurt to defend his water, and suddenly started to eat into Oxford's lead. As the crews came round the long, insidious final bend still in Cambridge's favour, Oxford found that little bit extra and held out, getting home by three-quarters of a length in 20 minutes 54 seconds – just two seconds between the crews. It had been a titanic struggle, deemed by all the critics to have been nothing short of magnificent.

Judging by the photographs of the crews seconds after they crossed the finishing line, Sandy was completely rowed out. He lies slumped over his oar in a state of utter exhaustion. He had given his usual 110 per cent.

News of the result was received on the ice factory roof via messenger and scenes of great jubilation could be heard as the Irvine party celebrated. The triumph, and the relief, in the Oxford camp were immense. It was their first win since 1913, also won by three-quarters of a length, and was to be their last until 1937. That evening the two crews joined seventy other old Blues for the Boat Race Dinner at the New University Club, an annual tradition renowned for its excesses.

Not only was the outcome of the race a great triumph for Oxford but Merton took enormous pride in the win. It was to be a quarter of a century before Merton College could boast another rowing blue and it was not until 1952 that a Merton man was in the winning boat. That year there were three and one of them was C. D. Milling, son of Geoffrey Milling, who was able to conclude a piece of family business and achieve what his father was deprived of in 1923. For the record the Race, rowed in a blizzard, was the closest and arguably most exciting Boat Race of the century, when Oxford won by a canvas, or ten feet.

After the victory of the Boat Race and the heady celebrations on the Saturday evening, Sandy joined Odell on the Sunday for an excellent lunch in Whitehall. Very much the toast of the party, he was in splendid form, turning a deaf ear to any of Odell's dire warnings about the hardships he and Milling might encounter on the Spitsbergen voyage. He was delighted, too, at the prospect of spending the Easter weekend climbing in North Wales in the company of Odell, Geoffrey Summers and his brother Hugh. From the lunch they wandered over to the Metropole Hotel, where they had tea with Dick and Geoffrey Summers and their stepmother, Marjory. Sandy returned to Oxford for further post-Boat Race celebrations while other members of the party dispersed in all directions, the Summers crowd heading back up to North Wales to make preparations for the climbing team's arrival at Highfield.

Born in 1891, Geoffrey Summers was Dick's eldest brother. He inherited from his mother a remarkable musical talent and distinguished himself by being the first amateur pianist in Britain to play Rachmaninoff's Second Piano Concerto in public, a work that makes enormous demands on the soloist. He spent all his working life in the family steel works, as was expected of him, but he was never at ease with the cut and thrust of business: at heart he was sensitive, an artist. He had learned to climb while he was a student at Cambridge. Initially suggested to him by his doctor as a diverting pastime, he was soon almost as devoted to the sport as he was to music, and became a very able rock climber. He met Odell at the Alpine Club and over the years they became close friends although he was never in the same class of mountaineer.

Odell left London on Maundy Thursday afternoon. Sandy had already arrived by train from Oxford and was installed at Highfield when he and his wife Mona arrived. After a good dinner and an excellent 'brekker' the following morning, the Odells, Geoffrey and the two Irvine brothers left for Capel Curig. Then, as now, Capel Curig was the major destination of all climbers in North Wales. From there the Snowdon range is easily accessible, as is the Carneddau range and, slightly further afield, the splendid rocks of Cader Idris, which boast some of the most spectacular mountain scenery in the area.

Odell was a meticulous diarist and kept careful jottings of each key place they passed, every familiar view he saw and everybody he met. They drove, via Ruthin, passing by the great shadowy hulk of Moel Famau and down into the Vale of Clwyd and across the Denbigh moors to Betws y Coed and then on to the Royal Hotel in Capel Curig where they were to be based for the weekend. They were a very congenial and cheerful party when they met up in Capel with Woodall, an old friend of Odell's, who was also spending his Easter climbing. It was a fair bet that Odell would meet several acquaintances and friends over the course of the weekend, so small was the climbing world at the time, but Sandy was nevertheless very impressed by the fact that people recognised him. That afternoon they made a brief excursion to clamber on some rocks near Capel and came back to the Royal for dinner.

The following morning they set off in glorious sunshine to climb the Great Gully on Craig yr Ysfa. The Great Gully was described by the Abrahams in their pre-First World War book on the rock climbs of North Wales, as a 'lengthy expedition of exceptional severity'. This was a far more technical climb than either Sandy or Hugh had ever done before, so Odell led and gave instruction. He noted in his diary: 'found great chimney v. wet & difficult, & after 2 failures to get above chock-stone, Sandy got up it with great difficulty a fine effort for 1st lead! I led remainder to top of climb: we all got v. wet in gully; took about 5 hrs, but v. fine climb.' Odell was clearly impressed by Sandy's ability to overcome the difficulties of the gully, referring to it in his obituary notice in the 1924 *Alpine Journal* as 'a brilliant lead for a novice'.

The following day the weather was not as beautiful as it had been on the Saturday, but the team, this time including Mona, was not daunted. They drove via Beddgelert, past the Pen-y-Gwryd hotel in Snowdonia, a hotel frequented by mountaineers both then and now, where the Odells had spent their honeymoon. The hotel's bars are full of climbing memorabilia and photographs of famous climbers who have stayed there. When I visited it recently with my father we were delighted to see a photograph of Sandy at Everest Base Camp in the bar.

The party had planned to walk and climb in the Cader Idris group which they approached from Dolgellau, a road that meanders along the shore of Llyn Trawsfynydd. They left the car on the road and went up the track to Llyn y Gadair from where they climbed a difficult buttress called the Cyfrwy Arête, a superb climb and always thrilling. It took about four hours to climb to the top, where they had lunch looking down an almost vertical drop onto Llyn Cau. There, according to Odell's diary, it hailed on them. On the summit of Pen y Gadair (2927 ft) the weather picked up and they were afforded magnificent views as they descended via Fox's path to the west of the lake Llyn y Gadair and back to the car. The whole excursion took a good twelve hours and they didn't get back to Capel until midnight.

On Easter Monday they drove to Pen-y-Pass which, in the pre-First World War years had played host to Geoffrey Winthrop Young's climbing parties in which George Mallory had frequently been included. From there they climbed Route II at Lliwedd in the Snowdon massif where they met Winthrop Young, David Pye and two other well-known Alpine Club members, Shott and Bicknell.

On Tuesday on their return from the hills they found a large Summers party at Capel who had arrived for dinner. Doris, Marjory and Dick Summers, who was presumably buttonholed to drive the ladies from Flint, left Capel Curig with Sandy after the meal and motored back to Highfield. Odell and Mona stayed on and left the following morning after breakfast, catching the train from Chester. Sandy had passed the test as far as Odell was concerned and moreover had impressed him with his strength, determination and agility.

Odell very quickly became a role model for Sandy. He had the knack of making people feel comfortable and Sandy responded to his gentle but perceptive humour. He was always happy to share his vast experience and as a superb raconteur he found a very willing and avid listener in his young protégé. What struck Sandy about Odell more than his climbing record and the contacts he had in the mountaineering world, two of whom – George Abraham and Arnold Lunn – he was subsequently to meet and who played a major role in his life, was Odell's ambition. Not only was he about to embark on a second Spitsbergen expedition but he was also on the short list as a member of the climbing party for the 1924 Mount Everest expedition and this did not fail to register with Sandy.

In the spring of 1923 Willie had taken a lease on Ffordd Ddwr Cottage, Llandyrnog which the family used as a weekend retreat. Sandy couldn't pronounce the Welsh spelling of the name so immediately christened it 'fourth door', a name which stuck for the two years the family had the house. How this tiny half-timbered seventeenth-century cottage accommodated the family and the children's university friends remained a mystery until I came across a photograph of the cottage with two bell tents standing in the field immediately in front of the house. The family regularly attended Sunday worship at St Tyrnog's church and the rector, the Reverend William T. Williams, was not only another Willie, but quite a figure in the locality. He was known as Pink Willie by virtue of his prominent red nose and was a keen supporter of the Irvine family, congratulating Sandy in the summer 1923 parish magazine on his rowing Blue and Evelyn on her hockey Blue. Sandy was staying in Ffordd Ddwr before he left for Spitsbergen and his adventures on that expedition, as well as on the Everest one, were closely followed by the locals. They took quite as much pride in their 'son' as others.

It was at about this time that Marjory, now twenty-five, really set her sights on Sandy. She had known him as a regular and entertaining visitor to Cornist as a friend of Dick's since early in her marriage to HS. A natural flirt and one who adored the limelight, she had begun to find Sandy increasingly interesting. In addition to his striking good looks and charming manner there had been added the heroic win over Cambridge in the Boat Race and with all its attendant publicity. It was, for Marjory, an intoxicating mix and one she was unable to resist. Sandy was surprised, delighted and flattered by her attentions and over the spring and summer of 1923 the flirtation blossomed into a none-too-discreet love affair. She loved to be seen with him and, to Dick and Evelyn's horror, turned up all over the place in his company. Marjory went to Henley where she conspicuously joined Sandy and his Merton friends; she took him out to the theatre in London, she joined in picnics and walks in Wales, not caring what anyone thought of her, and was a frequent visitor to Highfield, Geoffrey Summers's home, for Sunday lunch with Sandy. In the attitude to morals that prevailed in some circles at the begining of the last century, the most important criterion was the eleventh commandment, 'thou shalt not be found out'. But they were. Marjory unashamedly ignored the constraints and responsibilities of being married to an influential businessman. She threw discretion to the winds and, without a thought for the consequences, pursued Sandy single-mindedly and with abandon, in full view of the family. Her behaviour was seen as outrageous and deeply shocking.

Preparations for the Spitsbergen expedition took up a good deal of Sandy's time during the summer of 1923. In a frequent exchange of

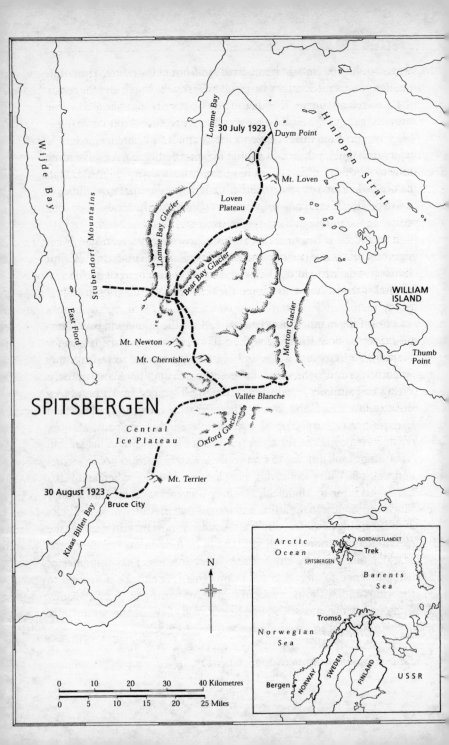

letters he received instructions from Odell about equipment and clothing. Sandy's aneroid barometer and compass were the subject of much of the correspondence. The barometer required calibration and the compass had to be filled with 60 per cent absolute alcohol since the usual 40 per cent would freeze in the Arctic. Odell, utilizing Sandy's organizing skills, put him in charge of getting Milling properly kitted out with Shackleton[6] boots, crampons and skis and reminded him that the boat was leaving two days earlier than originally planned.

Odell himself was busy with his own preparations and also with the testing of the proposed oxygen apparatus that the 1924 Everest expedition would be taking with them the following spring. He had been appointed oxygen officer for the expedition and June 1923 found him climbing with Percy Unna, a climber-scientist and member of the Mount Everest oxygen subcommittee, on Crib Goch in North Wales assessing the kit.

George Binney was hoping that his expedition would be able to carry out survey work in the hitherto unexplored regions of the ice-capped island of North Eastland. The only maps in existence dated from the eighteenth century and were known to be inaccurate. In his expedition prospectus, a closely typed sheet of foolscap, he stated the aims of the expedition:

Exploration (if Ice conditions are favourable) of the many islands of the Franz Joseph Land or East Spitsbergen Archipelago or the coastline of North East Land.

It is further hoped to continue the work of the exploring party of the 1921 Oxford University Spitsbergen Expedition. They attempted to traverse from West to East Spitsbergen but were unable to complete it. It would be possible, working from the East Coast, to complete this important piece of work. Any observations the expedition can make on the coastline of North Eastland will be of importance, as practically nothing is known of portions of this coast.

Full data of the ice conditions and of the temperatures and such errors as are discovered in the charts (which are by no means perfect) will be recorded and placed at the disposal of the Admiralty on the return of the expedition.

Details of the natural history, glaciology and geology follow with the

6 Sir Ernest Shackleton, Antarctic explorer 1874–1922.

last paragraph alluding to the hunting and shooting of polar bear, walrus, whale, seal and reindeer. 'The expedition will first attempt to reach Franz Joseph Land. If headed off by the ice pack, we will make for the East Coast of Spitsbergen, and, given favourable conditions, attempt the circumnavigation of North Eastland (from East to West) and reach East Spitsbergen from the North through the Hinlopen Straits.'

The plan relied heavily on the weather and the state of the ice pack being in their favour but Binney's experience in 1921 had led him to caution: 'I have stated the possibility of the expedition work, but decisions can only be made on the spot. It is useless to formulate an accurate plan beforehand.' It was an ambitious venture for a small expedition team with only four to six weeks at their disposal.

Each member of the expedition had to pay £200 [£6000 in today's money] towards the cost of their second-class travel, their share in the charter of the ship and 'adequate food throughout the expedition', although alcoholic drinks were not included.

There was much interest in the expedition, particularly from the press, and Binney was called upon for interviews and, from the expedition itself, dispatches. Before leaving he told a journalist: 'The expedition is fully equipped for scientific work in the fields of survey, ornithology, geology, and the study of glacial conditions, and a collection will also be made of flora and fauna.' He added, 'It will be necessary to depend to some extent on "shooting for the pot", and it is hoped that reindeer and polar bears may be found as well as seal and walrus. In fact, the expedition has undertaken, if possible, to capture a walrus for the Zoological Gardens.' They could not however rely on the pot shot, and the sledging party, especially, had to cater for extreme conditions when they might be prevented from reaching the ship and therefore have to survive for a longer period on their rations. As they sailed from Newcastle on the SS *Leda* they had with them four and a half tons of provisions, enough food for one year, in part organized by Willie Irvine, who was acting as agent to the expedition. The press was particularly interested in the consignment of bull's eyes (peppermint sweets) which 'have a real value in the Arctic, as they are nutritive and stimulating in cold weather'.

Amongst the provisions that had been donated to the expedition were

Australian tinned meat, Oxford marmalade and sausage, biscuits from Reading, Grapenuts, and a consignment of port. Quite what a modern-day quartermaster planning a trip to the Arctic would think of that selection of foodstuffs I have no idea. They were also well prepared with large quantities of Pemmican, which is an emergency ration food comprising dried meat and fruits pounded and bound with fat. It keeps for a long time and is useful as it contains much nutriment for little bulk. Reliable sources assure me that it tastes horrible. In addition there were porridge, cocoa, prunes and raisins, sugar, brandy and tobacco. Other essentials that had been donated to the expedition, Binney reported, included a complete wireless telephony transmitting and receiving set, a portable gramophone, and a set of épées for fencing, adding 'which is about the only strenuous sport that can be indulged on a 100-ton sealing sloop'. The press was quick to pick up on the gramophone and A. T. Wilder's Hawaiian guitar and were delighted at the prospect of what might be transmitted via the wireless set.

Despite the amusement at the expense of the party, it was an expedition that was credited with having a serious aim and, on one occasion when Binney's dispatches were not getting through owing to problems with the wireless, there was very real concern expressed in the press for the safety of the members.

In a move that was to prove to be the death knell of her first marriage and deeply shocking to the family, Marjory decided to accompany Sandy as far as Tromsö. Her infatuation with him had gone further than it had with any of her previous flirtations with Army and RAF officers. She persuaded her friend, Dora Fox, described by my cousin as another '*femme fatale*' to join her. They saw the trip to Norway as a great and amusing adventure – the two of them with twelve young men to entertain. The contingent that left from the north-west of England comprised Sandy, Geoffrey Milling, Geoffrey Summers, Marjory and Dora.

They left Chester, missed their connection in Manchester but were fortunate to find that a later train would get them to Newcastle on time for the evening sailing. The expedition members were travelling steerage but the women had first-class cabins so special arrangements were made for the whole party to eat together in the first-class dining room aboard the ship. Geoffrey Milling was not amused by the state of his cabin and complained, in his diary, that it was 'a filthy hole smelling like a rabbit hutch and surrounded by drunken Norwegians'. But he soon cheered up at dinner when he discovered that Dora was entertaining and amusing company. Sandy was equally scathing about his berth: 'cabin was minute & smelt like a badger house, Bunks as hard as nails.' However, as he was making night-time forays to a first-class cabin he spent his time on the SS *Leda* in rather more comfort than his friends. When I was reading through Sandy's Spitsbergen writings in Merton College Library, I was very amused to see he had made a mention of this in his notebook, although it was omitted from his diary. They arrived at Bergen two days later and boarded the *Midnatsol*, in which they would sail to Tromsö. The accommodation on this boat was much more to their liking, Sandy sharing a comfortable cabin with Odell and Ian Bruce. As they sailed up the coast they stopped at Lodingen and then Svolvaer, where Sandy and Odell climbed the highest peak south-west of the town, which afforded them glorious views from the top.

The following day they arrived in Tromsö where they met their sealing sloop and, after a farewell dinner given by the ladies in the Grand Hotel in Tromsö, the adventure began in earnest. All the men had enjoyed having the ladies along to add a bit of colour and entertainment to the boat trip. Odell noted that the dinner was a 'very jovial occasion'; Milling wrote 'Marjory Summers and Dora Fox saw us off – I was very sorry to leave them. They have done a great deal to make life amusing so far this trip. Dora, especially, is first class.' Sandy made no mention of his feelings in his diary but drew a beautiful, fluid pencil sketch of Marjory's head in profile in his notebook for that day. Was he in love with Marjory or did he just see the affair as an entertaining diversion? From the drawings and other notes in his diary I suspect that she had, if briefly, captured his heart.

The job of shifting boxes from one boat to another and checking stores was something that took up a great deal of time on the expedition. Sandy, Milling, Binney and Odell spent over twelve hours on 21 July counting, checking, repacking. Sandy packed 2240 biscuits by hand, Milling noted. The *Terningen*, their sloop for the next six weeks, was finally loaded and ready to sail at 1 a.m. on 23 July. It was not a particularly auspicious start as the mist was 'so thick the ship's compass could not be swung properly'; then Sandy, A. T. Wilder, and Odell had to spend some time fixing and adjusting the wireless. In vain. As soon as they reached the open sea they encountered a huge swell with high winds and the aerial blew down almost immediately. The rough sea took its toll on the expedition members and they all retired to their bunks for four days, 'sick as hell and doped out on opium'. When the storm abated and the sea became calm they awoke to find themselves in a new world of startling beauty. Binney wrote in his dispatch the following day:

All were soon on deck, even the worst sailors among us, to see the wonderful first glimpse of a mysterious land of ice and snow and jagged mountain peaks. The first impression to the mind of a newcomer to this strange part of the globe is one of awe at the grandeur of the ice and snow, and the thought that it is all new and thousands of years behind the world we know in geological formation and development. The mountains are reminiscent of the Alps but the barrenness and bareness is new. Glaciers bigger than the biggest in Switzerland sweep down right into the sea.

Odell, visiting Spitsbergen for the second time, was still moved by the extraordinary beauty and vastness of the scenery. One senses that he was deeply fascinated by every aspect of the Arctic. He notes with real enthusiasm that Binney had found a beetle in a warm spring, which was identified by Elton as being the furthest north such a beetle had ever been found and only the third such beetle to be found in Spitsbergen. On 28 July they dropped Longstaff, Elton, Brown, Wilder and Frazer on the Reindeer Peninsula for hunting. Wilder shot two reindeer and Longstaff found sanderlings' eggs. The reindeer meat was cooked and made a good meal on the boat.

Whenever they had a moment to themselves during one of their frequent stops up the coast, Odell, Sandy and sometimes the two Geoffreys (Summers and Milling) would leave the main party and climb some rock, crag or glacier bank in the immediate vicinity. The climb they made on a glacier on 28 July was the first time Sandy had experienced ice climbing and despite falling into a crevasse[7] made good progress. Some

---

7 A crevasse is a deep crack in the glacier that is caused by the ice moving over terrain.

larger crevasses are easy to spot, but others open and close relatively quickly and as none of them knew the ground they were covering, the crevasses would have added some spice to the adventure. Milling, a novice climber, was rather overawed by the technicality of climbing using ropes, but he was enthusiastic, if wary of the crevasses, and enjoyed the rock section towards the top of the climb.

Up to this point the expedition had enjoyed the relative comfort of the boat, which was warm and dry, and they had had access to good food. Despite sea sickness during the first few days and the broken aerial, everything else had gone very much to plan. Their luck changed when they arrived at Whalenberg Bay which they found to be blocked with ice and plans for landing for their journey into North Eastland were frustrated. Anchored just north of the Eastern Foster Isles, they discovered, however, that they could land on the New Friesland side just south of Cape Duym. Sandy and Odell left the boat after lunch to reconnoitre and returned convinced this would be a good place for the sledging party to land. That afternoon, 30 July, they made their landing on the ice, using an unreliable and faulty motorboat to ferry the sledges and stores to the shore. Before they finally set off they returned to the sloop for a dinner of eider duck and reindeer and were then rowed ashore towards midnight by Binney and Geoffrey Summers, who took a cine-film of the landing.

They set up camp not far from the landing spot and went to bed in glorious sunshine at 4.15 a.m. There were four of them in the sledging party: Odell as geologist, Frazer as surveyor and Geoffrey Milling and Sandy as cooks, assistants, camp secretaries and for providing the often required brute strength.

Although August is deemed to be the best month for getting to Spitsbergen from the point of view of the accessibility through the ice pack, it is a notoriously bad time of year for mist. On the positive side, there is sun for almost twenty-four hours a day, so the expedition could make use of the clearer night-time sunshine and sleep through the mistier daytime light.

For the first ten days of the journey they worked and travelled by night and slept by day to get the best of the weather. During the day the mist and fog tended to descend and made their survey work as well as their travel difficult. By night, as the temperature dropped, the mist would clear and they would have bright light by which to trek and work. The camp had to be set up each 'evening' and struck each day after breakfast, and to begin with this process took several hours until they got themselves organized. They had two sledges each weighing over 500 lb to which were lashed boxes of food, equipment, two tents plus a spare, sleeping bags, clothes, cookers, skis, crampons and cameras. At the outset they used crampons to walk on the snow and ice. A crampon is a device that fixes to the bottom of a boot for walking on hard-packed snow and ice. In the 1920s the crampon was made of two articulated metal plates that attached to the underside of the boot by means of leather straps. The front plate had six or eight spikes about 3 to 4 centimetres long and the back plate four spikes. They were a fiddle to put on and had to be accurately fitted to the boots for maximum effect. One of Sandy's jobs on the boat had been to see that each sledge party member had crampons that fitted and to ensure that ski bindings were correctly adjusted to their ski boots.

He quickly took responsibility for overseeing that the supplies were checked, that all the equipment was kept in working order and the tents were properly erected each day. He made long lists in his notebook detailing the exact contents of the food boxes, so that if they decided to leave one sledge behind and proceed with the other, as they did on several occasions, they would not find themselves without something vital. He seems to have succeeded, as nowhere in the diaries is there any complaint about a lack of pemmican or raisins. He was frustrated, however, by several defects in the equipment they had and made a list in the front of his notebook for future expeditions to include socks that don't shrink and felt for under his sleeping bag.

They were living off a diet of pemmican and dried fruit, with biscuits for pudding. Geoffrey Milling was put in charge of the cooking and he took on this often unpleasant task without complaint. Water was no problem for them but snow had to be melted if they were unable to find a camp site by a stream. When they were confined to their tents by wind or snow they would take it in turns to crawl out of the tents, collect snow, fire up the cooker and prepare food and drink for the others.

After the first few days they realized that their progress on foot with crampons was slow. Both the sledges had sails and they tried erecting them and using the wind to help them cover ground more efficiently, but the going was rough and the ice 'hummocky' which meant that the only real method of progress was to pull the sledges behind them. Sandy wrote in his diary that the worst aspect of pulling the sledges in the early part of the journey was the fact that the ice had melted in the sun and the ground was very wet underfoot with frequent morasses or bogs; 'Exceedingly heavy going in soft snow & bad hummocks with sledge constantly bogged down made progress very slow ... all the glaciers look very black & many morasses kept our feet very wet & cold.' Odell also noted the bad going and wrote: 'Our Shackelton canvas boots let the water in badly and proved quite useless for this part of the journey over lower glaciers.' If the sun didn't come out when they set up camp it meant that they had to put on wet socks and boots the following day. When the weather was bright, however, they could hang their clothes out to dry and the camp quickly took on the look of a shambolic laundry room with boots hanging from the skis, underwear on the guy ropes and socks strung between the tents.

Despite the discomfort they were experiencing, the mood of the party was cheerful. Both Odell and Frazer were rewarded regularly with excellent finds for their geological and survey work. The views were breathtaking, when the mist cleared, and even Sandy, whose diary style is economical at best, allowed himself the occasional outburst at the wonder of the scenery: 'We left the sledge out in the glacier & climbed the summit we had chosen by a very steep scree slope. The view from the top was marvellous with the sun close to the horizon & a wonderful Alpine glow on all the snow summits.' Whenever they spilt up into pairs to work Odell and Sandy would team up for the geological study, while Milling and Frazer concentrated on the survey work, often disappearing for hours on end up some summit to photograph and take aneroid readings of the landscape.

After a few days of hiking on crampons, Odell decided that the party would be altogether more efficient on skis. Neither Sandy nor Milling had ever stood on skis before, but Odell and Frazer were proficient and encouraged them to try. The first few attempts ended in much hilarity and a considerable amount of wet clothing as Milling and Sandy floundered and tumbled whenever the slope went even gently downhill. But they soon got the measure of their skis and both made forays off from camp on more than one occasion just for the sheer pleasure of ski running. Their skis were very long by today's standards, about 230 centimetres, and were made of hickory, so that they were light and flexible. The 'binding' or fitting for the boot consisted of a very basic leather strap that was attached to the front of an aluminium plate on the middle of the ski. The heel of the foot was free. The leather straps were relatively strong but Sandy had to carry out running repairs on the skis throughout the trek. Milling, particularly, had problems with broken straps which was both frustrating and potentially dangerous. I found Sandy's Spitsbergen skis in April 2000 and although they look basic they are astonishingly light and still flexible, despite having spent the last seventy years in a disused squash court. When climbing on skis, they attached seal skins whose hairs prevented the skis from sliding backwards. Nowadays skins are artificial and are stuck to the bottom of a ski with very sticky glue. In Spitsbergen they had to tie the skins to the skis using thin rope which meant that if they were not tight they would slip off, which could be off-putting on a difficult piece of snow.

Early on they made a significant geological find – a lake with a strange feature which Odell described in his diary: 'From this point was visible another lake across a low ice-col to east of lake (drained) and on the surface of its waters Sandy noticed a whirlpool with the water churned up in great commotion and several smaller ones.' Odell realized that the whirlpool marked the outlet of the drainage from beneath the ice col and the lake above: 'The distance between the two lakes was about 1.5 miles and accounted for the great pressure of the water, which caused the whirlpool. The lake drained out into a rushing river, which ran into the Hinlopen strait.' Sandy and Frazer took photographs and Binney later hailed this discovery as one of the most important of the Spitsbergen expedition.

The weather was erratic and after 150 hours of glorious sunshine the snow on the neighbouring glacier had melted, leaving the snow in a very sticky condition which made progress slow. They had hoped to reach the rock carpet, which would afford dryer conditions, but were unpleasantly surprised to find some very deep morass into which Odell and Sandy fell waist-deep. As they were both wearing their skis they could do little but flounder around until Milling and Frazer arrived to pull them out. Soaked through and extremely cold, they pitched their camp on the snow and spent a very cold, wet night in their sleeping bags.

The following day started well enough. They were trekking towards the rock carpet and saw, as the mist cleared, their way across the heavily crevassed glacier to their goal. The colours of the rock cliffs varied from pinks and greys to browns and blacks. Odell was in his element and he and Sandy made copious notes about the rock formations until the mist came down again and they were obliged to resume their journey. They had found a flat spot to camp and decided to return for the second sledge which they had left some four miles back.

During the long return for the second sledge, it came on to snow very thickly and it was not until 7.30 that Milling sighted it as we were moving extended out in line owing to the snowy atmosphere. After struggling through the very worst morassed ground plastered with sticky wet snow, we were obliged, owing to very bad clogging of the sledge and our skis to leave it again at 9 and make our way back the remaining 3 or 4 miles with the very worst of sticky snow obliging us to walk a good deal of the way.

It took Sandy and Odell two and a half hours to get back to the camp. Frazer returned an hour later and Geoffrey Milling, who had broken a ski strap, finally limped into camp at 1.30 a.m., four and a half hours after they had abandoned the sledge.

The matter of the marooned sledge was of great concern to the party, particularly to Odell who was at a loss to see how it could be rescued. While he and Frazer continued with their survey work, Milling and Sandy made their way back through the morass to the site of the stricken sledge. Odell recorded the mission: 'As a day could be saved by their doing so, Sandy and Geoffrey went off back beyond Camp 5 and spent a desperately strenuous day bringing No. 2 sledge up to Camp 6. The snow was fearfully sticky and the sledge sank deeply in: they took 4½ hrs in bringing it in, and were thoroughly tired out.' It was this superhuman effort, more than any other, which convinced Odell that

Sandy would prove to be a useful member of the Mount Everest expedition. He had shown not only ingenuity but also brute strength and persistence. He used this example in his recommendations to the Mount Everest Committee, pointing out that he really did not know how the two of them had achieved it. Sandy, with characteristic understatement, noted: 'After a very heavy day's work we got the sledge back but felt that we never wanted to see the damn thing again.' Milling explained the rescue effort in more detail. They had found it impossible to pull the sledge on skis and even on foot, as the runners had sunk too deep in the soft snow, but in the end at Sandy's suggestion they placed their own skis under the sledge between the runners, thus converting it into a Canadian sledge. His solution worked but even so they had an awful struggle to get home on foot and finally arrived at 9.30 p.m. (four and a half hours solid straining). 'Going up the hills was very hard work indeed. We were both very tired when we got in.'

As Milling and Sandy struggled with the sledge, Frazer and Odell set off on their own to continue their scientific work. They climbed up the glacier above Camp 6 and were rewarded with a marvellous view of Mount Chernishev, the mountain first scaled and thus named by the Russian expedition of some thirty years earlier, and one of their goals. From there they could see a range of peaks and identify three other geodetic beacons, Mount Loven, Black Mountain and Thumb Point, 'and so by resection established our position beyond question from the survey panoram. Photogs: this was a great coup!'

The following day Odell and Frazer caught up on their sleep while Sandy and Milling checked the stores. They were half-way through their journey and felt so confident in their supplies that they celebrated the reclaiming of the No. 2 sledge and Odell and Frazer's survey work of the previous day by opening their only pot of marmalade. That afternoon they succeeded in making the wireless work and were able to pick up Relf's time signal from the *Terningen*. A corner had been turned in more ways than one and they all felt triumphant at their various achievements.

At the next camp there was a little excitement in the form of a friendly Arctic fox that was nosing around the tents when Odell woke the following morning. Sandy was dispatched to the sledge where he collected his rifle and shot the poor creature. He and Milling then spent a mucky half-hour skinning it, which turned out to be a far more difficult task than either had anticipated. Milling was excited and thought that the fur would be valuable and insisted that they should keep it to sell when they got back to Norway. In the absence of any materials with which to cure the skin it soon began to smell dreadfully and had to be jettisoned. Milling, *chef extraordinaire*, cooked the fox but succeeded in persuading only Odell to eat it with him. Frazer and Sandy were both highly sceptical and preferred to stick to the pemmican.

On 16 August Frazer and Milling climbed Mount Newton, the highest peak in Spitsbergen, standing some 5880 ft above sea level. The same day Sandy and Odell took a different route and climbed an unnamed peak that had an imposing 1800 ft rock precipice which they proceeded to scale, reaching the 5500 ft summit after 'some pitches of considerable difficulty'. All in all they had had about 2800 ft of rock climbing. Odell, who had an encyclopaedic memory for climbs from the past, was quick to compare the climb with the Tower Ridge on Ben Nevis. 'The view from the top in every direction was stupendous, but above all generally to the westward where close at hand lay the group of rocky towers and summits: one huge rock peak rose steeply to a sharp gendarmed spitze, in appearance very like the Italian side of the Matterhorn, and looking impregnable from the east side ... The scene was as fine as any amongst the higher Alps.' The descent was via a steep snowfield, down over several hundred feet of easy rock and then along a steep ice precipice to the slope at the bottom of which they had left their skis.

At Mount Chernishev they discovered that the maps the Russians had prepared during their survey work were inaccurate. Frazer was pleased to be able to correct these and took a series of photographs for his survey under ideal conditions. Odell was keen to visit the site of the Russian geodetic survey so the four of them climbed up to the beacon where they found part of an iron Russian flag which had blown down. They kept the fragment as a souvenir deeming it to be irreplaceable. Sandy found a case with a max/min thermometer, which recorded a minimum temperature of −38.6° C. The max. column was broken so they could not accurately determine the maximum temperature. They also found a copy of a Russian newspaper from March 1901 and some other news-sheets. They replaced the thermometer and newspaper and left their own message which read: 'Visited by the Topographical party of the Merton College (Oxford) Expedition' which they each signed and dated. They were in fact the first visitors to the site since it was set up by the Russian Arc of Meridian Expedition in 1901.

All this time they were receiving radio messages from the *Terningen* which was now about seventy miles away from their current site. They had eight days to make the journey which they judged to be about enough time to cover the distance. They set off from Mount Chernishev in high spirits, finding a campsite that evening on a piece of moraine opposite the Oxford Glacier, which had been the focus of the 1921 Spitsbergen survey, and named one of its tributaries the Merton Glacier and the bay formed by its base Merton Bay.

The weather, however, had turned dramatically and they were buffeted by hurricane winds and blizzards for two days and three nights that kept them pinned in their tents. It gave Frazer and Odell the opportunity to write up their notes but Milling and Sandy became increasingly concerned about the distance they still had to cover before they met up with the *Terningen*. During the time they were holed up they exchanged stories of past adventures. Odell had a fund of wonderful tales which amused and impressed them all. He was a great raconteur and told many stories of his Alpine adventures. He then related an incident when he and Mona had been walking in North Wales a few years earlier and had encountered an intrepid young motorcyclist who had asked them the way to Llanfairfechan. Sandy recognized himself in the story and produced from his pocket his wallet with the press cutting to back it up. When they had recovered from their mirth, and with their fund of tales now exhausted, Odell began to talk about the forthcoming Mount Everest expedition of which he was a member. He found a very willing audience, particularly in Sandy, who questioned him on every aspect of the expedition he could think of. Odell had only recently returned from a couple of days in North Wales with Percy Unna, when they had tested the proposed design for the 1924 oxygen apparatus. Sandy was immediately fascinated and he and Odell spent hours discussing the apparatus. He made sketches in his notebook of details of the valves and flowmeters that were evidently presenting problems. He made several useful suggestions and it must have dawned on Odell fairly quickly that Sandy would be just the man to have helping him with the oxygen. His strength, resilience and good humour had been tested to the limit over the last few weeks, so on that count he was well suited, but more importantly, from Odell's point of view, he was clearly something of a mechanical genius and would be able to take over the responsibility for the capricious apparatus.

The conditions that confronted them when they emerged from their tent on the morning of the third day were as bad as any they had encountered on the early part of the journey: 'The snow was the very worst for ski-pulling adhering in large clods to our ski and making the worst of travelling. We were all very stiff and out of condition after three nights and two days in inactivity in a very damp tent.' In addition, Odell had strained a muscle in his shoulder shortly after they had left their last camp and was unable to assist with the towing of the sledges, which made far more work for the other three men. After several hours of trudging along in the snow and fog the view began to clear and they were rewarded with a brilliant view of Klaas Billen Bay, their final destination. Sandy and Milling erected the sails onto the sledges and made excellent forward progress in the strong wind, although controlling the sledges on ski was rendered difficult by the condition of the snow. There were several mishaps but no calamities. Odell and Frazer were skiing slightly ahead of the sledges with the object of finding the best route. 'The mist cleared and the delicate pinks and ultra-blues of the horizon and sky, the pure ivory white of the fresh snow and the deep blues and browns of the surrounding crags made a scene of the utmost beauty and rarity and probably only to be seen in a region such as this.'

After running in tandem some distance and having fairly frequent spills, the sledges being blown over with the freshening wind, they lashed them together broadside-on with the sails swung out on either side for stability, and Sandy and Milling managed them, while Frazer and Odell skied separately. They found the glacier relatively smooth and all but the widest crevasses were filled with snow making their progress quite easy. They pitched their final camp on a rocky outcrop above Billen Bay in glorious sunshine. 'The view was grand in the extreme with the N. face of Mt Terrier right opposite, the imposing group of Urmston Mt Robert & Cadell to the right of it, and beyond the dark stormy waters of Ice Fjord a perfect glimpse of the mountains at the back of Advent Bay drawn out to Mount Starachin at the entrance to Ice Fjord, 60 miles away, reflecting the golden evening sunlight.'

An hour after they crawled into their sleeping bags a terrific storm blew up with hurricane force winds which snapped the guy ropes on Sandy and Odell's tent causing it to collapse on top of them and trap them. They were rescued by Milling and Frazer who braved the storm and, after a very heavy struggle, succeeded in righting the tent and making it secure. They then lay awake for the next nine hours as the storm raged, wondering whether the tent and poles could survive the onslaught. They were amazed that the fabric of the tent was robust enough to withstand the battering and Sandy was impressed when Odell informed them it was made of the same material, aeroplane fabric, as used for the higher Everest tents. Sitting in a tent, miles from rescue, is an alarming experience. There are many accounts of how people have survived such storms and they all share the same theme – the tremendous noise of the wind snapping at the fabric, tugging at the ropes and wondering, just wondering when the storm will abate.

At about 9 a.m. the storm blew itself out and the party emerged tired and dazed to a wild day with angry storm clouds hugging the surrounding summits. Despite their relief at having survived the night intact they were sad to leave their last camp and head for the relative civilization of the *Terningen*.

They arrived at the Mount Terrier moraine towards evening after a painful journey across morasses, hummocky ice and gaping crevasses through which they had to weave a careful course. Sandy spotted the *Terningen* in the distance and fired off several rounds with his rifle in the hope that they would be noticed. It was at about this time that Longstaff, scouring the moraine with his telescope, trained it on the party. Contact. As they made their way over the ice and dirt coves Odell noted that they had hardly changed their position since 1921, amazed at the very slow progress of the Nordenskiold glacier. They found a 1921 jam tin beside one of the hummocks. A little further on they found an abandoned sledge with tins with Russian writing on them. They concluded that this would have been the sledge left by Vassilier and Backlund on their journey to Cheydinnes in 1901. Odell added: 'Sandy took bearings from the sledge's position onto known points in order to compare it with the position at which actually abandoned by the Russians and so obtain a measure of the rate of flow of the glacier over the period.'

About a mile on they spotted a man on the glacier, who turned out to their relief to be Longstaff. He was soon joined by Binney, Summers and Bruce and, eventually, Elton. The meeting that followed was an emotional one with exchanges of stories and news of discoveries. With extra hands to assist they were able to cover the remaining bad ground to the shore in two and a half hours, their arrival at the motorboat captured on cine-film by the camera-ready Summers.

At the shore Binney regaled them with port, digestive biscuits and chocolate which they all found 'delicious to an amazing degree' after a month on a diet of pemmican and dried fruit. As they were loading up the motor boat and dinghy they were alarmed by a series of dramatic ice falls from the glacier, some of which caused miniature tidal waves that threatened almost to upset the boats. An hour later they were safely aboard the *Terningen* after a beautiful run down Adolf Bay in the motor boat, and were sitting down to a splendid dinner in their honour.

After four days' sailing, catching up on sleep and food, playing bridge, shaving, getting stores and equipment sorted, they arrived in Tromsö where Binney and Summers arranged for them to take one step closer to civilization, organizing rooms in the Royal Hotel, where after hot baths they were entertained by Geoffrey Summers to a champagne dinner in honour of his and Milling's birthdays.

By rights this should have been the end of the expedition but they had a three day wait in Tromsö before their ship left for Bergen. Odell had planned to tackle a serious rock climb on Jaegerrasstind, a peak in the Lyngen Alps. A team of four climbers, Odell, Sandy, Summers and Milling, took a small boat down the fjord to where they disembarked, had breakfast on the shore and set off at 5 a.m. for the mountain. It was a walk of about five miles through forest and over boulders. When they arrived at the foot of the rock face, 1000 feet above sea level, they were presented with a fifty pitch climb to the 5500 ft summit. Odell and Sandy took it in turns to lead up the rock face while Summers and Milling followed. It would be putting words into Sandy's mouth to say he was frustrated by the slow progress of the group as a whole on the face, but twice in his notebook he records his and Odell's climbing rates to be considerably faster than those of the other two. After twelve hours of strenuous climbing up difficult and often treacherous rock, they were forced to concede defeat and turned to descend, only three hundred feet from the summit. Odell lectured them on the importance of a sensible turn-around time and on the significance of conserving sufficient energy for the descent, a critical and valuable lesson for Sandy. The descent was hard work and took over five hours, scrambling over boulders and down slippery tracks, through the forest and back to the shore where they all fell asleep waiting for the boat to collect them and take them back to Tromsö.

The Spitsbergen expedition had been a great success for Sandy. He had had a taste of many of the types of hardships he would encounter on the Mount Everest expedition and had shown himself to be, in every area, an excellent team member. His mechanical expertise had been called upon when it was left to him to fix the aerial aboard the *Terningen*, but also *en route* whilst sledging when many small running repairs were effected without the slightest problem. He had proved himself to be fit, able and above all to exhibit at all times excellent humour despite the cold and the damp, the frustrations of hauling the sledges across difficult ground and living in the primitive conditions under which he was only able fully to undress and dry out on one single occasion. If Odell had needed any convincing that Sandy was the right person to recommend for inclusion in the 1924 team, he had had ample reason to feel his choice had been fully validated by Sandy's performance on the sledging party. Moreover, during the long hours they had spent holed up in their tent towards the end of the expedition, when he and Odell had discussed at great length the subject of the oxygen apparatus, it became clear that in Sandy he had discovered a man who would be capable of helping to produce and maintain functioning apparatus.

Although a place on the 1924 Mount Everest expedition was not in Odell's gift, he knew that any recommendation he might make to the committee would be considered. There was the added bonus for Sandy that Tom Longstaff, on whom he had already made a very good impression was appointed a member of the independent selection committee

87

that considered, in the Autumn of 1923, the make-up of the climbing team.

Sandy did not need to be asked twice and Odell offered to put his name forward if someone could be found to second the proposal. Clearly Longstaff was out of the question because of his place on the selection panel. No one in Sandy's circle would have had any clout with the Mount Everest committee itself, but Odell, once again, was able to produce a useful contact for him in the shape of George Abraham, the Keswick photographer whom he had known for over a decade. Odell recommended to Sandy that he should make contact with Abraham, whom Sandy knew only slightly in his capacity as a photographer. He agreed to do this and asked Odell in what other ways he should prepare himself for the expedition. As his only experience of snow had been in the Arctic, Odell suggested that he might consider going to the Alps in the winter for some skiing and climbing in order to learn more about snow and ice conditions. Again he had a useful contact and put Sandy in touch with his old friend and the doyen of British skiing in the 1920s, Arnold Lunn.

Equipped with these names and a list of reading material, Sandy returned to England from Spitsbergen as fired up as he had ever been in his life.

4

The Fight with Everest

I have never known a man so entirely dominated by the spirit within him.
E. F. Norton, on Mallory

When I first began to consider writing about Sandy Irvine I realized that I would have to tackle the subject of the greatest Everest legend of all time, George Leigh Mallory. His and Sandy's names have become inextricably linked as a result of what befell them on 8 June 1924, but the lives of the two men had no bearing on each other until they met in Liverpool in February of that year. When Mallory first climbed in the Alps, Sandy was only two years old. My greatest concern, however, was that I would find myself standing in judgement over Mallory and blaming him for the death of my great-uncle. In fact I now do not hold him responsible for Sandy's death because I believe that by the time they made their final climb in the attempt to reach the summit Sandy, ever his own man, was possessed of the same determination to climb the mountain as Mallory.

George Mallory's name is so intimately entwined in the story of the early Everest adventures, his presence so great and his spirit so dominating that he cannot be dismissed with a brief résumé of dates and achievements. In his adult life he was consumed by two over-whelming and ultimately conflicting passions – his love for his wife and his obsession with Everest. At least three biographies of Mallory exist and he features in several other books, so that his life is as well documented as Sandy's is not.

George Leigh Mallory was the elder son of the Revd Herbert Leigh-Mallory, a devout and conventional man, who was rector of the parish of Mobberley, a Cheshire village about twelve miles due south of Manchester. He was born in June 1886 and was followed by a sister and brother, his older sister Mary having been born in 1885. His childhood was spent in Mobberley, from which time there exist a number of stories about his fearless climbing pranks. At seven he was banished to his room at tea time for unruly behaviour and was shortly thereafter discovered climbing about on the church roof. 'Walls, roofs and trees seemed to be his natural playground. No very unusual one, it is true, but ... at this early age he was scarcely affected by any sense of personal danger.' Other anecdotes survive that point to his undertaking activities with the minimum margin of safety. This trait in his character inclined him, later in life, to catch trains with a matter of seconds to spare, infuriating his friends but pleasing him as he had not wasted any unnecessary time. He was described by his earliest biographer, David Pye, as a 'dashing rather than a good driver of motor-cars'.

In September 1900 he won a scholarship to Winchester College where he turned out to be a good pupil, an able athlete and a talented gymnast. His academic forte was in mathematics but he took up History with a view to obtaining a scholarship to Cambridge. His judgement was sound and in 1905 he was awarded an Exhibition to Magdalene College, Cambridge.

His school days at Winchester brought him into contact with Graham Irving, his housemaster and one of the first men to adopt guideless climbing in the Alps. In 1904 Irving invited Mallory and his friend Harry Gibson to join him at his summer home in the Alps. Mallory was eighteen. He had no climbing experience at all and had shown no interest at Winchester in matters to do with mountaineering, but after two exciting climbs with Irving including a traverse of Mont Blanc, he was enthused and converted to the cause. From that moment climbing became one of the dominating forces in his life. It gave him release in times of strain, a challenge when one was lacking in his working life and, in the end, the avalanchine passion that cost him his life. The following summer he was again invited to join Irving, this time in Arolla, with two other schoolboys, one of whom was Guy Bullock.

After that summer Mallory went up to Cambridge and it was a few years before he was able to go back to the Alps. At Cambridge he developed his ideals as an aesthete and became involved in debating and political discussions, which he relished. He had a glittering circle of friends, many of whom had connections with the Bloomsbury set. In addition to his academic and political interests, Mallory continued with sport at Cambridge, rowing in the Magdalene College boat in the Easter terms.

In 1909 he was introduced by a mutual acquaintance to Geoffrey Winthrop Young, ten years Mallory's senior and at that time at the peak of his Alpine career. Not only was Young regarded as the foremost Alpine mountaineer of his generation, he was also credited with being responsible for encouraging British rock climbing and held regular 'meets' in North Wales when he would invite prospective and seasoned climbers to join him. They would stay in the Pen-y-Pass hotel in Snowdonia and spend long days on the cliffs while the evenings were devoted to socializing and impromptu theatricals. Mallory was quickly included in Young's inner circle although he was not apparently as at ease with the sociability as Young. What he shared with the older man, however, was a deep love and understanding of the mountains. This perhaps is one of the clues to Mallory's personality. He climbed with feeling, above all.

He joined Young in the Alps in the Summer of 1909 where the two of them did several training climbs before setting off with Donald Robertson for a traverse of the Finsteraarhorn by the difficult southerly arête. There were several anxious moments during the climb, including an instance when Mallory, accidentally forgetting to attach the rope to himself and delicately perched on a tiny foothold, was surprised by a clatter of rocks when Robertson slipped as he was attempting to reattach the rope. Mallory turned round to see what was happening and Young closed his eyes, sure that the next thing he would hear was Mallory tumbling down the 5000-foot glacier. Mallory, however, had supreme balance, and remained safely on the rock face, apparently completely unconcerned by the incident. Young wrote later, 'he was as sure-footed and as agile in recovery as the proverbial chamois'. The security of the rope meant little to him. The fact that he forgot to tie on when making that climb is an example of his absent-mindedness, something he was noted for even on the Mount Everest expeditions. In one of the last notes he sent down from the high camp on 6 June 1924 he wrote that he had left his compass in the tent at Camp IV. Such forgetfulness may be an endearing trait on the one hand but in the context of mountaineering it can be dangerous in the extreme.

On leaving Cambridge he worked in various temporary jobs and spent a few months in the South of France perfecting his French. Eventually he settled down and accepted a post at Charterhouse School as an assistant master. He believed in the 'civilizing force of education' and encouraged the boys in independent thought. He promoted extramural activities and taught about world affairs and literature, all of which were considered extracurricular, but to which he attached great importance. All this time he was climbing regularly in Wales and in the Alps. In 1911 he made an ascent of Mont Blanc which was, for him, as much of an emotional experience as it was a feat of mountaineering. He wrote a long article in 1914 entitled 'The Mountaineer as Artist' which was published in the *Climbers Club Journal*. In this article he distinguished between two types of climber: 'those who take a high line about climbing and those who take no particular line at all'. He described the importance of climbing to the former type, of which he regarded himself as a member, that it is more than just an athletic pursuit: 'Every mountain adventure is emotionally complete. The spirit goes on a journey just as does the body, and this journey has a beginning and an end, and is concerned with all that happens between these extremities.'

In 1914, when taking part in an amateur dramatic production in Godalming, he encountered the Turner sisters, whom he had previously met at a dinner party. Their father, Thackeray Turner, was a local architect and had built a beautiful home in the style of Lutyens in Godalming. Mallory became a regular visitor to the house and enjoyed not only the company of the three girls, Marjorie, Ruth and Mildred, but also that of Turner himself. They would have long discussions about art history, a subject that interested him deeply since his meeting and subsequent friendship with the English impressionist painter Duncan Grant. When the Turners invited him to join them in Venice for the Easter holiday he leapt at the chance. Venice was glorious, and Ruth Turner captured his heart. Within a week of returning to England he proposed to her. They were desperately in love and married in the July, only a few weeks before the outbreak of the First World War, spending their honeymoon in

Cornwall. Ruth's beauty, Mallory claimed, was Botticellian: she had a rounded, tranquil face with large blue eyes and wore her hair in a style which reminded him of the Pre-Raphaelites. As a personality she was honest and completely lacking in guile. His friends were as enthusiastic as he was and agreed they made a good-looking as well as ideal couple. They settled down to life in Godalming and Mallory continued with his teaching. Ruth herself was a gifted rock climber but the birth of their children prevented her from joining Mallory other than very infrequently, so that his climbing was essentially his private pursuit, although he did not exclude her from his thoughts and decisions about it.

Teaching was a reserved occupation and it was not until 1916 that the headmaster of Charterhouse permitted Mallory leave to go to the front where he served as a gunner in the Royal Garrison Artillery. Although he enjoyed the campaigning and organizational aspects of the army and was relieved that he was not fainthearted about the horrors he beheld, he was nevertheless sickened by much that he saw. He came back to Britain to have an operation on an old ankle injury, sustained in a climbing accident at Thurstaston quarry in 1909 after which he had not sought proper treatment. Following his recovery he returned to France for the last few months of the war, when he found he had more time to write, think and read than he had had before. In the meantime two of their three children, Clare and Beridge, had been born and Ruth had her hands full caring for the girls and organizing their new house in Holt.

After the war Mallory returned to teaching but was never as content as he had been before. He continued with his climbing but the discontent grew and he knew that he would have to seek a greater challenge. In the spring of 1920 he was climbing in North Wales with Geoffrey Winthrop Young, who was trying to learn how to climb again, having lost a leg in the war. Young had heard that there was a planned expedition to Everest and even contemplated going himself but then realized that the proposal was wholly unrealistic. He talked to Mallory about the expedition and encouraged him to consider the possibility of leading the climbing party. The seeds of an idea were sown although when the invitation from the Mount Everest Committee arrived his initial reaction was to refuse out of concern for Ruth. On receiving word of Mallory's refusal, Young

visited them in Holt and after twenty minutes of talking up the pos-
sibilities that would follow if he reached the summit Mallory and Ruth
were convinced, and Ruth told him to go to Everest.

It was not until 1852 that the mountain recorded simply as Peak XV
was even understood to be the highest mountain in the world. The
British Survey in India was occupied in the nineteenth century with
surveying and mapping India and the Himalaya. As successive peaks
were measured there was growing interest in which mountain might
prove to be the highest. The story, founded no doubt on fact but which
has taken on a somewhat mythical status, is as follows. The Bengali chief
computer, a man rather than a machine in those days, rushed into the
office of his superior, Sir Andrew Waugh, exclaiming: 'Sir! Sir! I've
discovered the highest mountain in the world.' After a series of lengthy
analyses of the computations by means of a series of triangulations, Sir
Andrew Waugh felt confident enough to announce, in 1856, that the
Survey could confirm it had established that Peak XV was 'probably the
highest mountain in the world', standing 29,002 feet above sea level.[1] Its
closest rival in the Karakoram, K2, had been assessed at 28,156 feet.

This important revelation brought with it the desire to give the mountain a suitable name. Ignoring the generally accepted tradition of adopting local names for geographical places, Sir Andrew suggested that the
mountain should be named after his illustrious predecessor, Sir George
Everest. Sir George, during his tenure at the Survey of India, had insti-
gated most of the work of establishing the Great Arc of the Meridian.
Ironically Sir George was against the idea of the naming of Peak XV
after himself, but nevertheless the mountain soon became known as
Mount Everest. Its Tibetan name, Chomolungma, 'Goddess Mother of
the Land',[2] was ignored.

By the 1890s there were serious discussions amongst British mountaineers and explorers about the problems that climbing Mount Everest
might pose. Prior to that it was not known whether man could climb

1 Everest's height was later calculated to be 29,028 feet, so the computer had been extraordinarily accurate. Modern-day calculations have revised this still further upwards and
Everest's summit is sometimes recorded as 29,035 feet or 8850 metres.
2 Chomolungma is translated variously as 'Goddess Mother of the Land', 'Mother Goddess
of the World' and 'Mother Goddess of the Snows'.

so high or whether indeed human life was sustainable above 25,000 feet. It seemed clear to the main parties involved in this speculation, amongst them Capt. Charles Bruce and Francis Younghusband, that any attempt to climb the mountain would have to be preceded by a reconnaissance mission to map and chart the immediate environs of Everest and to plot a possible route to the summit. Relations with Tibet and Nepal were particularly fragile prior to the First World War and the then secretary of State for India, John Morley, vetoed a proposal put forward by Lord Curzon, Viceroy of India, to seek permission to mount an expedition to approach the mountain.

By now the seeds of interest had been sown and several people were occupied with contemplating seriously the possibility of climbing Mount Everest. In 1913 Capt. John Noel took leave from his Indian regiment to make an illicit reconnaissance of the mountain by means of a route through Tibet. He was able to get within forty or fifty miles of the mountain before he was turned back by armed guards, and was very nearly court-martialled for entering a foreign country without permission. Fortunately his service was required in the First World War and the court martial was dropped. Noel's plan was to make the foray and report back his findings to Col. Rawling who planned an expedition to the mountain the following year. This expedition had the blessing of the Alpine Club and the Royal Geographical Society, but it was stopped by the events of the Great War.

After the war, relations between Britain and Tibet were not improved, but the desire to take an expedition to the mountain had reached new heights. In 1919 Francis Younghusband was appointed President of the Royal Geographical Society. He later wrote of the 'spark which set flame to the train'. There was a meeting in London that year of the Royal Geographical Society. Captain Noel was asked to deliver a lecture on his reconnaissance trip of 1913. 'He made no reference to anything more than approaching the mountain: he made no suggestion of attempting to reach the summit.' The lecture was followed by a discussion in which Capt. Percy Farrar, then President of the Alpine Club, announced that the Club 'viewed with the keenest interest the proposal to attempt the ascent of Mount Everest'. It was the impetus that was required to reassess Britain's relations with Tibet and to put forward the proposal of a serious reconnaissance expedition to Mount Everest. The Alpine Club, Farrar proposed, would not only make available what financial aid it could but would be prepared to suggest the names of two or three young mountaineers who, he felt, would be qualified to deal with any 'purely mountaineering difficulties that were likely to be met with'.

Younghusband, who was sitting next to Farrar at the meeting, got to his feet. He reminded the meeting that he and Charles Bruce, then Captain, now General Bruce, had considered twenty-six years previously the proposition of 'going up' Mount Everest. He vowed that during his presidency of the Royal Geographical Society, he would make 'this Everest venture' the main feature of his three-year term. He felt that his in depth knowledge of both the Tibetan government and the government of India would put him in a particularly good position for initiating such a project. He also felt the combined strengths of the RGS and the Alpine Club would be able to draw on the greatest expertise that was available at the time.

Action followed quickly. The Mount Everest Committee was formed, taking members from both the Alpine Club and the Royal Geographical Society. Younghusband had on more than one occasion to defend his position as Chairman of the Mount Everest Committee. Purists regretted that the formation of such a committee was required and felt that it would have been altogether more sporting for the mountain to be climbed by an individual on a personal mission. R. G. Irving, the schoolmaster from Winchester, who had first introduced Mallory to climbing, was a particularly stern critic. His objection was that the climbers on the Mount Everest expeditions were selected by a panel. 'The Everest expeditions are not the result of individual enterprise. The selection of the climbers and the payment of the cost are the responsibility of men of whom few have taken part in the actual climbing of the mountain.' Written as this objection was, after the death of Mallory and Sandy, it is possible that some of his misgivings stem from the belief that the climbers felt a pressure on them to succeed. Had they initiated the venture themselves, they would have only had to make mountaineering decisions and not concern themselves with the possibility that they might be letting the expedition down. He went on to regret the publicity that was now surrounding mountaineering, comparing it with the spotlight shone on the cricketers and footballers of the time. 'By all means let us encourage men to go on their own responsibility to climb the Himalaya and any other mountain, but do not let us set the ring for them as we have begun to do. Our great footballers, our great cricketers have become public entertainers, and we must accept the fact. Mountaineering is altogether unfitted to follow such a trend.'

Younghusband acknowledged that it might well have been more desirable for Everest to be climbed by a team of climbers that had initiated the expedition themselves but there were overwhelming reasons for that not working. First and foremost, Everest was not easily accessible, situated in one of the most secluded countries of the world, a country which rarely opened its borders to foreigners of all descriptions. Moreover, the Tibetans held the mountains in high regard as places of the gods, and they did not welcome the proposition of these holy sites being violated by foreigners. The British government was respectful of Tibet's deep sensitivities, so much so that even after the Mission to Lhasa in 1904 the India Office in London felt unwilling to ask permission from the Tibetan government for a British explorer to enter Tibet. Younghusband and the other members of the Mount Everest Committee felt, however, that whatever the India Office and the Tibetan government might not feel able to agree to on behalf of an individual, they might well consider a representation from such serious scientific bodies as the Royal Geographical Society and the Alpine Club. This was perhaps the overwhelming reason for the formation of the Mount Everest Committee.

Another, more practical reason, was that of organization and finance. Sending an expedition half-way round the world to explore unmapped territory leading up to the highest mountain in the world was a very expensive and complex proposition. The Mount Everest Committee was at its best thoroughly realistic. It realized that one if not two expeditions would have to be dispatched before the summit was finally reached. Younghusband wrote in 1936:

Ideally it would have been delightful if a band of happy mountaineers, accustomed to climbing together on holidays in the Alps, would have undertaken the tremendous task of tackling Everest. But in practice this was not feasible. At any rate, no such band came forward. And even if it had, the probability is that it would have been incapable of giving to the enterprise that sustained continuity of effort which the committee of a permanent society can provide. Thus it came about that the attack on Mount Everest was organized by a committee and not by an individual.

At the time of the first Everest expedition the highest point on earth was seen by many as the last great adventure. Both the Poles had been gained over the past two decades and the 'third pole', as some people chose to term Everest, was an adventure of equal importance and, moreover, a manifestation of the spirit of human endeavour. The challenge from the start was the unknown factor of altitude. It was not known if man could survive at an altitude of 29,002 feet; indeed balloonists who had aimed to reach such heights had died from lack of oxygen at 26,500 feet. Mount Everest was already an enigma – it had cast a spell and the committee felt bound to attempt to break the spell if it was possible to do so.

The committee invited George Mallory and George Ingle Finch, both widely regarded as two of the strongest Alpinists of the day, to make up the core of the climbing party. Finch and Mallory had great mutual respect but little affection for one another. From the outset Finch seemed to be at odds with the committee and, in the event, he was prevented from going on the 1921 expedition on slightly spurious grounds of his health. Despite his own misgivings about Finch's health and, to be honest, his ability to get along with him, Mallory was very concerned by the lack of strong Alpine climbers on the 1921 expedition. He privately considered it unlikely that either Alexander Kellas or Harold Raeburn would get above 24,000 or 25,000 feet, and after Finch was dropped Mallory was desperate about the prospects of getting to any height on the mountain. He finally succeeded in convincing the committee to include his old climbing partner and friend Guy Bullock, who was available at short notice, and the party set off for India.

When the first British expedition left Darjeeling in 1921 no European had been within forty miles of the mountain and nothing was known about Everest other than its height, latitude and longitude. The committee concluded, therefore, that the first expedition should have as its objective a preliminary reconnaissance of the region. With this in mind a team of surveyors, mountaineers, medical officers and interpreters was assembled under the leadership of Lt. Col. Charles K. Howard-Bury. Mallory with Guy Bullock represented the climbers on the expedition. Dr A. M. Heron from the Geological Survey of India accompanied Maj. Henry T. Morshead and Maj. Edward Wheeler, both from the Survey of India. Dr Alexander Wollaston was the medical officer and naturalist. Dr Alexander Kellas was a key member of the expedition: he had extensive knowledge of travelling in the Himalaya, having climbed over a period of seven years in Kashmir, Sikkim and the Garhwal Himalaya and had been the first mountaineer to ascend three of the great peaks seen on the Sikkim stretch of the march through Tibet: Chomulhari, Pauhunri and Kangchenjau. He was the only member of the team who had given serious thought to the possible routes up Everest. Prior to 1919 Kellas had been a chemistry lecturer at a London medical school. He and the celebrated scientist Professor Haldane had worked together and Kellas had conducted experiments in pressure chambers, concluding that bottled oxygen might well provide a help to climbing at altitude. He had made studies of the problem of acclimatization and was in fact the world's expert at the time on mountain sickness and on the problems of lassitude that affect climbing and other performance at high altitude. He was planning to undertake experiments using the gas as an aid to climbing on this expedition.

Tragically the expedition was robbed of Kellas's experience. He died of heart failure on the last high pass on the trek across Tibet, before the expedition had even reached base camp. His death was a tremendous blow to the expedition and Mallory personally was appalled by his loss. He had greatly looked forward to getting to know Kellas better and to benefiting from his unique Himalayan experience.

Howard-Bury had not been the first choice of the Everest Committee for expedition leader. They had wished to appoint General Charles Bruce but he could not be spared from the British Army at the time. Howard-Bury, however, travelling to India at his own expense, had been instrumental in gaining permission from the Dalai Lama[3] for a British expedition of climbers to go to Everest. This was rightly considered to

3 The spiritual leader of Tibet.

be a real coup after years of abortive applications via the India Office and the committee felt deeply indebted to him and his efforts. As this first mission had as its brief the reconnaissance of the area as its primary objective, the Everest Committee concluded, that it would be better to employ Howard-Bury in 1921 and to keep Bruce in reserve for 1922, when a climbing expedition would almost certainly be launched. Howard-Bury was, at forty, some five years older than Mallory. He had been brought up by his cousin the Viceroy of India and had developed at an early age a great passion for travel. He was widely respected as an excellent linguist as well as being a good photographer, a naturalist and a keen plant collector. His Victorian upbringing coupled with his career in the British Army had turned him into a strict disciplinarian. Mallory was wary of him and wrote to Ruth after their first meeting: 'He is well-informed and opinionated and doesn't at all like anyone else to know things he doesn't know. For the sake of peace, I am being careful not to broach certain subjects of conversation.' With Harold Raeburn, the Climbing Leader, Mallory also failed to form a satisfactory relationship. Before the expedition had even left England he had been exasperated with Raeburn's desire to cut down on the amount of climbing equipment, most of which Mallory considered to be essential. Raeburn did not see the reason for taking with them adequate clothing nor making provision for the extreme cold they would encounter at great heights. From the outset, Mallory believed the expedition to be fatally flawed. In the event, Raeburn began to exhibit worrying symptoms shortly after the death of Kellas and Wollaston decided he should be taken down quickly – the expedition could not afford another fatality. Raeburn's departure further weakened the climbing team, but Mallory persevered.

From Kampa Dzong, some forty miles from Everest, he gained his first sight of the mountain and the frustrations he was feeling with his fellow team members were instantly swept away as he stood, awe-struck, contemplating its size. He recognised Everest's neighbour, Makalu, and described the mountains in a letter to Geoffrey Young: 'That to the left must be Makalu, grey, severe, and yet distinctly graceful, and the other, away to the right – who could doubt its identity? It was a prodigious white fang excrescent from the jaw of the world.' Mallory was captivated.

The spell of Everest had caught his imagination and his enthusiasm began to shine through in his letters to Ruth. He reported to her: 'I felt somehow a traveller. It was not only that no European had ever been here before us, but we were penetrating a secret: we were looking behind the great barrier running north and south which had been as a screen in front of us ever since we turned our eyes westwards from Kampa Dzong.'

Later that day Mallory and Bullock climbed up a little hill above Chiblung and waited patiently for another glimpse of the mountain. He was not disappointed:

Suddenly our eyes caught ... a glint of snow through the clouds; and gradually, very gradually, in the course of two hours or so, visions of great mountainsides and glaciers and ridges ... forms invisible for the most part to the naked eye or indistinguishable from the clouds themselves, appeared through the floating rifts and had meaning for us – one whole clear meaning pieced from these fragments, for we had seen a whole mountain range, little by little, the lesser to the greater until, incredibly higher in the sky than imagination had ventured to dream, the top of Everest itself appeared.

Once the excitement of the first sighting began to fade, Mallory's mind began to focus on the problem of how best it could be tackled. He began to consider which approach would lead him to a place from which he could plan an assault on the summit. The real job had commenced.

Howard-Bury dispatched Mallory and Bullock with a team of Sherpas and porters to reconnoitre the approach to the mountain from the glacier at the end of the Rongbuk valley that he named the Rongbuk Glacier. Mallory ascended the glacier to near its source but was confronted by 'the most forbidding, utterly unclimbable cliffs'. There appeared to Mallory to be only one chink in the mountain's defences, a gap which later became known as Chang La or the North Col. This col, however, could not be reached from the source of the glacier so Mallory was forced to retreat and approach the mountain from the east side. From here he climbed up the ice fall to a height on the North Col of 23,000 feet from where he was able to survey the problem of the summit of Everest from a closer vantage. He reported to Ruth in a letter: 'For a long way up those easy rock and snow slopes was neither danger nor difficulty, but at present there was wind. And higher was a more fearful sight. The powdery fresh snow on the great face of Everest was being swept along in unbroken spindrift, and the very ridge where our route was marked out had to receive its unmitigated fury.'

By the middle of August Mallory and Bullock, who had by this time been joined by Morshead, found what they had been looking for, a breach in the mountain's defences. On 18 August they spotted from their point on the Kharta Glacier the East Rongbuk Glacier which ran north under the north-east face of Everest. A month later the weather, which had been stormy and rendered climbing impossible, cleared to give them another chance at the peak. Towards the end of September they ferried stores and made a camp at 22,000 ft, below the Col that Mallory had christened the North Col. Once again the weather was against them, this time in the nature of a ferocious wind which impeded their progress and forced them to descend. Nevertheless, the climbing route for the summit had been spotted and Mallory wrote to Ruth, 'It is a disappointment, there is no getting over it, that the end should seem so much tamer than I hoped ... As it is we have established the way to the summit for anyone who cares to try the highest adventure.'

Despite his mixed feelings Mallory was forced to admit that several valuable lessons had been learned from the 1921 reconnaissance expedition. One of the principal lessons was that they had approached the mountain at the wrong season, that is to say during the monsoon. It was soon realized, and is now taken for granted, that the best season for climbing Everest is in the Spring, after the winter cold has lessened and before the monsoon has begun. The reconnaissance mission had, in general terms, been a success. A possible route up the mountain, to the North Col at least, had been established and there was great optimism within the Mount Everest Committee that a substantial attack on the mountain in the spring of 1922 might well lead to success.

With extraordinary energy and efficiency, an expedition was put together for the spring of 1922 under the leadership of Gen. Charles Bruce. On account of his age Bruce would not be considered a member of the climbing party but he was a valuable member of the team nevertheless, as his own experiences in the Himalaya were considerable. He was charged with the responsibility of directing operations, organizing the expedition and, in particular, collecting local porters and enthusing them with an *esprit de corps*, a task for which he was most admirably suited. Charles Bruce was described by many of his contemporaries as a boy at heart. He was widely credited with having introduced shorts to the British Army, believing them to be less of an obstacle to climbing and scrambling over rough ground than trousers which were so easily holed at the knee. His humour was schoolboyish and it endeared him greatly not only to his fellow team members but also to the Sherpas, with whom he dealt with firmness but affection. The dispatches he wrote for the *Times* were frequently laced with repartie and his telegrams to the Mount Everest Committee were sometimes considered to be too flippant.

Under the leadership of Bruce the committee put together what they believed to be a very strong team. This time George Ingle Finch was to be included, as was Mallory, considered indispensable to the operation. The climbing team was further strengthened by the inclusion of two other formidable Alpinists of the day, Maj. (later Col.) E. F. Norton and Dr Howard Somervell. Younghusband considered these four men to be at the absolute 'zenith of their powers' and held out high hopes for the success of the team. Two other members of the 1921 expedition were included in 1922, namely Morshead and Gyalzen Kazi, an interpreter in 1921 and subsequently the Sirdar or head of the Sherpas in both 1922 and 1924. General Bruce's cousin, Capt. Geoffrey Bruce, was brought in to be one of the three transport officers; the veteran climber and explorer Dr Tom Longstaff was invited to be medical officer and chief naturalist; Dr Arthur Wakefield as another medical officer. Bruce appointed Lt. Col. Edward Lisle Strutt as deputy leader to the expedition and Colin Crawford and John Morris to help Geoffrey Bruce with transport matters. The predominance of climbers as opposed to surveyors on this expedition pleased Mallory and he felt more confident of their chances of success. Although he was no great friend of Finch he respected his climbing abilities and felt he would be a strong member of the team. Mallory also instinctively liked and trusted General Bruce who, he felt with good reason, would prove to be a supremely efficient expedition leader, which would free Mallory to concern himself only with matters to do with the mountain.

One of the most significant changes to the expedition was the decision by the Everest Committee to supply it with bottled oxygen. The two scientific members of the expedition, Finch and Somervell, both strongly favoured its use and were convinced of the benefits of using supplemental oxygen at altitude. They had both taken part in experiments at Oxford University in decompression chambers. This involved them exercising, stepping on and off a chair carrying a 35-lb load, in a decompression chamber where the pressure was lowered to simulate the effect of an altitude of 23,000 feet and their performance was monitored. Finch performed well, but Somervell 'appeared to waver after his fifth step'. He denied feeling any ill effects but 'his insistence was taken as a sign that he was exhibiting the quarrelsome characteristics known to be one symptom of hypoxia [oxygen deficiency], and oxygen was forcibly administered.' But the tests were crude and the sceptics were loath to attach any great importance to them. Finch noted in his diary that Somervell had suffered during the decompression tests at an altitude of 23,000 feet and concluded that he would advocate the use of the artificial gas only above that altitude.

The proportion of oxygen in the air is unchanged at altitude, remaining a constant 20.93 per cent. What changes is the atmospheric pressure, which decreases as the altitude increases. This causes problems for the body, which has difficulty making the necessary gaseous exchanges in the lungs. At 18,000 feet, roughly the altitude of Everest base camp, there is only half the atmospheric pressure that is found at sea level. At Everest's summit, 29,028 ft, the pressure drops to only one third of that found at sea level, and at this level the body is unable to survive for any great length of time. The level above 25,000 feet is therefore known, dramatically but accurately, as the Death Zone. Such exact information was not available in the 1920s but the scientists were well aware of the problems of performance at high altitude. There had been studies into oxygen depletion at altitude in the late nineteenth century conducted on balloonists. This research was known to the Mount Everest Committee and Hingston, the 1924 expedition doctor, refered to it at some length in his post-expedition paper submitted to a joint meeting of the

Alpine Club and the Royal Geographical Society in October 1924 and later published in *The Fight for Everest*. He noted that balloonists in Paris in 1875 made a rapid ascent to nearly 28,000 feet with catastrophic results: 'they were provided with oxygen but unable to use it. Tissandier [the balloonist] fainted at 26,500 ft, and when he recovered consciousness the balloon was descending and his companions were dead. The balloon had reached an altitude of 27,950 ft. This was a rapid ascent with no acclimatization. The result was death between 26,000 and 28,000 ft even when sitting quietly in a balloon.' Such a rapid ascent does not of course allow for acclimatization, another major factor in performance at altitude, but it did lead the scientists of the day to conclude that they were uncertain whether breathing would be at all possible on the summit of Everest. Further study into the subject had been undertaken by the Air Force whose pilots were suffering considerably as a result of oxygen depletion. Professor G. Dreyer, who had been a consultant to the Air Board on the subject of the use of oxygen at high altitude, had expressed his views even before the 1921 Reconnaissance expedition left Britain: 'I do not think you will get up without it', he had pronounced, 'but if you do succeed you may not get down again.'

We now know that it is possible, as proven by a number of climbers over the years, most notably Reinhold Messner and Peter Habeler, who made the first oxygenless ascent to the summit in 1978, that it is possible to reach the summit of Everest and return safely without the use of supplemental oxygen. As early as 1924, a record height of just over 28,000 feet was achieved by Norton and Somervell without oxygen, which record stood until Messner and Habeler's ascent. However, all this was to come after the 1922 expedition.

The use of bottled oxygen, or artificial air, was a deeply contentious issue from the outset, and there was ignited a furious debate that raged for many years. The pro-oxygenists argued that the mountain could not be climbed without it whilst the anti-oxygenists believed it to be unsporting to make use of an artificial aid to climb the mountain. Mallory belonged to the latter camp although he was less outspoken than some critics in 1922, commenting that climbing with such a weight and a mask over one's face held little charm. There are still those who will argue that the only true ascents of Everest are those made without oxygen, but it is widely recognized that it is by no means possible for everyone attempting the summit to succeed without it.

The first symptom of oxygen deprivation is an increased respiratory rate. The body fights to gain sufficient usable air and the heartbeat rises to 140 beats per minute. This, for many, is peak heart rate and thus the act of merely breathing exhausts the climber, for exercise can only effectively be carried out when the heart rate is below peak, although there are certain endurance athletes and elite climbers able to go on performing at maximum heart rate. The little research that had been carried out prior to the 1922 expedition had led to a basic understanding of the value of acclimatization but a real understanding of the problems of altitude did not exist. This led to a misreading of the symptoms of high altitude sickness and there was little comprehension of the effects of dehydration.

In 1922 the highest point reached to date was 24,500 feet, some 4500 feet lower than the summit of Everest. Scientists were still sceptical as to whether it was possible to go higher and survive in the thin air. Following the Oxford tests in Professor Dreyer's decompression chambers, Finch was convinced it was imperative that the expedition be supplied with oxygen. He was annoyed by what he regarded as 'slipshod thinking' by the anti-oxygenists, pointing out in a slightly spurious argument that the climber made use of several adventitious aids such as warm clothing, caffeine and anti-glare sunglasses – so why not oxygen? He concluded: 'if science could prepare oxygen in tabloid form or supply it to us in thermos flasks that we might imbibe it like our hot tea, the stigma of "artificiality" would, perhaps, be effectively removed. But when it has to be carried in special containers, its whole essence is held to be altered, and by using it the mountaineer is taking a sneaking, unfair advantage of the mountain!'

He had an ally in Percy Farrar on the Mount Everest Committee and it was agreed to set up an oxygen subcommittee, which would comprise Finch, Farrar, Somervell and another climber-scientist, P. J. H. Unna. The oxygen apparatus supplied by Siebe Gorman for the 1922 expedition was adapted from the standard apparatus used by the Royal Air Force. It was cumbersome, heavy – weighing some 33 lb – and complicated to use with tubing over the shoulder that frequently caught and snagged in front of the climbers' stomachs when they were ascending steep pitches. In addition, the heavy oxygen bottles were prone to serious leakages. All in all the apparatus did not hold any great attraction for its users and Younghusband was not at all convinced that the benefits outweighed the disadvantages of having to carry so great a weight. He wrote later: 'I confess that when I saw and lifted the complete outfit for a climber I was aghast at the idea of anyone being saddled with such a load. But if the men who would have to be carrying it were not deterred it was not for me to raise objection.' Arthur Hinks, a Fellow of the Royal Geographical Society and Secretary to the Mount Everest Committee, was an outspoken sceptic. Hinks was a geographer but had little, if any, knowledge of field work and what was involved in mountaineering. He frequently put people's backs up with his opinionated comments, seldom more so when he wrote, anonymously, in 1922:

A section of the climbers had convinced themselves or had been convinced that they would never reach the summit without it [oxygen]. The committee, feeling bound to supply whatever in reason might be demanded, cheerfully faced the large expenditure required. It is more than likely that some of the climbers will find it impossible to tolerate the restraint of all this apparatus, and will develop new and interesting varieties of the 'claustrophobia' that afflicts men shut up in pressure chambers or the diving dress. And this will be a good thing, because it seems to us quite as important to discover how high a man can climb without oxygen as to get to a specified point, even the highest summit of the world, in conditions so artificial that they can never become 'legitimate' mountaineering.

Farrar was infuriated that Hinks had gone beyond his remit and published such comments but Hinks was unabashed. He wrote to Farrar in April of that year: 'I should be especially sorry if the oxygen outfit prevents them going as high as possible without it. The instructions laid down by Dreyer say clearly that oxygen should be used continuously above 23,000 feet. That I am convinced is all nonsense. Wollaston agrees. If some of the party do not go to 25,000–26,000 feet without oxygen, they will be rotters.' Farrar retorted in a letter to Hinks that he was of the opinion that oxygen was not 'any more of an artificial aid than food.'

Such public differences of opinion within the committee did nothing to assist the pro-oxygenists' cause. There was an air of disquiet about the oxygen apparatus which pervaded throughout the expedition, to the extent that when Finch and Bruce reached a higher point with oxygen that year than Mallory, Norton and Somervell did without, his and Bruce's achievement remained largely ignored.

Finch was appointed oxygen officer to the expedition and took his duties seriously. He instituted oxygen drills on the boat to Bombay, which did not particularly endear him to Mallory. He claimed that it would take at least two weeks to learn how to use the apparatus properly, something Mallory dismissed in a letter to Ruth as fantastic nonsense, believing it would require only two days at the outside. Finch soldiered on with his oxygen drills during the trek across Tibet, frustrated that they usually took place after a long march when the climbers were tired and wanting rest. He bitterly resented the others' resistance to what he saw as the key to their success on Everest. Not only was he having to deal with his fellow climbers' aversion to the thought of climbing with the heavy apparatus, but he was troubled by its lack of reliability. The cylinders leaked badly and the rubber tubing worn around the front continually snagged on rocks during experimental climbs. General Bruce was highly wary of it, although he did arrange to have it ferried up the mountain as agreed, but wrote home to Hinks: 'Finch is working very hard at oxygen arrangements and getting people trained in the proper use of primus stoves etc, but I myself am rather terrified at the oxygen apparatus. It seems to me to be so very easily put out of order and also so liable to be damaged by hitting against rocks, or by catching its indiarubber tubing on rocks; also the change of bottles on steep slopes when the apparatus has to be taken off and readjusted by very weary and hungry men seems a danger.'

The 1922 expedition met in Darjeeling, as the 1921 expedition had done, and set out on the long trek through Sikkim and Tibet to Everest base camp on 22 March, travelling by foot or on ponies. The march took six weeks. The weather was very cold and they frequently encountered blizzards. Several caught colds and on one occasion General Bruce ordered a rest as he was so concerned for their health. Mallory was particularly concerned about the doctor, Tom Longstaff, who was showing worrying signs of ill health, and had in the back of his mind the death of Kellas the year before. Fortunately Longstaff recovered sufficiently and reached Base Camp on 1 May with the others, where they began to prepare for their assault on the mountain.

There are two recognized ways of climbing a mountain. One is known as Alpine style and the other as Siege style. The former requires the climber to carry with him everything he requires for an ascent and descent. The latter, which has been more or less uniformly adopted for climbing Mount Everest since the 1920s, requires the party to 'lay siege' to the mountain. Camps are established gradually *en route* for the summit and the climbers make forays from Base Camp to increasingly higher camps in order to acclimatize and give themselves the best chance of success on summit day. This also gives the porters time to carry food, equipment, tents and bedding to the high camps in preparation for a final push. There have been some notable Alpine-style assaults on Mount Everest, one of the most famous being that of Reinhold Messner in 1980 when he climbed the North Face of Everest alone with no support from Sherpas and with no fixed camps to aid him.

In 1922 Bruce had decided that at least five camps would be needed on the mountain in addition to the Base Camp at 17,800 feet. For the whole of May loads were ferried between Base Camp and Camps I, II and III and cooks were installed at each camp and the stores of food, oxygen and bedding were sent 'up the line', carried by teams of Sherpas and, frequently, by the climbers themselves.

The original plan had been for Mallory and Somervell to make an attempt on the summit without oxygen, followed by an oxygen attempt by Finch and Norton. Stomach troubles had been a recurring theme at Base Camp and Finch, suffering from dysentry, was laid low in his tent for several days. Bruce and the climbers were concerned that the monsoon would soon be on them so the plans were changed. Mallory, Somervell, Norton and Morshead took a team of nine porters up to the North Col from where they planned to set off early the next day and to climb into the uncharted territory of the upper mountain.

The night before this first attempt Mallory wrote to Ruth, 'I shall feel happier, in case of difficulties, to think that I have sent you a message of love ... It's all on the knees of the gods, and they are bare cold knees.'

The plan was to set up Camp V at 27,000 feet from where they would make their summit bid. In the event they had a very difficult time of it with bad weather and high winds and Camp V was established at 26,000 feet on precarious platforms manufactured out of stones which they dug out of the frozen ground. After an extremely uncomfortable night Norton, Somervell and Mallory left Camp V. Morshead, who was feeling too ill to continue, elected to remain in his tent and await their return. The terrain was treacherous, tilting slabs covered in snow, and their progress was woefully slow as they struggled to breathe in the thin air. By two o'clock Mallory realized that their mission was hopeless and elected to return, collect Morshead and descend to the North Col. Mallory concluded, as he told the Royal Geographical Society and Alpine Club joint meeting in London later that year, 'It would have been an insane risk to climb to the utmost limit of one's strength on Mount Everest and trust to inspiration or brandy to get one down in safety.' They had nevertheless set a new height record of 26,985 feet, nearly 400 feet higher than the record of the time.

Finch, meanwhile, having recovered from his illnesses, was determined to make his own summit attempt with oxygen and enlisted as a climbing companion Geoffrey Bruce. Although Bruce had no mountaineering experience Finch considered him to be strong, athletic and have the right mental attitude. The two of them and a non-commissioned officer, Lance-Corporal Tejbir, set off with porters and spent several days at Camp III preparing the oxygen apparatus. Finch made one or two forays testing out the oxygen and was delighted with the speed of their progress using the bottled gas. On 24 May they left for the North Col and, having reached it at 8 a.m., set off to make a new camp, higher, Finch hoped, than the previous high camp of Mallory's party at 26,000 feet. High winds prevented them reaching this height and they had to settle for a camp 500 feet below. All that night and the following day they were pinned in their tents by the fierce winds but at last the wind abated in the afternoon and Finch decided that the following day would be their summit attempt. Tejbir was unable to struggle beyond 26,000 feet but the other two carried onwards and upwards, reaching a height of 27,300 feet. At that point Bruce's oxygen ceased to flow and Finch saw him stumbling dangerously. He grabbed Bruce by the shoulder, saving him from falling backwards into oblivion and led him to the relative safety of a small ledge, giving him his own oxygen while he rigged up a T-piece to enable them both to breathe from his set. Bitter though it must have been for Finch, it was obvious that the two men could not possibly continue upwards and he was deeply concerned that Bruce was at the limit of his strength. They roped up and set off back down to Camp IV where they arrived 'deplorably tired' at about 4 p.m.

With two successive height records attained, one with and one without the use of supplemental oxygen, it might have seemed sensible to call it a day. All the climbers, with the exception of Somervell, had suffered in one way or another from frostbite, enlarged hearts and a variety of other complaints. Mallory, who was suffering from a frostbitten finger, was nevertheless determined to put together another team for a final summit attempt. Although he never admitted it, he was probably galled that Finch had climbed higher than he had and was determined to have another crack at the summit, unable to turn his back on the mountain until climbing was rendered impossible by the onset of the monsoon. Very much against the advice of Tom Longstaff, who declared all the climbers unfit to climb, Mallory and Somervell sought a second opinion from Dr Wakefield, which he gave in their favour. Quickly they collected together as strong a team of Sherpas as they could muster and set off with Crawford, who had not been involved in either of the earlier attempts and was therefore fit. They climbed to Camp III which they found in a terrible state, the tents full of snow and the stores all buried. By 5 June, when further snow fell, they were seriously questioning their decision, but on 6 June the weather cleared and they decided to press on the following day. On 7 June the weather appeared to be holding. The three men lead fourteen porters on four separate ropes up towards the North Col. Mallory was aware that the snow was in an unstable condition and was at pains to test the condition of it along the first part of the route. It seemed to be satisfactory and so they pressed on. Shortly after lunch he heard an explosion like gunpowder and knew it instinctively to be an avalanche. The avalanche had broken a little above them and enveloped the whole party in tons of snow. Those men on Mallory's rope were only relatively lightly covered and were able to extricate themselves but the roped group of nine were hurled a hundred feet down the face and over a sixty-foot ice cliff. The fall alone had killed most of them and the first roped party were able only to extricate two of the nine men alive, they having sustained relatively minor injuries.

Mallory and Somervell were devastated. 'Why, oh why', lamented Somervell, 'could not one of us Britishers have shared their fate?' When Mallory returned to England his spirits were low. Not only had he been beaten by the mountain but he had also the burden of guilt for the deaths of the seven porters to bear. He felt it very acutely because almost more than any other man on the expedition, with the exception of General Bruce, he had been concerned for the welfare of the porters. To Ruth he wrote: 'The consequences of my mistake are so terrible; it seems impossible to believe that it has happened for ever and that I can do nothing to make good. There is no obligation I have so much wanted to honour as that of taking care of those men.' Mallory sought to assure his friends in the Alpine world that the accident had not been due to recklessness and received support from Geoffrey Young and Young-husband, but the event cast a shadow over the 1922 expedition. In the weeks that followed Hinks was quick to blame Mallory for the disaster but others found the case far less clear cut. Bruce, as expedition leader, had been under pressure to achieve results this year and many people felt that this too had contributed to the decision to make a final attempt. Mallory concluded that probably the main cause of the accident was his ignorance of the snow conditions: 'one generalizes from too few observations.'

He was unable to put Everest from his mind as the committee in London had arranged for him to give a series of public lectures both in Britain and, later, the USA. Public interest in Everest had grown to such an extent that it was almost inevitable that there would be another expedition to the mountain – the only outstanding question was when? A post mortem of the 1922 expedition was held and the lessons learned were recorded and analysed. General Bruce felt optimistic that another assault could and should be made. He was a great advocate of the porters and attributed much of what he felt to be the success of the 1922 expedition to their strength and ability to carry loads to camps as high as 25,000 feet.

Hinks was keen to send a party back in 1923 but others were in less of a hurry, pointing out that work needed to be done on the oxygen apparatus and, more importantly, funds would need raising for a third trip to the Mountain. It was therefore agreed to set a new date of Spring 1924.

In the summer of 1923, soon after Mallory returned from his three-month lecture tour of the USA, he was offered a position at the Board of Extra-Mural Studies in Cambridge. It was the type of break he had been waiting for and he threw himself into the role of assistant secretary and lecturer to the Board with his usual energy and dedication. As soon as he was installed he and Ruth began to make plans to move herself and the children to Cambridge, where they would settle down and begin a new life.

5

Walking on Metaphorical Air

'Subject to Medical Examination I have been finally accepted so I'm again walking on metaphorical air.'

A. C. Irvine to R. F. Summers, 26 October 1923

Sandy returned from Spitsbergen towards the middle of September 1923 and headed straight for Cornist Hall to see Marjory. Dick was also at Cornist when he arrived. He had spent the summer motoring in Switzerland, the excuse for the visit having been that he wished to consult a doctor about his fear that he had contracted tuberculosis. He had not, in the event, and thus he had spent a very happy month with his friend Keith Robinson driving over as many Alpine passes as they could find. On this visit he had met and fallen in love with a young Danish heiress called Thyra and he took great pleasure telling Sandy all about her. She had swept him off his feet.

Marjory was delighted to have the two of them for company, life having been very dull since her Norwegian trip, and she immediately threw a big party to celebrate their return. One morning, shortly after his arrival at Cornist, Sandy was seen coming out of Marjory's bedroom in the early hours of the morning by Mr France, an old friend of HS. It was a deeply embarrassing moment for them both. Nothing was said but France immediately sent a telegram to HS which read, 'Sorry to say things are not going well at Cornist.' Finally, HS was persuaded to take notice of the gossip surrounding his young wife. Marjory had overstepped the limit of what he could accept; she had become recklessly indiscreet in her pursuit of Sandy's affections and HS asked her to leave Cornist, instituting divorce proceedings against her in the spring of 1924. He made a very generous settlement on her of £3000 [£90,000] per annum for the rest of her life on the condition that she would not come within twenty miles of Chester. She agreed and the divorce was finalized in 1925. In the days when divorce was comparatively rare, Marjory's behaviour had been outrageous and embarrassing. The whole matter of HS's second marriage was seen by his wider family as an 'unfortunate' episode. The subject was never discussed, in fact, it was suppressed to such an extent that my father did not learn until he was in his teens that HS had even remarried, and of Marjory's affair with Sandy he learned even later. Evelyn told him that Marjory was a thoroughly bad lot and that it was she who had made all the running in the relationship. Dick was always rather more generous towards Marjory as he'd found her entertaining as an adolescent but the affair between Sandy and her had placed him in a difficult and embarrassing position, not least as his brother Geoffrey had appeared to condone the relationship and was always delighted to see Marjory and Sandy at Highfield.

Marjory married again three times. First a colonel at the Tower of London, then a Mr Trebers who drank heavily and finally a fellow officer of Trebers's, Murray, whose name she bore at the time of her death in Kirkcudbrightshire in the late 1950s. Upon her death the money she had received from HS was returned to the family and divided between the grandchildren. It was known as Majory's Millions. She had spent very little of it and some people in the family believed that right to the end she retained a measure of love and sympathy for HS. Others point out less generously that her other husbands were as rich as or richer than HS and that she had no need for the money. Elsa Trepess's opinion of her friend Marjory was that she 'was just a rather shallow person, very pretty, never vicious, never wanting to pay anyone back. She was a butterfly.'

Sandy maintained contact with Marjory until he left England in February 1924. She joined him at a college dinner in November 1923 and they met fairly regularly in London at the Jules Hotel in Jermyn Street where she had lodgings, spending three days there at the beginning of February 1924. He only mentioned her once in correspondence after she left HS and that was in a letter to Odell when he refered to a telephone conversation in which she asked Sandy to pass on her love. What the state of the relationship was towards the end must be a matter for speculation. Sandy received a letter from her in May 1924 and replied the same day but that is the only mention of her again. I personally think he viewed her as a delightful diversion and, probably in the end, as something of a liability. For him there could never have been a future in the relationship. In the days when such things mattered far more than they do today, Marjory simply wasn't the right type of girl and he would have been under great pressure from the family to end the relationship and find the right sort of partner, one who would be acceptable to them all.

As Dick and Sandy were both due to return to their respective universities towards the end of September, Dick suggested that they should have a couple of days motoring in the Lake District before they left the north for the Michaelmas term. This suited Sandy's needs perfectly as he was anxious to get in contact with Odell's friend, George Abraham, as soon as possible to put in motion a recommendation for the Everest expedition. In an adventure born of very much the same spirit as Sandy's Foel Grach motorbike escapade in 1919, Dick planned an attempt to make the first crossing in a motor car, in both directions, of Wrynose and Hardknott passes. Sandy contacted George Abraham in Keswick who, it transpired, had driven from Eskdale to Little Langdale via the passes in June 1913. His daughter, who had accompanied him with her younger sister and mother on that journey, recalled her shock at seeing 'car rugs and mats going out wholesale to give a grip to the wheels on the atrocious surface, and of dodging from the back to the front of the car to lay the next mat or rug for further progress.' Abraham was so enthusiastic about Sandy's suggestion that he offered to join them and to record it in photographs. He also brought his two daughters with him.

By any measure the crossing of Wrynose and Hardknott passes in a 1920s car was a fairly ambitious undertaking. The road from Langdale to Eskdale rises steeply from almost sea level to the top of Wrynose pass, marked by the Three Shire Stone at 1277 feet, down through Wrynose Bottom at 763 feet and then over Hardknott pass, also 1277 feet and down into Eskdale. The road is now metalled and has fewer hairpin bends than it had in the 1920s when it was merely a drover's track, partly grass and partly large loose stones, but it is still only passable in good weather conditions and is often closed for weeks in the winter. Within this area the fells are some of the highest, roughest and grandest in Lakeland. They are volcanic in origin and there is much naked rock in evidence. The views are breathtakingly spectacular and the drive of some eleven miles is one of the most exciting drives in the Lake District.

After motoring up from Cornist, Dick and Sandy spent the night in Keswick, dining with Abraham. Sandy made a good impression and talked to him at great length about the excitement and adventure of the Spitsbergen expedition. He described the climbs he and Odell had done, emphasizing how he had enjoyed the ice climbing and adding that it was his most fervent hope that he would be considered for the Everest expedition. Abraham agreed to write to his friend, C. E. Meade, who was a member of the Mount Everest Committee, and put Sandy's name forward.

The following day five of them drove from Keswick to Ambleside in Dick's Vauxhall 30/98 and from there into Little Langdale from which valley the passes lead. The weather was fine but there was a chill wind and they were all wrapped up in heavy coats, hats and scarves. At the foot of Wrynose Sandy helped Dick to fix chains to the rear tyres of the car as the drover's road was not only steep and winding, with hideous 180° bends, but also extremely slippery. Dick relied on Sandy's mechanical knowledge for the excursion and knew that if anything went wrong with the engine or any other part of the car he would be able to depend on his friend to fix it. In fact everything went smoothly but the photographs show Sandy sitting in the back of the car with the two girls looking decidedly nervous on the steeper sections of the road. Bill Summers, the family's expert on cars, reminded me that the car had no brakes on the front wheels so, despite the chains, it would have been a fairly 'hairy' ride, especially on the downhill sections. Dick added front brakes to the Vauxhall in 1924 but I do not know whether that had anything to do with the Wrynose and Hardknott crossing. Abraham's elder daughter, Enid Wilson, recalled: 'the most lasting recollections of that trip – much less strenuous than the first – was of the superb driving and performance of the car, and of the evening light as we came back down Wrynose into Little Langdale.'

The following day they drove over the Kirkstone pass down to Ullswater where Abraham photographed them parked beside the lake.

Reading between the lines of her letter, I get the impression that Enid was rather taken with Sandy, 'the last (but far from the least) member of the crew'. The dozen or so photographs taken *en route* are some of the most evocative images in the family's collection. Abraham succeeded in capturing the beauty of the scenery with the little car appearing often only as a tiny dot on the steep tracks. Dick was always very proud of the photographs and kept a full set of them in his desk until the end of his life. It was clearly the highlight of that year's motoring for Sandy who wrote later: 'Dick I'll never forget those 2 days last vac – the most enjoyable of any I can ever remember.' Sandy returned to Oxford with the promise from Abraham that a letter would be sent to the Mount Everest Committee sooner rather than later.

One of the questions that has been in the back of my mind for a long time is why Sandy was ever considered a possible candidate for the 1924 expedition. He was so much younger than any of the other expedition members and although he had exhibited great skill and determination in the climbs he had done with Odell, he was sorely lacking in real mountaineering experience and his height record to date was 5800 feet, some 23,200 feet lower than the summit of Mount Everest. There was nothing to lead anyone to be confident that he would perform well at altitude, nor did the fact that he climbed well up gulleys, chimneys and castle walls mean very much in terms of ice climbing in the Himalaya. I suspect that it was Odell who influenced the committee's decision, convincing them that on the mechanical front, at least, he was as good as Finch had been in 1922.

The Mount Everest Committee certainly had a significant problem finding climbers with relevant experience and of the right age as the Great War had robbed England of a generation of young men. Those men who had experience of climbing in the Himalaya were very few and far between in the 1920s, and the majority of them had been there in the 1890s and the early 1900s, and were thus in their forties and fifties. The committee deemed these climbers to be too old to be considered for an assault on the mountain, so they went about finding the strongest Alpinists of the day.

When it came to putting together a team for 1924 the Mount Everest Committee decided, on the experiences of 1921 and '22, to set up a committee of twelve which included in their number George Mallory, Tom Longstaff, General Bruce and Percy Farrar. It was agreed that they needed to send eight climbers and began to look around, once again, for suitable candidates. By the summer of 1923 the list included Howard Somervell, Noel Odell, Benthley Beetham, Edward Norton and George Mallory. That Mallory would be invited was a given, although it was by no means certain that he would accept and indeed he left the question open until late in the Autumn of 1923. Norton and Somervell had proved themselves to be immensely strong climbers and very good at acclimatizing. Norton was also considered to be an excellent organizer and his strengths in that area were put to good use when he was appointed deputy leader under General Bruce. Geoffrey Bruce, the General's nephew, had had no mountaineering experience prior to 1922 but he and Finch had set a height record of 27,300 feet and it was decided he too should be included; Finch, however, would not be asked to go back. The committee was divided. Finch had proven, argued some, that given fine weather, Everest could be climbed using oxygen. Indeed Finch was a fierce advocate of the use of the gas and some members of the Committee, including Younghusband, had a real antipathy towards the clumsy apparatus and, by extension, to its chief advocate. There were other problems with Finch who, acting as a free spirit as was his nature, had embarked on a series of lectures about Everest in flagrant contravention of his agreement with the Mount Everest Committee who held the right to decide who would lecture and where. There followed an untidy scuffle between the committee and Finch which ended in his backing down, but certain members did not feel kindly towards him. Besides, he wore his hair long, and that told them something about his attitude. To their shame the committee members dithered on the subject of Finch for many months but in the end his name was dropped.

The committee had chosen Odell as he had a great deal of Alpine experience and was deemed to be a strong team player, having been on the Oxford University Arctic expeditions to Spitsbergen of 1921 and 1923. Benthley Beetham, a schoolmaster from County Durham, had been Somervell's regular climbing partner in the Alps and his record fully justified his inclusion. John de Vere Hazard, also a fine Alpinist, was a friend of Morshead and had served in India as a sapper. Other new recruits were Edward Shebbeare of the Indian Forest Service, who was appointed transport officer under Geoffrey Bruce, and Maj. Richard Hingston as medical officer.

Abraham was as good as his word and put Sandy's name forward in a letter to Meade, on 10 October 1923: 'You will probably remember our talks about Everest etc at Jerwalt last June. There is a young friend of mine, A. C. Irvine, who is very anxious to go out next year. He is an ideal chap for the job & if, as I understand, you are on the Selection Committee I have every faith in recommending him.' He goes on to say that he knows Odell will be doing everything he can to include Sandy, 'as they went through the real stiff work of the recent Spitsbergen expedition together.' He concludes: 'Of course this is a purely personal matter, but as you do not know Irvine, I felt that a note of this kind might be useful. He is up again at Oxford now, where on the athletic side he is exceptional – a good tempered youngster of wonderful physique.' Such a ringing endorsement of Sandy's enthusiasm and talent did not go unnoticed and Meade forwarded the letter to Hinks, noting: 'I can only say that I know and like what I have seen of Abraham and that his opinion carries weight with me as far as it goes (as you know it does not go as far as India).' Meade's opinion may not have gone as far as India but it went as far as the Mount Everest Committee.

The choice of Sandy as the final and youngest member of the climbing party was defended on the grounds that the committee believed they needed a young, strong man to complement the skills of the older and more experienced climbers. He had an ally on the selection panel in Tom Longstaff who spoke up for him. After the decision was taken to issue the invitation Mallory wrote to his friend, Geoffrey Young: 'Irvine represents our attempt to get one superman, though lack of experience is against him.' Even so it was always considered a contentious choice and the committee and General Bruce went to some length to defend their decision to expose someone 'so young' to the rigours of Tibetan travel and to the dangers of high altitude mountaineering. One should not forget, in all this, Sandy's own passionate enthusiasm for the venture. If he was inexperienced and young, he was nevertheless utterly dedicated to the expedition and determined to be included and to perform well. It was inconceivable to him from the outset that he would not be one of the climbers tackling the summit. This might be put down to youthful arrogance and enthusiasm but it was far more deep-seated than that. For Sandy the only possible outcome of any race was to win. This was as true in the rest of his life as it was in his rowing. Following the success of the Spitsbergen expedition he was desperately keen to pursue further expeditions; he had become completely captured by the excitement and adventure which such ventures afforded. The Everest expedition was to be the fulfilment of all his ambitions and he threw himself into the project with all the energy at his disposal. Sandy was built for bravery and once focused on an objective, he pursued it relentlessly until it was conquered. Moreover Everest presented him with the chance to prove himself, as much to himself as to anyone else. It was in his eyes the ultimate goal.

One of the considerations he had to take into account were the feelings of his family. Although technically 'of age', being twenty-one, he did not need the consent of his parents, he felt out of a sense of duty and love that their permission should be sought. He talked to them in early October and they asked for time to consider the request. In the past people have suggested that Willie and Lilian had no idea of the risks that their son would be taking if he were to climb high on Mount Everest, but I feel it is disingenuous to suggest that they were naïve. I feel certain that Willie knew as well as any well-informed layman could what might be in store for Sandy. The experiences of the 1922 Everest expedition had been well documented and he would certainly have read of the difficulties the team had encountered, the problems and effects of climbing at altitude and of the accident in which the seven porters had died. The fact that both he and Lilian sought guidance through their prayers shows me how very seriously they took the request. Lilian wrote later to Hugh:

Often I have thought of the future & prayed that this same God who has been my Guide and Friend all my life and on whom I have relied in all our decisions, will be my children's Guide and Friend too. That is why I have never had any regrets or questionings about the right or wrong of letting Sandy go up Everest – it must be the answer to our prayers when we prayed earnestly about our decision to give him permission.

They gave him their blessing and, thus equipped, he pursued his application with even greater vigour.

On 24 October 1923 Sandy received an invitation from the Mount Everest Committee to join the 1924 expedition. The letter arrived at a time of unprecedented emotional turmoil in Sandy's life. On 19 October he received the news that Dick Summers had proposed to and been accepted by Evelyn. The announcement came like a bolt out of the blue and completely knocked him off his stride. He had been totally unprepared for this development, having only recently talked at length with Dick about his relationship with the Danish girl, Thyra. The cocktail of emotions that coursed through his veins was so intoxicating that he gave vent to his feelings in a series of letters to Dick and Evelyn that give some indication of just how deeply he felt the shock and dismay at the announcement. He felt betrayed and jealous. Why had his best friend not confided in him his plans for the engagement? How could his beloved sister, of whom he thought the world, have betrayed his trust? Evelyn had been his friend, his playmate and suddenly he was forced to regard her as a woman and to admit she had a life of her own. He didn't like it. Such irrational, immature but completely comprehensible thoughts were spinning round in his head when he wrote to Dick that evening in a state of drunkenness: 'If I am construing your letter correctly and there seems only one construction to put on it, I think you are a bloody fool. There is only one possible thing to be said for it, and that is that I would get another opportunity to wear my Top Hat that I paid £1.10.6 for.' He was certain that neither Willie nor HS would hear of the engagement and that all his brothers would be equally outraged. Dick, after all, had been around since 1917 and it had never crossed any of their minds that he would ever be anything more to anyone in the family than Sandy's best friend. Besides, he was only twenty one and had still two years of study left. No, it was unthinkable! 'I may have sobered down sufficiently by Sunday to be really serious with you, but at the moment I am walking metaphorically on air – not an advert for Eno Epsum or ANDREW his liver salts. Have a good night's sleep, a cold bath, read your morning paper and think twice, then again, and you will be nearer the mark. Spheroids to you, Sandy.' The allusion to walking on air is a reference to the fact that he was waiting to hear whether his name had been accepted by the Mount Everest Committee and I am sure this contributed to his heightened sense of emotion.

The next day he had sobered up and wrote a poignant and honest letter to Evelyn in which he poured out all his thoughts and anxieties.

Sorry if I appeared a bit blunt on the phone, but I was quite bowled over by Dick's letter. I suppose I should congratulate you – but I think it is Dick that needs the congratulations more than you … I must admit I don't feel at all happy. I'm probably in a pessimistic mood but there it is. I like Dick beyond words but – Oh I can't say it all in a letter – what it comes to is that he needs changing completely and even then he wouldn't be half good enough … Oh E, it's all very upsetting. I better not say more, I may only spoil your pleasure. I know Dick is everything that could be desired – I like him more than any man I've ever met – there isn't a kinder or more generous soul in all the world but you'll have to make a real man of him before I'll feel really happy about it.

That was one of the fundamental problems for Sandy: Dick was not in his opinion a real man. The early loss of his mother had left him anxious and insecure, emotionally weak where the Irvines were strong. Sandy feared that it would be Evelyn's role in the marriage to wear the pants. In a way he was right but what he failed to appreciate was that she knew what she was taking on.

Sandy could only fret that his sister was being 'wasted' on his friend. He wrote: 'There is only one sister in this family & we can't afford any experiments with her. I suppose I shouldn't interfere in other people's business but a brother cares more for a sister than all the other brothers put together & I frankly am not happy about it yet – I always pictured someone totally different – a man – a real rough rider who really knew what life was.' Was he not modelling his ideal man for her on himself? I believe he was, in which case he would have been pushed ever to find someone to live up to his expectations. Not only did Sandy feel betrayed, rightly or wrongly, by Dick and Evelyn's engagement, but perhaps more significantly he feared that Evelyn had been chosen as second best after Dick's friendship with Thyra had ended so abruptly. His own relationship with Evelyn had become somewhat strained after the affair with Marjory had developed. Perhaps he saw now that the delicious naughtiness of the affair was but temporal and Evelyn had found real love, something which had eluded him in his life. Possibly his outspoken dismay had something to do with his embarrassment at the fact that his indiscretion compromised her in her future father-in-law's eyes.

A week or so later he wrote back to Dick a rather more measured if equally emotional letter:

My dear Dick, If you are both the same next year there is no objection in the world. I was quite naturally very bowled over when I heard – My first thoughts were naturally I think a) you were too young to think of marrying b) E had not met enough men as she has always been tied to Mothers apron strings. You seemed to have shown no outward signs ever + E had always laughed at the idea as ridiculous when I had suggested it – so I thought it might be a case of 'I must marry someone soon'.

He went on to agonize over the fact that he would lose them both as absolute friends and worried that Dick's money would spoil Evelyn, although he did admit that it had not spoiled Dick in his opinion.

Dick I hope you don't mind my saying all this – it may sound as if I've got a grudge against you – well since the first game of Fives at Salop [Shrewsbury] I've never had a better friend in the world! To think you <u>ever</u> doubted my friendship – perhaps it sounded like it in my letter but I thought you knew me better than that. I never in my life will be able to repay you for all your kindness & the good times you have given me. If you doubt my friendship after all that you make me out one of the most degraded bounders that ever bounded. I'm always your best & truest friend though there may have been times when I haven't shown it outwardly.

He signed off: 'Subject to Medical Examination I have been finally accepted so I'm again walking on the metaphorical air.' And then in a thoroughly schoolboy manner he concludes the letter with a postscript that has always caused a very wry smile when used by anyone in the family: 'I haven't time to read this through again so forgive any errors of punctuation, alliteration or constipation.'

Despite the ending, this letter was written from the heart and gives an unequivocal and resounding endorsement of the importance he attached to friendship and family. The dilemma for Sandy was that friendship and family met in this engagement and it is that which threw him so badly off course. The thought of losing both his best friend and his sister hurt him more than he could handle: he would never again have access to their undivided affections. If ever there was a revealing moment to show Sandy's vulnerable side it is here. He felt himself being eased out of the picture by the two people he cared for most in the world and the panic that that potential loss instilled in him was immense. Over the week between the two letters he wrote to Dick he had rationalized it in his mind, but this episode gives a once only glance into his heart, into the insecure soul that dwelled within. The letters from Sandy caused both Evelyn and Dick terrible hurt. Relations were already strained in view of the Marjory affair and to have Sandy expressing his opinion so directly and openly both confused and upset them. They were quite unaware that their engagement would cause him so much pain and distress. Although by December Dick and Evelyn joined him at a dinner in the Georgian room at the Hotel Metropole in Oxford, Sandy's outburst had cast a shadow over his relationship with them both. With Dick I don't think he ever had a complete rapprochement.

With this shattering experience behind him, Sandy turned his attentions to his other obligations. First there was the forthcoming Everest expedition; after the medical examination he sent a telegram to his parents which read, 'Have passed the vet alright – Sandy'. Then there was the small matter of his college work and, finally, he had committed himself to coaching the Trial VIIIs in preparation for the 1924 Boat Race. It is absolutely in character that Sandy should not allow a new and alluring opportunity to divert him from what he considered to be his duties and he threw himself into the coaching with his usual gusto. In a manner typical of his empirical attitude towards life, he was frequently seen pedalling up and down the towpath along the Isis on a tricycle. A somewhat unusual method of transport for someone as athletic as Sandy was explained by Patrick Johnson, a friend of his at Merton, in a letter to Bill Summers in 1986. 'This saved the trouble of getting on to and off a bicycle; – Sandy could simply leap off, demonstrate the point he wished to make to the crew and spring back on to the tricycle to continue pedalling and keep up with the boat. Johnson pointed out that 'when in motion, Sandy kept one wheel off the ground.' To pedal along the tow path on a tricycle balanced on two wheels required a degree of skill not given to all, but as Sandy saw it, his life was made simpler by adopting this mode of transport. This somewhat eccentric bahaviour did not escape the notice of the local press who were rather more bemused by it than his friends, who were, I presume, more used to Sandy's foibles.

In the meantime the Mount Everest Committee was bombarding Sandy with paperwork. There were agreements for signature, clothing lists and instructions as to equipment he would need, documents from Captain Noel about the filming of the expedition and sundry other communications. Soon after he signed the agreement he made contact with Percy Unna, the member of the oxygen subcommittee charged with making arrangements for the equipment to be ready in time for February. Unna had been forewarned by Odell that Sandy was handy with mechanical matters and it did not take Sandy long to persuade Unna to let him have a 1922 oxygen set which he took back to Oxford and began to work on in the labs there, although parts of it frequently found their way into his rooms. One of his fellow students recalled him cocooned in his room, clouds of pipe smoke billowing from the door, 'struggling with a somewhat imperfect oxygen apparatus'. He examined the mechanism of the set very carefully and then dismantled it completely in an effort to reduce the complexity of the workings and to make the apparatus lighter and more user-friendly. In the 1922 set the oxygen bottles had been carried upright in the frame attached to the climber's back with a complicated number of valves and tubes that were only able to be exchanged by another climber or by the climber taking the set off and altering it himself. Sandy wrote extensive notes on the 1922 set and referred to the design thus:

With the present form of Mount Everest Oxygen Apparatus the cylinder valves are at the top of the back & so can only be turned when the apparatus is standing on the ground. This arrangement also requires that 2 auxiliary valves be carried in such a position that the climber can easily turn from one cylinder to the other. The weight of these auxiliary valves is quite a consideration & might be eliminated if the cylinders were inverted, so putting the cylinder valves in a convenient position to be used by the climber wearing the apparatus.

He concluded that by inverting the cylinders much of the tubing could be done away with and would have the added advantage that the climber could jettison a used bottle from his back pack without having to take it off. Such a simple alteration to the design would considerably reduce the weight, complexity and vulnerability of the apparatus, doing away with the fragile tubes that were apt to get in the climber's way and get damaged during a scramble. He worked up the drawings during November and, with Unna's blessing, sent the revised designs to Siebe Gorman with his notes attached.

To my absolute delight a full set of the oxygen drawings Sandy had sent to Siebe Gorman, plus his handwritten notes to accompany them, turned up in the May 2000 find. The drawings are exquisitely and minutely observed and the notes fluent and comprehensive. Not only had he given the oxygen set a great deal of his time and attention, but he had really got to grips with the system and the suggestions for modifications he made were done so with the confidence of somebody who really understood the nature of the problem. Unfortunately the Siebe Gorman correspondence has been lost over the years, but the company was clearly irritated by Sandy's recommendations, feeling that comments from a twenty-one-year-old chemistry student could not be taken seriously. Whether or not they communicated this to Sandy I have been unable to find out, but by the time he met up with the oxygen apparatus in Darjeeling and saw that his suggestions had been ignored he was extremely indignant.

Sandy visited Unna three times in London in the February of 1924, twice to discuss the oxygen apparatus and once to talk about primus stoves which, it became evident, were also to be his responsibility on the expedition. Unna clearly liked him enormously. After Sandy's death he wrote to Willie asking to be forgiven for promoting the venture which led to the tragedy. He wrote: 'The first time one met him one could not help thinking that there was the man one would like to have as a life long friend and be proud if one could do so.' On one of Sandy's London visits he dined with Unna and his sister, who was equally impressed by his dashing appearance and modest manner. Sandy and Unna were very much of the same turn of mind and talked at length about the equipment that would be required for the expedition. Unna was delighted to find someone who took this responsibility so seriously and gave him leave to spend money on additional equipment and tools that he thought might be required. One of the first things Sandy did was to put together a tool box, getting details of washer, bolt and screw sizes and types from Siebe Gorman, amongst others. He knew full well that there would be running repairs to all manner of equipment on the march and he tried to ensure that he had the right tools and enough spare parts to feel sure that he would be able to do these. Here was Sandy focusing his mind very clearly and, given that he had only Unna's and others reports of previous mishaps and malfunctions to go on, it is quite remarkable that he was as successful as he was in preparing an adequate kit; this to the extent that nobody who brought an article to him for repair during the long march and the weeks on the mountain was ever let down. The only thing he failed to mend satisfactorily was his own watch.

In addition to their discussions about the oxygen apparatus, Unna and Sandy spent some time considering the possible inclusion of a brazing lamp, in addition to the other primus stoves that would be required on the mountain. Sandy argued for the inclusion of the lamp which would be helpful if any welding were required. Unna gave permission for these special primus burners to be made only at the very last minute, and Sandy directed Condrup Ltd to make him two on 26 February with instructions that he needed them in Liverpool two days later. They were duly delivered, but only after two of Condrup's men had worked through the night on his behalf.

During the last few weeks of the Michaelmas Term at Oxford Sandy was working and living flat out. He was the toast of several clubs and attended at least one dinner a week. He was elected to the Oxford University Mountaineering Club and the president, in a rather droll obituary, wrote, 'I never climbed with him; in fact the only climb I ever saw him do was from a box at the Winter Garden Theatre onto the stage.' Everyone at Merton had heard of the success of the Spitsbergen expedition and was very proud to know that he was to be included in the 1924 Everest expedition. Several people voiced their opinions and concerns about his undertaking, but he brushed them off, replying that if he had to die there would be no finer death than in an attempt to conquer Everest. This was not just sheer bravado; the lessons of the history of British exploration were still fresh in people's minds. Sandy knew precisely the risks he was taking and he did it with zeal and commitment.

One tradition at formal dinners was for the men, during the port drinking, to circulate their menus for signature. At the Merton College Spitsbergen Dinner given on 8 December 1923 all the members of the expedition signed Sandy's menu with a variety of messages of good luck. His Shrewsbury friend Ian Bruce drew a sketch of Everest with a motorbike close to the summit, a reference to his motorcycling exploits on Foel Grach four summers earlier.

The next event for his calendar was a skiing trip to Switzerland over Christmas. At the beginning of November he took up Odell's suggestion and wrote to Arnold Lunn in Mürren. He asked Lunn several questions about winter snow conditions and told him that he was anxious to learn to ski in the shortest possible time in order to prepare himself for Everest by studying snow and ice in the high Alps. Lunn replied that he would be delighted to teach him and invited him to Mürren for three weeks over Christmas and New Year. Sandy sent Lunn a telegram announcing that he would arrive on 23 December at 3.40 p.m. and would make his way to the Palace Hotel where he was to be staying and where the Lunn family lived.

Mürren (5400 feet) is situated just above the great cliff that overhangs the Lauterbrunnen valley in Switzerland. Access to the village in the 1920s was via a steep funicular railway from Lauterbrunnen (2687 feet) via Grütsch (4885 feet). It was widely regarded as one of the grandest railways in Switzerland. Mürren was a favourite Alpine centre for eminent Victorians and, in the early twentieth-century, it was the cradle of Alpine ski-racing. Arnold Lunn spent a good proportion of his adult life in Mürren and was deeply emotionally attached to the mountains. It was this instinctive love that he shared with Sandy and which for him singled out Sandy as a mountaineer in the making.

The British were the first to introduce skiing into the Bernese Oberland and it was a travel agent, Lunn's father, Sir Henry Lunn, who was the first to popularize winter sports. He succeeded in persuading the local hoteliers to open their hotels for his clients as early as December 1902, and in 1910 he opened Mürren as a winter sports centre. Arnold Lunn wrote in his memoirs: 'I arrived in the Oberland exactly one year after the first pair of ski had appeared in Grindelwald. In my life-time I have seen skiing evolve from the pursuit of a few eccentric individuals into the sport of masses.'

When Sandy arrived in Mürren in 1923 British skiing was no longer in its infancy. The origin of Alpine skiing was in Norway where cross-country skiing was considered to be the sport. The Norwegian attitude to downhill sections is embodied in the official instructions issued in the early part of the twentieth-century by the Norwegian ski association to competitors taking part in cross-country racing: 'When going downhill one should regain breath and rest as much as possible. Avoid falling as it both fatigues and lowers the spirit.' In 1924 the rigorous approach to ski discipline was at the point of being superseded by intrepid young men and women, who, rather than slavishly following the curriculum which taught stem kick turns, telemark turns and Christianas, were eager to ski straight downhill at speed. There is something in the mentality of the British that forces them to challenge accepted ideas, whether in pursuit of sport or risk. It was obvious that skiing around the mountain rather than down it simply wasn't going to be of lasting interest to the British skier.

In 1921 Sir Kenneth Swan and Arnold Lunn were entrusted by the Ski Club of Great Britain with the organization of the world's first downhill ski race. The following year Lunn astonished the Alpine world by setting up a slalom race in Mürren where the competitors were expected to weave in and out of poles on a set course. Slalom had been practised in Norway, using trees, but not in a serious race capacity. It was a full eight years after Swan and Lunn organized the National Championship that another country decided to adopt the idea of downhill ski-racing.

By the winter season of 1923/24 there were several ski-races on the calendar, which were proving increasingly popular with the young British contingent who met together in the Public Schools Alpine Sports Club. In January 1924 the Kandahar Ski Club was formed and Sandy was elected one of the first members. Another early member of the club was Tony Knebworth, a contemporary of Sandy's from Oxford. Knebworth knew Sandy slightly as he was at Magdalen with Hugh and had come across Sandy at a lunch the previous summer. The club existed to promote downhill and slalom ski-racing and to campaign for their international recognition by the Fédération Internationale de Ski (FIS) and took its name, at the suggestion of Sir Henry Lunn, from Lord Roberts of Kandahar, a great general with a distinguished career in India and a friend of Lord Lytton, Tony Knebworth's father and President of the Public Schools Alpine Sports Club. The Kandahar downhill ski race was first run in 1924 when Tony Knebworth won the Challenge Cup.

During Mürren's first winter season (1910–11) there was no railway up to the Allmendhubel, so the skiers had to climb up for the skiing. It was not until after the Second World War that the Schilthorn cable railway was constructed. From the Schilthorn summit you can ski down to Mürren and also to Lauterbrunnen, a vertical descent of 7200 feet, making it one of the longest downhill runs accessible from mechanical transport. In 1923/24 the Allmendhubel still provided the only ski lift in Mürren. That year there was a great deal of snow and the runs down into Mürren were in excellent condition. But Lunn was at heart a skier who preferred the 'off piste' and he observed in his book the *Bernese Oberland* that 'the best ski-ing, like the best things in life, have to be paid for in the currency of climbing'. Sandy's determination to try glacier skiing, even at his relatively novice level, is another example of his taste for adventure and his desire to pit his will against the elements rather than taking the tamer option of skiing 'on piste'. The real beauty of skiing away from the pistes is that you are alone, far from the crowds and often in a scene of such sublime beauty that it is difficult to go back to the hurly-burly of the ski village. Sandy had already developed a deep passion for the mountains in Spitsbergen and I have no doubt that he would have returned to the Alps regularly had he lived.

When he arrived in Mürren Sandy had almost no experience of skiing. It is true that he had spent part of the Spitsbergen expedition on skis, but this had involved mostly traversing on the level and dragging heavy sleds. When situations had arisen permitting him to ski in Spitsbergen for pleasure rather than as a mode of transport he had greatly enjoyed it and could readily see the appeal of skiing downhill. Lunn found him eager, enthusiastic but a complete novice without any knowledge of even the most basic turn. He was delighted with Sandy's progress and wrote: 'He spent his first day on the practice slopes. I showed him a Christiania and a Stem Turn, and after a couple of attempts he brought off both turns. He is the only beginner I have ever known who brought off at his first attempt a downhill Telemark, or rather a step Telemark, which is by the way a far easier turn for the novice to master than the ordinary downhill Telemark.' Sandy pushed himself hard and turned out to be a diligent pupil, mastering all the basic turns he required to take his elementary test. 'The test was started on the steep slope just above the half-way station of the Allmendhubel. Irvine took this straight and his time was thirty seconds. The next candidate took five minutes,' Lunn observed.

Sandy was staying, along with a hundred or so other winter sports enthusiasts, including Knebworth, at the Palace Hotel in Mürren, owned and run by Lunn. In view of his elevated status as a member of the Everest expedition, he was accorded the honour of a place at the Lunn table in the dining room. This was of considerable embarrassment to him and Peter Lunn, Arnold's then nine-year-old son, recalled that he 'kept away from all praise if he could and would not let anybody get into any skiing book the fact he was going on Everest'. Dinner was a formal affair and Sandy initially found himself somewhat overawed by the company. Lunn persisted with Sandy and eventually succeeding in breaking through the barrier of his shyness and was delighted to find that Sandy proved to be fine company with an attractive, hidden sense of humour.

When he first joined our table, he resisted all attempts to draw him into general conversation, but once his shyness had worn off, he proved excellent company. His humour was latent, but only needed a sympathetic environment for its full expression. He had a knack of recalling things which had tickled him so that their humour was not dissipated in the telling. Many people who can see the funny aspect of life do not possess the necessary technique for recapturing the humour of an incident which they have witnessed. Very pathetic are their attempts to reinforce an unconvincing narrative by assuring us with an emphasis which becomes more poignant as their failure becomes more marked, that if we'd been there we'd 'have screamed with laughter.' Irvine never failed to recapture and to convey to his audience the essence of those things which had tickled his fancy. He had an odd way of laughing. It was a silent laugh, visible but not audible, a long low reverberating chuckle which lit up his face with sunny merriment. And as his normal expression was grave, the contrast was all the more striking.

Two weeks into the holiday Sandy entered the Strang-Watkins Challenge Cup for slalom running. He elected to take part in order to gain experience and was not expected to do well as there were several skiers in the field who were known to be stronger and had considerably more skiing experience. One of the other competitors, an Englishman by the name of Emmet, won the Alpine Ski Challenge Cup, an open slalom race, a few days later.

Once again Sandy surprised everyone including Lunn, who recorded: 'Irvine did not do very well on hard snow, but on the soft snow section he ran down with a combination of dash and certainty which would have been surprising in a man who had been skiing for ten seasons, and won the Cup. A few days later he passed his Second Class Test, within three weeks of learning his first turn. His must be a record.' Sandy was delighted with his win and wrote enthusiastically to Odell: 'I was awfully pleased with myself and put it all down to getting used to the feel in Spitsbergen.'

He was not in the least concerned that he spent a great deal of his time falling, something which quickly earned him the nickname of the Human Avalanche. 'I took the Nose Dive straight my 2nd day', he told Odell in the same letter, '& Lone Tree my 3rd & stood which shook some of the expert skiers to the core.' Sandy was in his element, captivated by the beauty of the Alpine scenery. 'Aren't the mountains wonderful?' he enthused, 'Just asking to be climbed and real Spitsbergen colouring in the evening.' He wrote to Arnold Lunn on his return to Oxford in January 1924: 'When I am an old man I will look back on Christmas, 1923, as the day when to all intents and purposes I was born. I don't think anyone has *lived* until they have been on ski.'

Lunn was convinced that Sandy would have made a very great ski racer and even conjectured that he might have been chosen to race for the British ski team against the Swiss universities in the 1924–25 season.

'I have seen some hundreds of beginners emerging from the rabbit stage, but in the whole of my experience I have never met a more remarkable beginner than "Sandy" Irvine. He was blessed with complete fearlessness, with great physical strength, and, above all, with a genius for the sport. In a few years,' Lunn claimed, 'he would have been in the same class as the very best Swiss performers.'

However, skiing was not just about racing and passing tests and Lunn conceded that Sandy was first and foremost a mountaineer. I find this an interesting observation on Lunn's part, and I suspect that he, as a very experienced mountaineer, recognized and acknowledged those characteristics he attributed to mountaineers to be burgeoning in Sandy. 'He would have played an important part in that crusade which we all have at heart, the crusade for transforming ski-runners into mountaineers, and mountaineers into ski-runners.' Lunn held Sandy in great affection, regarded him almost like a son, and he had very high hopes and beliefs in what his protégé would have achieved had he lived. Peter Lunn told me when we met in the summer of 1999 that he had no recollection of his father writing at such length or in such terms of praise about anybody else.

Sandy was staying in a room at the Palace next to Peter. They met both at dinner and on the slopes and Peter formed a very strong and positive opinion of him. My cousin Ann always said that Sandy, whom she had known as a child, had a lovely manner with children. He had the ability to talk to them as if they were as important to him as grown-ups and this always made a very strong and positive impact on them. Peter well remembered being allowed to join his parents at dinner one evening and sitting next to Sandy whom he quizzed at great length about all the technical equipment that was going to be taken on the Everest expedition.

Arnold Lunn observed the conversations and wrote: 'I remember the grave courtesy with which he listened to the eager questions of my own small son, who was interested in the Everest expedition and in the scientific aspect of oxygen, etc. He hurled a succession of questions at Irvine with all the ruthlessness of a small boy who has at last discovered a patient victim. Irvine replied with as much care as if he had been giving evidence before a committee of oxygen experts.' Peter followed the events of the Everest expedition with enthusiasm and recalled his surprise and delight when Sandy sent him three long letters from Everest, giving detailed accounts of the progress he was making with the oxygen apparatus. The letters were taken away from Peter for safekeeping and, tragically, were lost during the Second World War. I found a letter from Arnold Lunn to Willie Irvine written after Sandy's death in which he said he was enclosing copies of these letters from Sandy to Peter. For a moment I had real hopes that they would be amongst the papers but sadly they were not. However, the great generosity and kindness which Sandy showed towards his young friend has never been forgotten and Peter Lunn has hanging in his Buckinghamshire kitchen a large black and white print of himself and Sandy together after the Strang-Watkins Challenge Cup, in which Sandy had taken first prize and Peter third.

One of the plans Sandy had had before arriving in Mürren was to do some climbing in winter conditions. This, he felt, would give him additional valuable experience for the Everest expedition. The winter of 1923 experienced exceptionally high snowfall, which made for excellent skiing but thwarted his desire to climb. He made several attempts to mobilize guides and others, but without success: 'I couldn't get any actual rock climbing though I tried hard', he told Odell, 'nobody would come with me as the weather was so bad ... and it was too prohibitive to climb alone with two guides.' Finally he succeeded in attaching himself to a group of very strong skiers who, in the care of Alpine guide Fritz Fuchs, had planned a descent of the largest glacier in Europe, the Aletsch. The tour was organized by a man called White from nearby Wengen. The group consisted of Fritz Fuchs, Sandy, Tony Knebworth, White and two others. Of them all Sandy was the weakest skier but the strongest climber: it was a companionable party that left Mürren at the end of January.

They skied down from Mürren to Lauterbrunnen and caught a train to Wengen from where they took another train up to Kleine Scheidegg, the middle station below the awe-inspiring Eiger North Face. There they had lunch, staring up at the great face which, in 1924 was still unclimbed. From there they boarded the Jungfraubahn, an electrically as opposed to steam-operated railway, in its time a pioneering engineering feat of staggering advance. When it was first approved in 1891 a furnicular railway to the top of the Eiger was proposed but plans were rethought and the railway, which was commenced and built by Adolf Guyer-Zeller in 1894 went only as far as the Jungfrau Joch. The looping tunnel through the Eiger and Mönch mountains has a maximum gradual gradient of 25 centimetres per metre which allows for progressive adjustment of the human body to high altitude. Coming out of the top station at the Jungfrau Joch at 3454 metres (11,333 feet), the top of Europe as it is often described, is still one of the greatest wonders in the Alps. There you are confronted by a scene of near perfect beauty, a world of snow and rock peaks with the great Aletsch glacier sloping gently away like an enormous tongue of ice licking the sides of the mountains. Tributary glaciers feed into the Aletsch, folding into the great frozen river. In 1924 this perfect world was barely disturbed by man, the snow still virgin, many of the peaks yet unclimbed. Little wonder Sandy was filled with a sense of awe and wonder. Fifteen years earlier George Mallory had sat in the Concordia hut overlooking the glacier, lying in the August sun, sleeping and dreaming. A very different but equally wonderful prospect from the mid-winter impressions Sandy formed.

The route from the top station to the Egon von Steiger Hütte is via a run called Concordia, a gentle slope, and then a climb on skis of some three hours, for which they would have required skins on the bottoms of their skis. At the bottom of the Concordia Sandy took over the lead from Fuchs, setting a formidable pace. Going uphill on skis is tiring work but Sandy was more experienced at this than the others. It was the downhill which stretched his abilities. Fritz Fuchs took over the lead as they reached the field of crevasses that criss-cross the slopes beneath the hut. There was a certain amount of hilarity amongst the party as they tried to avoid falling into oblivion and struggled to master the uphill kick turn, a fiendishly difficult manoeuvre to the unpractised. It involves changing direction by 180 degrees, often on a steep slope, crossing one ski above the other. Perfectly executed it is an elegant turn, but for those less practised a cat's-cradle of skis, sticks and knees is more often the result. The views from the climb are breathtaking and they were all impressed by the isolation of the glacier. They arrived at the hut in the late afternoon, elated but exhausted. Sandy, being physically the strongest and the most used to skiing up rather than down, found the uphill section exhilarating: Tony Knebworth described it as 'an awful sweat'.

During the course of my research into the Aletsch glacier trip I contacted a close friend, Fiona Morrison, who is an experienced ski tourer, and asked her whether she had any information on the Egon von Steiger Hütte. She emailed me back to say that she and her husband were just off to Switzerland to do a ski tour but she would have a look in her books and, failing that, would ask their guide. They had planned to make a tour from the Jungfrau Joch and had booked to stay in a Dutch-owned hut called the Hollandiahütte in the mountains above Wengen.

A few days later I had an excited phone call from Fiona. She, her husband Eivind and their Scottish guide, Willie Todd, arrived at the hut only to discover a plaque mounted above the door identifying it as the Egon von Steiger Hütte. In a year when coincidences cropped up in the most extraordinary places this was without doubt the most out of the way of all. They had made exactly the same tour as Sandy and his companions, starting at the Jungfrau Joch, skiing down to Concordia and then 'skinning' up to the hut. Fiona and Eivind made the climb on skis up to the Ebenfluh which Sandy had hoped to take but was stopped by the blizzard. I was particularly pleased to have this piece of news as it helped me to piece together, with the aid of Fiona's photographs, a whole picture of the glacier outing in January 1924.

The Egon von Steiger hut is no different from other huts which can be found in the High Alp. The *raison d'être* of the huts is to provide basic shelter for mountaineers who are attempting a climb or ski tour that takes longer than a day. It obviates the necessity for camping or bivouacking in the mountains. The huts are generally basic, providing sleeping accommodation on bunks, a central space for eating and sitting in the evening. The general rule of thumb for these huts is that they are supplied with firewood stacked outside, a stove and a few pots. Hut etiquette dictates that you leave the hut in the state you found it, clean, tidy and with a pot of melted snow ready for the next lot of incoming climbers or skiers who will be thirsty and in need of liquid before almost anything else. That hasn't changed in over a hundred years.

When Sandy and party arrived at the hut they found it extremely cold: 10° F or −21.5° C inside. But they soon got a good 'blizzard fug' going in there from the fire and pipe smoke and one of them, Mac, made a heart-warming cheese soup which they devoured with relish. Unfortunately Fritz Fuchs had consumed half the brandy they had brought with them on the ascent, so they were a little short of alcohol, but good spirits prevailed and there was a great deal of joking and laughter that evening. Sandy's plan was to rise at 3 a.m. and climb up to the Ebenfluh on ski before setting off down the glacier. I get the impression that the others thought he was being somewhat overzealous and, according to Tony Knebworth, they were relieved to discover that at the appointed time it was snowing and blowing a blizzard. Fuchs decreed it would be insane to attempt to climb in such conditions so they returned to their blankets and slept on until 7.30 a.m. Tony Knebworth recorded: 'We ate a huge breakfast and tidied up the hut, and eventually got started down at 9.05 a.m.'

The blizzard had ceased, the wind abated and the weather was beginning to clear as they left the hut but it was bitterly cold in the shadow of the peak. Typically the mountaineer elects to climb or ski in the early morning when the snow conditions are stable and before the sun has warmed the slopes and increased the risk of avalanche. The state of the snowslab can vary in very short distances and it was important to the inexperienced party with Fuchs that he took control of where they skied.

Skiing on a glacier is a very different experience from skiing on piste, and neither Tony Knebworth nor Sandy had ever done it before. The first and most important requirement for the safety of the skiers is a detailed local knowledge of the glacier. For the recreational skier this is best found in a local guide who knows intimately the mountain, the glacier, the snow conditions and the route to the valley. Fuchs explained to the group that they would have to follow his tracks exactly, stop above him and obey his instructions. Only thus could he guarantee that none of them would fall into a crevasse. This type of skiing was not entirely to Tony Knebworth's taste, as he wrote to his father, Lord Lytton, on his return to England:

I will give you my views on glacier skiing. In the first place, the snow is probably bad because it is either crusty from the sun or wind-swept, and even if it's powder it's very slow because it's so cold. With us it was a bit of everything, but mostly wind-swept crusty stuff, which we didn't go wild about. Fritz said it might have been much worse. In the second place you don't know where you are, or what you might fall into. You've got to follow the guide and not deviate from his line, or you may hit a 60 ft drop, which is an infernal bore. You can't just run down doing telemarks, because you catch the guide up at once, even if you wait until he's out of sight before starting. So that I feel there is no dash about glacier running – it's all kick turns and 'daren't fall down' sort of running.'

If Knebworth was frustrated by the skiing, Sandy was in his element in the mountains. This had been the aim of the skiing trip for him and he wrote to Odell enthusiastically about his experience, concluding: 'I had a hell of a good time on the glacier and climbed the snow peaks with maximum rapidity.'

They made the run in two hours and arrived in a village called Blatten (but which they nicknamed Blotto) where they found an excellent pub. Here they celebrated their descent with a large quantity of *vin de pays* and a home-brewed brandy, all for two Swiss francs. One of the locals in the pub refused to believe they could have made the descent in two hours when his own personal best time had been two and a half hours. More brandy, more celebrations! Fuchs told them later that the man was no great skier, but that served only to make them more cheerful. Knebworth recalled: 'We entertained the village, and sang songs to them for about an hour – in fact had a real good orgy, and then went on and tried to ski.'

The run down to the Goppenstein from the village of Blatte is, fortunately, not a difficult one, a gentle run down a snow-covered track. 'Fortunately' because they were all, by the time they left the pub, blind drunk. 'It's the funniest feeling in the world trying to ski when you're blind [drunk]. The snow comes up and hits you in the face! Old Fritz went off first, waving one ski round his head, and sitting down every few yards. One had no idea of the contours or the bumps or anything, and it felt too queer for words. I got down to Goppenstein at about 1.30. Mac and John Carlton at 1, Fritz about 1.15 and the other two at about 2.0 or 1.45.'

The whole run from the top of the glacier to Goppenstein was supposed to take some seven hours. They had done it in three and a half. 'Fritz said he'd never done it so fast before' recalled Knebworth cheerfully, 'and he was sweating like an old hog when he arrived. We could have done it twice as quick if we'd hurried on the glacier and been sober down the path.' They changed and bathed in Spiez and caught the 9.33 back to England 'with heavy hearts and a feeling that we shouldn't do it again for a year...'

If Mürren had been seen as a foretaste of things to come then Sandy was flying even higher than he had been before he left Oxford. With that trip behind him and a little more experience under his belt he was looking forward more than ever to getting on with the 'real show'.

Upon his return from Switzerland Sandy went back to Oxford for three days to make some final preparations there before leaving for Birkenhead. There was still much work to be done on the oxygen apparatus and he was disappointed not to have had a reply from Siebe Gorman about his suggestions for design modifications. He had arranged to go up to 20,000 feet in an aeroplane to get a feeling for the altitude. This was organized for him by Evelyn who, during her time at Oxford, had joined the predecessor of the Flying Squadron and had earned her wings flying Avro 504s. As these planes do not fly above 15,000 feet I have to suppose that it was not Evelyn who piloted Sandy's plane but one of her contacts at the flying school.

Shrewsbury School had invited Sandy to lecture to the boys at the end of January on his Arctic trip. Odell sent him his paper on the mountains of Eastern Spitsbergen but Sandy was not confident about the prospect of speaking in public and confided in Odell that he was 'just terrified'. But whatever he said at the lecture it went down well both with the boys and the masters. He presented the school with a copy of the 1922 Everest expedition book *The Assault on Mount Everest* which he signed and dedicated. After Sandy's death many of the masters who wrote to Willie alluded to his talk. Baker, his old chemistry teacher, wrote: 'When he last was here he more than ever endeared himself to us and won the admiration of all who listened to his lecture on his achievements in the far North. I felt as I listened to him that Shrewsbury had pride in so fine a son.' The headmaster went even further: 'There was a nobility and a selflessness in his whole bearing which deeply impressed us and with it all a reality of affection for each one of us which touched us unspeakably.' Harry Rowe, then the head of Sandy's old house, spoke for the boys in a letter that arrived the day Sandy sailed for India. He wished Sandy luck but cautioned: 'remember to bring back those two feet off the top of Everest, so that even though we may not have any Cups in Hall, we can at least put the summit of Everest on it, with a House-Colour ribbon round it!! Cheerio! And keep away from Dusky Maidens, & their allurements!!!' He finished the letter by illustrating the notice he had posted on the house board: *The following will represent Moores v. Everest in the Final of the Mountain Climbing Expedition: A. C. Irvine.*

6

Bound for Darjeeling: The Tittle-Tattle of Travel

'Techniques today are utterly different from those of the pioneer period in the Himalaya. It is unhistorical to look at the expedition of 1924 through modern eyes without making allowances for these differences.'

Herbert Carr, *The Irvine Diaries*

Much was made in the press after the discovery of George Mallory's body in 1999 of the woeful inadequacy of the clothing he was wearing: cotton and silk underwear, a flannel shirt, a long-sleeved pullover, a patterned woollen waistcoat (knitted for him by Ruth) and a windproof Shackelton jacket. On his legs he was wearing a pair of woollen knickerbockers and woollen puttees and on his feet hobnailed boots. Inadequate in terms of what is now worn on Everest certainly, but the fact remains that two men wearing similar clothing succeeded that year in gaining a height of more than 28,000 feet without using supplemental oxygen, a record that stood until 1978. And that is without knowing exactly how high Mallory and Sandy got with oxygen.

It is only too easy to stand in judgement from today's perspective but it cannot be forgotten that both the Poles had been conquered by 1912 and the conditions met by the polar explorers were at least as inhospitable as those the climbers met on Everest. The fundamental difference between then and today, as I understand it, is in the materials that they were using for clothing and footwear. The design of the boots, for example, has altered relatively little but nowadays leather has been replaced by a lighter and warmer man-made material. When I spoke to Rebecca Stephens, the first British woman to climb Everest, we talked at some length about the clothing from the 1920s. She has strong opinions as she climbed in the Alps, for a children's television programme, wearing hobnailed boots. She found them to be relatively comfortable and very reliable on slippery rock, where they had better grip in her view than the modern boot and crampon alternative which, although excellent on snow and ice, is less than perfect when it comes to rock and loose ground. The terrain above the North Col on Everest is rock rather than snow, so perhaps their 'woefully inadequate' footwear, which has been so universally derided, was not quite as bad as some people have made out.

They knew then that the best way to keep warm was to dress in layers and to wear silk or wool close to the skin. What they didn't have was down, goretex and polar fleece, but nor did Hillary and Tenzing when they made their ascent in 1953. I have talked to several high altitude mountaineers and they all agree on two things. First, the overwhelming advantage of today's clothing is that it is breathable and light: wool, gabardine and tweed can be very heavy and restrict movement. Second, if anyone were caught out for a night on the high mountain in 1924 clothing they would have no chance of survival. Nowadays there is a chance that a climber can survive for a night or sometimes more. But that is only of use if they can then be rescued or get down the next day under their own power. Where Sandy and Mallory died they had no chance of being rescued.

The 1924 expedition benefited from the best research and the most advanced equipment available at the time. Not only had they had the experiences of the 1921 reconnaissance mission and the 1922 assault to draw upon, but they had also made great advances on the clothing used in the Antarctic by the Scott Polar expedition of 1911–12 and in oxygen technology for which the research had been carried out by the RAF. Several of the appliances, articles of clothing and of course the tents had been specially designed for the expedition. They firmly believed they were wearing and carrying the best of the best, which indeed they were for the time.

The Mount Everest Committee had to organize every last detail of getting the supplies shipped out to Calcutta on time and in good condition. It was comparable to a military operation and with General Bruce and Colonel Norton in charge it ran as smoothly as a well-organised campaign. The committee issued a long list of necessary items annotated by Norton with his usual dry wit. Members were even advised to take their own saddles – not a piece of equipment much used by modern-day Everest climbers. The note reads, 'Tibetan saddles are the acme of discomfort' and goes on to give a name of a second-hand saddlery company in St Martin's Lane where such equipment can be acquired. The list ran to four pages and the budget for acquiring the equipment was £50, or about £1500 in today's money. The first items on the list were windproof clothing to be acquired from Messrs. Burberry, Haymarket ('ask for Mr Pink'), the Shackelton range of windproof knickerbockers, smocks and gloves. Norton added a note: 'a knickerbocker suit of this sort supplied to Major Norton was a great success last year'. The next item was Finch's eiderdown quilted balloon cloth coat which, years ahead of its time, was laughed at by the 1922 expedition team and was dismissed by Sandy with a simple strike of the pencil.

General Bruce was a big fan of puttees and persuaded the committee to issue them to the expedition as standard. The photograph taken by Odell of Mallory and Sandy leaving Camp IV shows them quite clearly. A puttee comprises a long strip of cloth, in this case the finest cashmere wool, that is wound spirally around the leg from the ankle to the knee. Not only were they warm and comfortable but Bruce was convinced they offered support to the leg as well.

Messrs Fagg Bros. in Jermyn Street supplied a felt boot with leather sole, which was to be made large enough to accommodate three pairs of socks. As this new boot was an experiment they were also advised to purchase a pair of Alpine climbing boots which the committee recommended they had 'nailed'. The leather sole of the boot had hobnails, but in addition to that, little metal plates about one centimetre long were driven between the inner and outer soles to give extra grip. Some of the 'nails' are serrated. Norton goes into great detail about these nails, not least as some believed that the conductivity of the metal caused the foot to get prematurely cold. He sets out his case at length, recommending a certain design and then suggesting a felt sole to be added between the welt[1] and the nailed sole but concluding, 'Boots should be sparingly nailed for lightness – every ounce counts.'

1 A welt is a strip of leather placed between and sewn to the edge of the sole and the turned-in edge of the upper in soling a boot.

When I read the reference to camp equipment I really began to get a feeling for how extraordinarily tough these men were. 'Camp bed is not strictly necessary; it is a comfort up to Phari and in the Kama valley in wet weather. A camp chair is a comfort in tent and for dining (the alternative being a ration box).' I find it a little difficult to conceive of sitting on a ration box for five months and I was glad to see that Sandy bought himself a camp chair. 'An X pattern bath and basin is sound; a bath between two is probably sufficient. A camp table is a luxury; a private folding candle a necessity', the list went on.

Under 'Miscellaneous' they were advised to take out a dinner jacket, to be worn with a soft shirt as opposed to a stiff collar, a big umbrella, also available in Darjeeling at a competitive price, and one packet of Dr Parke Davis's germicidal soap.

The expedition supplied the tobacco duty free to the team members and asked them to let Norton know which was their preferred brand. Sandy, who seemed very much to enjoy his pipe and was frequently photographed with it, appears to have foregone smoking for this trip: he makes no reference to it in his diary and letters, nor are there any photographs of him smoking. Finch had even argued in 1922 that he and Geoffrey Bruce had derived benefits from smoking at altitude, something I cannot conceive of anybody recommending nowadays.

Sandy spent three days in London at the beginning of February ordering his kit, being fitted for his boots and acquiring a saddle. He was staying at the Jules Hotel in Jermyn Street with Marjory. The final bill for his equipment, minus the tool kit, primus burners and spare parts for the oxygen kit, which he paid out of his own pocket, was about £75 (or £2250 today). He was finally reimbursed for his equipment plus the additional kit he had ordered on behalf of the expedition to the tune of £86 1s 1d in May 1924 which, he told Willie Irvine cheerfully, should help to reduce his overdraft.

With a sigh of relief Sandy returned to Birkenhead to spend the final month before leaving England with his family, although he made three further trips to London at Unna's request to finalize details about the oxygen equipment and stoves. He had collected the oxygen apparatus from Oxford and set to work on it in his workshop at Park Road South. Still having heard nothing from Siebe Gorman, he pressed on with his modifications, the realization dawning on him that he was in all probability going to have to effect some fairly major alterations as soon as he met up with the apparatus in its final form in India. He was also occupied with putting together the tool kit and ensuring that the primus stoves and burners that Unna had asked him to take responsibility for were up to standard. Unna had a great deal of faith in Sandy's mechanical capabilities and had given him a free hand in ordering the tools he thought might be required. Sandy sent his list to Spencer at the Mount Everest Committee saying that he regarded it as adequate for looking after the oxygen apparatus, primus burners and the ladder bridge. He added: 'they all pack in quite a small box and none are very heavy; the vice is not a large affair at all and would clamp onto a box or table or any old thing like that.' He had also recommended a pair of Bernard Revolving Pliers for punching holes in leather and a variety of stocks and dies which, he added quickly, would not depreciate in value and could be brought home intact.

Although Odell was appointed oxygen officer, Unna addressed all his communications on that subject and on all other matters to do with the stoves to Sandy, asking him to ensure Odell received copies of the letters. This was in part a shift in Unna's thinking but it was also necessitated by the fact that Odell was on his way to Persia on company business prior to his arrival in India.

Hinks had arranged for Sandy to travel from Liverpool in the company of George Mallory, Benthley Beetham and John Hazard at the end of February. Other expedition members would be travelling from different parts of the Indian subcontinent and of course Odell from Persia, and they would all meet up in Darjeeling at the end of March.

A dinner in honour of the four 'North Country' members of the expedition was given by the Wayfarer's Club on Friday 28 February at the Exchange Club in Fenwick Street. Willie Irvine and the Revd. Herbert Leigh Mallory were invited as guests of honour. Arthur Wakefield, a veteran of the 1922 expedition was also present, as were several members of the Alpine Club. Fifty years later, R. G. Plint, another guest, found his copy of the menu, which had on the front a sketch of Everest. He collected the autographs of the team members and his menu shows Beetham and Hazard's signatures at the base of the mountain but

Sandy in the back of Dick Summers' Vauxhall, September 1923. 'Lower hairpins on Hardknott Pass from Cockley [Beck] Bridge side.' The girls in the back are daughters of the photographer George Abraham

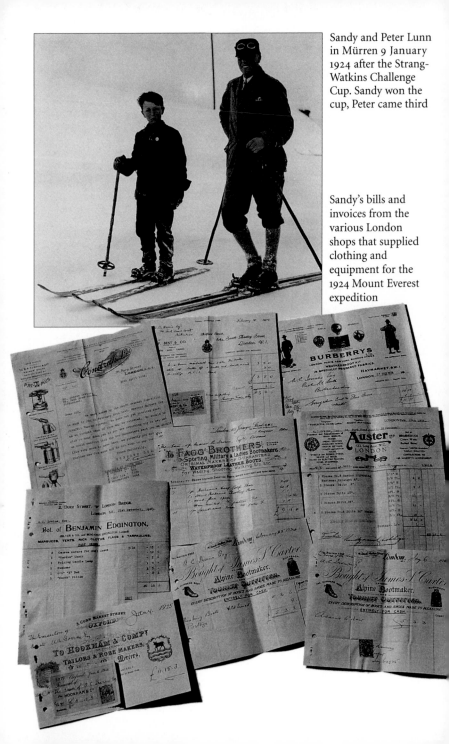

Sandy and Peter Lunn in Mürren 9 January 1924 after the Strang-Watkins Challenge Cup. Sandy won the cup, Peter came third

Sandy's bills and invoices from the various London shops that supplied clothing and equipment for the 1924 Mount Everest expedition

George Mallory and Sandy aboard the SS *California*

P.S. My name in Nepal. – (labels on all my boxes) is

अरबीन साहेब ।

My dear Mother,

Just a line to say all is going very well. We wasted no time getting

Letter from Sandy to Lilian written on Mount Everest Hotel notepaper illustrating his name in Nepali

A piece of cloth from his baggage bearing his name in both English and Nepali, returned to Evelyn in 1931 by Sandy's porter. In it Lobsang had wrapped 20 Himalayan garnets in memory of Sandy

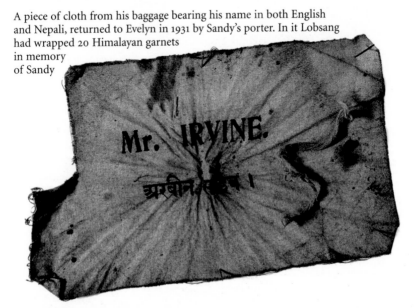

Evelyn aged 22

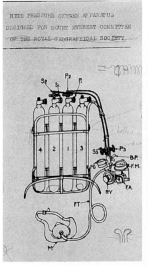

HIGH PRESSURE OXYGEN APPARATUS
DESIGNED FOR MOUNT EVEREST COMMITTEE
OF THE ROYAL GEOGRAPHICAL SOCIETY

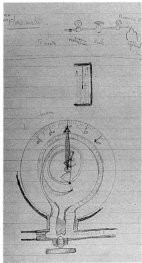

Oxygen Apparatus

Far left 1922 oxygen apparatus

Left Sketch of flow-meter made in Sandy's notebook when he and Odell were trapped in their tent by a blizzard in Spitsbergen, August 1923

Below Sandy's radical redesign of the 1922 apparatus which included inverting the cylinders and doing away with cumbersome and fragile pipework

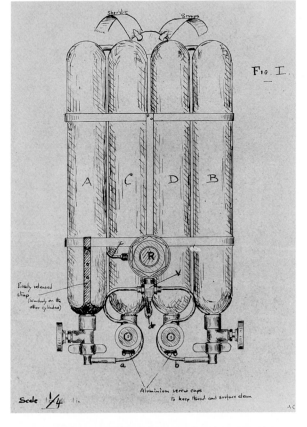

Fig. I.

Right Sandy photographed by Odell at Shekar Dzong on 24 April 1924 showing his Mark V oxygen apparatus which they tested on the rocks below the Dzong

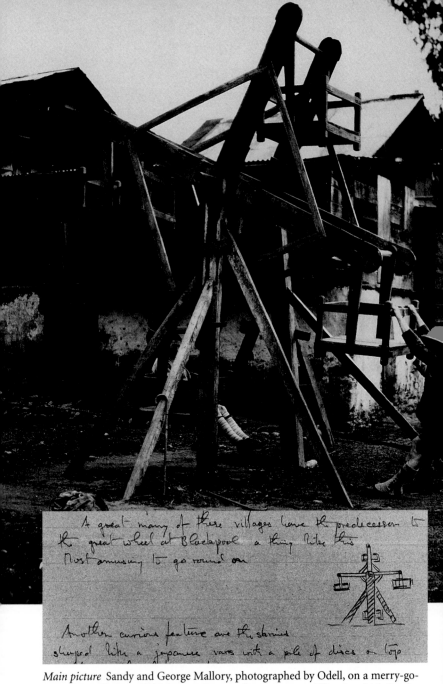

A great many of these villages have the predecessor to the great wheel at Blackpool a thing like this Most amusing to go round on

Another curious feature are the shrines shaped like a japanese vases with a pile of discs on top

Main picture Sandy and George Mallory, photographed by Odell, on a merry-go-round in a village in Sikkim. *Inset* Excerpt from a letter to Lilian in which Sandy sketched the merry-go-round they had encountered in several villages

Mallory and Sandy had signed their names across the summit. The local press had made much of the fact that Sandy and Mallory were both Birkenhead men and had already been fantasizing about the possibility of the two of them standing on the summit of the world together. The *Liverpool Post* had published the names of the 1924 expedition members on 11 January 1924 and ran the headline: 'MOUNT EVEREST EXPEDITION – TWO BIRKENHEAD MEN IN THE PARTY'. In the minds of the Liverpool press at least, the names of George Mallory and Sandy Irvine were already linked.

The following day Mallory, Hazard, Beetham and Sandy posed for photographs, leaning uncomfortably against a life-boat wearing light suits and deck shoes on board the SS *California*, somewhat dazzled by the interest their presence had aroused. The quayside was thronging with well-wishers and members of the press. One journalist from the *Daily Graphic* caught Sandy's attention and asked him how he felt about climbing Everest. 'It is the duty of the Alpine Club to climb as near as it can to Heaven!' he exclaimed with boyish thrill.

The Irvine and Mallory families turned out *en masse* for the send-off, caught up in the excitement and commotion. Tur stood on the dock beside his mother and brother, and muttered prophetically, 'Well, that's the last we'll see of him.' He was rounded on by Alec who told him abruptly to hold his counsel, but the words had been uttered.

Sandy had been overwhelmed with advice and good wishes from friends and family. Everyone felt involved in his adventure and they all felt enormous confidence in his ability to climb the mountain, even though there were at least seven other men who were far more experienced than he was in mountaineering. To all of them it was a matter of great personal pride that Sandy had been selected for the expedition and they were to follow its progress enthusiastically in the *Times* dispatches. Lilian handed her son an envelope as he embarked containing a letter in which she expressed her hopes for Sandy's success. She also permitted herself to give him a good deal of advice and to encourage him to live up to his reputation and not to let the family down. He was not unaware of these high expectations and in his first letter from the *California*, written the day after they sailed, he wrote to Lilian thanking her for the letter and promising to 'try & live up to it'.

The *California* was a 10,000 ton steamship belonging to the Anchor Line Company, based in Glasgow. A large majority of the crew were Glaswegians and there was some mirth on account of the accent which rendered them incomprehensible to a number of the passengers. The Master of the Ship was James Blackie, to whom the expedition members had a letter of introduction.

They finally set sail on the evening of 29 February after several hours of delay. Sandy's first letter was written at the end of their second day on the ship bound for Bombay. He told Lilian about the delays they experienced leaving Liverpool, where the ship was held up for several hours until the harbour master succeeded in finding enough tugs to tow them out of harbour in the strong cross-wind. That night was very rough but once they reached open sea the following day the wind dropped and the weather was calm: 'It has been fairly mill-pondish so far nevertheless the breakfast room was almost empty & the decks are strewn with very miserable looking people. We will be in the middle of the Bay tonight so I hope we don't have an expensive dinner.' Mallory reported at the same juncture that the sea was rough, so perhaps Sandy was comparing it with the stormy experiences he had had *en route* for Spitsbergen.

As usual his letter contained instructions to his mother about his personal effects which he appeared to have left scattered all over the house in Birkenhead. A suitcase he had borrowed from an Oxford friend would need to be sent back, cleaned and emptied ('I've left some bits of primus in it!') and his grandfather's hymn book, which he had left on the billiard table, he asked her to hide until his return. It evidently contained anecdotes and tunes, probably irreverent, that he didn't wish his grandfather to see by mistake. James Irvine was in his ninetieth year but he still exerted a very strong influence over the whole family and had taken Sandy aside before he sailed to give him some advice and warn him what to expect. In his typically dry style Sandy pointed out that what his grandfather had led him to expect on the boat turned out in fact to be the very opposite of the reality. 'He said I would hardly be on the boat before people would start singing hymns – people look more like a burial service than singing!'

The Mount Everest Committee had booked two first-class cabins on the boat, and although Mallory had suggested to Baldrey that he and Sandy might share a cabin, as they were both leaving from Liverpool, Sandy ended up sharing with Benthley Beetham and, by the spin of a coin, got the coveted bottom berth. Never able to resist tinkering, he told his mother that he had pulled the plug on their WC and it had not stopped running which, in his opinion, saved a lot of trouble but had been causing the crew endless headaches as they could not work out how to turn it off. 'Practically the whole of the ships crew have been in to try & stop it but none of them thought of turning off the tap just above!!'

The dining arrangements on the ship had also been prearranged and Sandy was at a table with Mallory while Beetham and Hazard were sitting together at another table. Dinner was a formal meal for which they were expected to dress in dinner jackets but with the concession that soft collar rather than starched collar shirts were acceptable. The seating plan was not changed until the ship arrived in Port Said, so they had plenty of time to get to know the other diners at their table. Two days into the journey Mallory wrote to Ruth giving his impressions of his fellow travellers. Beetham he found good-humoured and unselfish, 'I expect he'll be very useful altogether.' Of Sandy he wrote: 'sensible & not at all highly strung he'll be one to depend on, for everything perhaps except conversation'. If Mallory thought Sandy was short on conversation after just two days at sea, Sandy was equally candid about him, writing 'Mallory is far too energetic for so early in the voyage – he was up and dressed before I had even finished my morning tea & apple.'

When Sandy first met Mallory is a question that has vexed many of us for a very long time. I do not believe he would have written a comment like that to his mother if he had not already at least made Mallory's acquaintance and talked of him to her. Try as I might, I have not found anything that would indicate they had ever seen each other before the dinner at the Wayfarer's Club. Nevertheless, when I was looking through Sandy's correspondence with Unna I came across a reference in which it was suggested that Mallory and Hazard should visit the Royal Geographical Society to see the oxygen apparatus. Although there is no proof, I suggest Sandy met Mallory on one of his visits to London which coincided with the meeting Unna was keen to set up.

Mallory's remark about Sandy has been widely published in the accounts of the 1924 expedition and has been used further to underline the fact that Sandy was inarticulate and lacking in intellectual strength. The latter claim contains some truth, but his lack of conversation, initially at least, would have been on account of his shyness. Mallory wrote to Ruth about the people at the table early on in the voyage:

Next to me at the head of the table is a gentlemanly looking colonel with whom I don't expect to converse in any very interesting way and opposite are a youngish army doctor & his wife, good, enterprising, hard sort of people – hard I mean in the good sense –; she is Canadian by birth & doesn't love Canadians which is a mercy. Mrs Solly's friends, the Lennoxes (you'll remember he's in the Indian survey) seem pleasant people too. Anyway here we are all learning each other's languages, a process which may have gone some useful distance by the time we reach Bombay; then we shall go our separate ways and I shall never see any of this group again.

Poor Sandy! It is hardly surprising that he felt uncomfortable at dinner. There was no one his age at the table and almost certainly no one who shared his interests.

Arnold Lunn had commented that when Sandy joined them in Mürren it was initially difficult to get him to participate in the conversation at dinner. Once Sandy found his confidence, however, his company was greatly enjoyed by everyone and he had the ability to tell an amusing story well. He got over his shyness with Mallory but never felt confident to hold his own when discussing great works of literature or philosophical ideas. He had a very good eye for observation of his fellow men and was able to communicate that with fluency and often humour, both verbally and in his letters home. He was primarily a practical person and when it came to discussing the oxygen equipment he was eloquent and held strong views.

Sandy respected Mallory's knowledge of mountaineering and particularly his experience on Everest from the two preceding expeditions, and he was enthused by Mallory's determination to climb to the summit. In Mallory Sandy found someone who was as focused and determined as he, someone who went all out to achieve his goal and moreover someone who had set himself the highest goal in the world and was resolved to attain it. The two men had much in common, both from the point of view of their backgrounds but also in their aims and ideals. Mallory, like Sandy, valued friendship and loyalty very highly. He was at times impatient and intolerant, something Sandy understood well and a trait he shared. Above all else, he was physically immensely strong and at least as energetic as Sandy. People have sought in the past to try and assess why Mallory was drawn to Sandy and why he elected to make the climb to the summit with him rather than one of the other climbers with more experience, and there have even been some suggestions of a physical attraction on the part of Mallory. Peter and Leni Gillman wrote in their recent biography of Mallory: 'It is more likely that George saw in Irvine a reflection of his younger self, the enthusiastic, athletic undergraduate, eager for new experiences, determined to live them out. Through Irvine, George could also act out the counterpoint of his relationship with Geoffrey Young and his other senior mentors, this time with George initiating a younger partner into the ways of mountaineering.' I think that assessment is much closer to the mark than any other and there can be no doubt that Sandy adopted Mallory as a role model and went all out to impress him from the outset. The summit of Everest had became a goal of his own and although it never gnawed away at him as it did Mallory, he nevertheless set his sights no lower than 29,002 feet and he was determined to be chosen for a final assault.

In the meantime Sandy was content to enjoy the journey and to observe his fellow passengers. The Captain in particular amused him. Mallory had arrived on board with a letter of introduction from Hinks and the four expedition members were duly summoned. Sandy could not resist a dig. 'We have to go to the Captain's with an introduction after lunch – I long to hide his telescope – he never uses it but always rushes in and comes out with telescope under arm & paces the bridge in true nautical style if any one comes to see him. I suppose it's to stop people mistaking him for the steward.'

Although Mallory spent a great deal of his time in his cabin learning Hindustani and catching up on his correspondence, he did use the ship's gymnasium with Sandy and wrote to his sister Mary that he had 'a magnificent body for the job, and he is a very nice fellow'. Mallory was recognized by several passengers and word soon spread as to who he was and where he was heading. He found the attention, the questions and the requests for photographs a burden, so he kept himself out of the public eye as far as he could. Sandy was untroubled by the other passengers and spent most of his time out and about taking part in the deck activities. He played tennis and participated in the deck competitions about which Mallory was disdainful. However, Sandy did succeed in getting him to compete in a potato and spoon race in which he had 'brilliant success & was only knocked out in the final when one potato was really impossible'.

Of the other two men, Beetham and Hazard, Sandy made no mention on the voyage. Beetham was a schoolmaster from Barnard Castle School in Yorkshire. He was shorter than Sandy by several inches, dark haired and was described by Sandy in mid-May at Everest Base Camp, as looking like 'a mixture between Judas Iscariot and an apple dumpling'. Beetham was an agreeable companion and they seem to have got on fine as berth mates, sharing an interest in photography and nature. Sandy was fascinated by the natural environment and would have enjoyed learning from Beetham about observations of bird life he made from the ship. Beetham was one of the great hopes for the 1924 expedition and was expected to perform well on Everest. He and Howard Somervell had spent the summer of 1923 in the Alps, when Beetham had distinguished himself by making thirty-five ascents in as many days. He had also tested the oxygen apparatus designed by Siebe Gorman for the 1924 expedition by carrying it over the Eiger.

Hazard was also a climber. He was an engineer, a close friend and war-time colleague of Morshead, veteran of the 1921 and 1922 expeditions, and had served in India as a sapper. He kept himself very much to himself on the expedition and was only really able to get on with Odell, although he and Sandy did occasionally ride together on the march through Tibet. Sandy should have had a lot in common with Hazard, an engineer and therefore sharing many of the same interests, but the age difference and Hazard's character seemed to prevent any kind of relationship establishing itself. Hazard, sadly, became the fall guy on the 1924 expedition in the way Finch had in 1922. He was heavily criticized for more than one of his actions during May on the mountain. Somervell commented later that Hazard 'built a psychological wall round himself inside which he lives. Occasionally he bursts out of this with a "By Gad this is fine" – for he enjoys (inside the wall) every minute of the Tibetan travel, and even hardship. Then the shell closes to let nothing in.'

Sandy's next letter home was again full of enthusiasm for the voyage and for the beautiful scenery they passed. He had not been particularly impressed by the Rock of Gibraltar but the Atlas Mountains really caught his attention. 'The sea is a most marvellous blue here & the snow on the Atlas Mountains looked magnificent though they must have been 70 miles from where we passed if not more. We were in sight (quite close in places) of Africa for about 1 ½ days but now we don't see land again till Port Said at 2 p.m. tomorrow Sunday.' He added that he hoped the shops would not be shut there as he had no bathing suit and the crew had put up a canvas swimming pool on the after deck for the passengers who were not disembarking in Port Said. The fact that they were to be reduced in number by 200 pleased everyone as there would be far more room on board and Sandy considered they would be a 'very cool & jolly party thereafter'. In the absence of much else to report he told Lilian that one passenger so far had died but he had missed the funeral, which was a disappointment.

The ship docked in Port Said on Sunday 9 March. The shops were closed and no swimming trunks could be found. Sandy was not impressed by the town and wrote to Alec, 'Tell mother that Port Said is quite the ugliest, dirtiest least interesting town I've ever seen. Its only redeeming feature is that those long brown bean things that aunt Gertrude sent Hugh & E & me for swords when we were young grow on trees all down the main street.'

From Port Said the ship sailed through the Suez Canal and into the Red Sea. Here the temperature rose and the heat left them all feeling languid and limp. The ship was sailing at sixteen knots and the wind was the same speed with the result that there was no air on board and the cabins became insufferable in the afternoons. From the deck they were rewarded with marvellous displays of 'flying fish that looked like small swallows flying or rather gliding very close to the water and schools of porpoises quite 500 at a time, a fascinating sight especially as we got quite close to one lot. The Phosphorescence in the Red Sea was

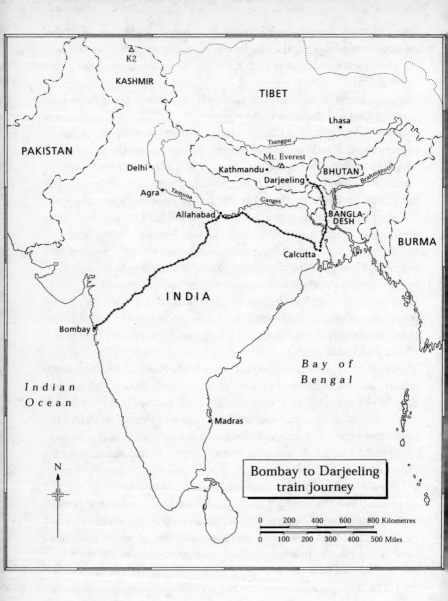

Bombay to Darjeeling
train journey

wonderful & I caught quite a lot in my bath once. No one fell over board', Sandy added, 'so the voyage was fairly uneventful – a mad man on board tried to commit suicide but unfortunately I didn't see it!'

Four days later they arrived in Bombay. The bustling, busy port intrigued Sandy. His senses were assaulted by a wealth of new impressions, as he wandered around, slightly dazed and finding his land legs after three weeks at sea. He took photographs of the dockers unloading the ship and watched with amusement as their heavy boxes of equipment were bundled onto groaning carts and pushed off towards the station. This was his first taste of India and he loved it. His next letter, written from Darjeeling, talked of the great adventure of the train journey across the country. The journey from Bombay took five days and the men slept on the train. The trip left some of them feeling tired and short of sleep. Sandy, however, did not seem to suffer at all and was in high spirits when he wrote to Lilian, 'Just a line to say all is going very well. We wasted no time getting here spending 5 nights only & all in trains between Bombay & here. The temperature was well over 100° F in the shade while we were crossing to Calcutta & 99 in the shade at Calcutta. It was wonderful to get out of the train at wayside stations at 11 or 12 p.m. & see India by a full moon & just cool enough to live in shirt sleeves.' The train, having no corridors, had to stop to allow the passengers to get off and walk to the restaurant car for their meals. The guard discovered one morning that Sandy had overslept and missed breakfast. To his great amusement the guard stopped the Bombay to Calcutta mail train while he got dressed and walked down to the restaurant car for his meal. As there were so few passengers on the train the four of them were more or less at liberty to choose where they would like the train to stop for their lunch or dinner, so they picked spots where the scenery was most beautiful or the wayside attractions the most amusing.

The highlight of the journey for Sandy was the ride from Siliguri to Darjeeling where the railway leaves the plains of India behind and rises into the mountains, entering into an entirely different world.

The last bit of train journey 6 a.m. – 11.30 a.m. climbing 7000 ft up to Darjeeling in a motor rail coach on a 2 ft gauge railway doing most terrifying curves & traverses of cliffs & swaying about the whole time was most delightful. Starting up through very impressive & terribly thick jungle quite impossible to penetrate without the greatest difficulty & all hung with creepers some quite smooth just like hundreds of cords hanging from the branches & some thick & wound together like enormous cables. All the way just enough clearance for the train & a cart track.

The colours, smells and the people made a deep impression on him. Every phase of vegetation was represented from coniferous evergreens to tropical jungle. The brilliant coral blossoms of the cotton trees were contrasted with the ever deepening blue of the sky as the railway climbed higher and higher. They passed bazaars and villages and, just beyond Ghoom, were rewarded with a first glimpse of the Himalaya. From there the train brought them into Darjeeling, the capital city of Benghal. At 7000 feet above sea level it is set in a forest of oaks, magnolia, rhododendrons, laurels and sycamores. 'And through these forests', Younghusband wrote a few years later, 'the observer looks down the steep mountainsides to the Rangeet River only 1000 feet above sea level, then up and up through tier after tier of forest-clad ranges, each bathed in a haze of deeper and deeper purple, till the line of snow is reached; and then still up to the summit of Kangchenjunga, now so pure and ethereal we can scarcely believe it is part of the solid earth on which we stand; and so high it seems part of the very sky itself.'

Sandy, Mallory, Beetham and Hazard arrived on Friday 22 March where they were to spend four days packing and sorting their clothing and equipment, meeting the other expedition members who had gathered from all over. They were staying at the Mount Everest Hotel and it was here that Sandy met up with Odell, who had travelled from the Persian Gulf. 'Odell is here in great form & looking very fit', he told Lilian. They immediately fell into reminiscing about the Spitsbergen expedition and Sandy confessed in his letter to Milling a week or so later that he was certain the other members had become heartily fed up of their banter and continual references to Milling and to Spitsbergen. It must have been a relief for Sandy to see Odell again and to be able to share with him all the impressions he had gained during the five-week journey from Britain.

This was Sandy's first opportunity to meet the other members of the expedition, several of whom knew each other from 1922. The expedition leader was General Charles Bruce, younger son of the first Baron Aberdare. He had been a soldier since the early 1880s and as a keen mountaineer had taken part in a number of early expeditions to the Himalaya between 1890 and 1910. He had long advocated the training of Indians in mountain techniques with a view to forming a body of porters and guides as were commonly used in the Alps in the nineteenth century. Charles Bruce was a man of enormous physical strength. His mountaineering feats were highly regarded until long after his death. His character was as large and rounded as his figure. Younghusband had once described him as 'an extraordinary mixture of boy and man ... you never know which of them you are talking to'. His *joie de vivre*, his perpetual good humour and enthusiasm were coupled with a singular competence and shrewdness. He was a no-nonsense leader and his meticulous planning and organizational skills were well known and widely respected. He was a unanimously popular choice of leader and was particularly liked by the local peoples with whom he had a good empathetic relationship. Bruce was a superb raconteur and at once put Sandy at his ease. He was a keen observer of human nature and had an ability to describe a situation with much humour, observing with obvious delight the idiosyncrasies of the human condition. Writing the expedition dispatches gave him enormous pleasure and he and his typewriter-operator, one of the transport officers, would frequently be heard laughing loudly 'as they sought just the right phrase to shock or baffle poor Hinks'. Bruce's attitude occasionally infuriated Hinks, to whom in 1922 he had famously quipped, when complaints were made about the expenditure he was incurring, 'Captain Noel will be arriving in Darjeeling with a box 40 feet long and I am currently scouring the country for an adequate mule.' On another occasion, when the expedition was running short of funds, he had written to Hinks: 'Please note that I am doing my best for this expedition. I have interviewed the Viceroy, I have preached to Boy Scouts, and I have emptied the poes in a Dak Bungalow. This is the meaning of the term General. They are cheap at home, they are more expensive out here. Hurry up with that thousand [pounds] please.' Bruce's boyish humour was infectious. He laughed uproariously at his own jokes and his 'ready fund of bawdy stories made him extremely popular wherever he went. It was said that his wheezy laugh was a tonic the length and breadth of the Himalaya.' Sandy loved these stories and sorely missed Bruce after he was forced to return to Darjeeling. Bruce had once described Sandy as 'our splendid experiment'. He wrote after the expedition: 'He rapidly ceased to be an experiment for we found that with a young body he possessed a mature judgment, combined with a very remarkable handiness and adaptability as a practical working engineer. All these valuable qualities, combined with infinite stamina and infinite unselfishness, made Irvine a very great asset to our party.' High praise indeed from Bruce.

Norton, the deputy leader of the expedition, was a distinguished soldier. He had been the great 'find' of the 1922 expedition and had proved himself to be a strong and able climber who acclimatized well. He was born in Argentina but was brought back to England as an infant. His education was at Charterhouse and the Royal Military Academy in Woolwich; he was commissioned in 1902 and fought in France during the 1914–18 war. After the war he commanded D Battery in India and it was here that he first came to the notice of General Bruce. As an adolescent he had spent much time scrambling over steep, loose ground on the slopes above the family chalet in Sixt in the Haute-Savoie. He and his brother would chase up the hills after chamois, mastering the difficult ground and often finding themselves on slopes onto which the local hunters would not venture. It was this which he believed made him feel confident on the tricky slopes above the North Col on Everest. He came from a family with a distinguished mountaineering background, his grandfather being the Alpine pioneer and President of the Alpine Club, Sir Alfred Wills, who had made the first ascent of the Wetterhorn in the nineteenth century. Norton was later awarded the Founder's Medal of the Royal Geographical Society and in 1937 acted as ADC to King George VI. In 1938 he commanded the Madras District and was appointed CB. He retired in 1942 as Lieutenant-General after a spell as acting governor and commander-in-chief of Hong Kong. Norton was summed up in an article which appeared in the *Times* in Spring 1924: 'Besides his ability as a climber, Major Norton, who was decorated with the D.S.O. and the Military Cross in the war, is known as a keen soldier and a devoted follower of the sport of pig sticking; he has a good knowledge of botany, a quick eye for the habits of birds, and knows how to paint them.'

Integrity was the essence of his character, Longstaff wrote after Norton's death in 1953. He was a charming companion and a born leader.

Norton had arrived earlier than the rest of the expedition in Darjeeling and Sandy did not have the opportunity to meet him properly until they were on the trek as he was forced to rush off to Kalimpong with Shebbeare, the transport officer, to receive and forward the heavy baggage as it arrived. Norton took his role of deputy expedition leader very seriously: he was a quartermaster without equal and his efficiency and energy meant that when the unthinkable happened and Bruce was invalided out he was able to take over leadership without a hitch. He had made several suggestions and alterations to the organization of the march since 1922, one of which was to redesign the mess tent, a very popular move which every member of the expedition commented on in their diaries and letters. The organization and the writing of dispatches home, which most people, particularly Hinks, conceded he wrote better than Bruce, took up a great deal of his time during the trek and so it was not until they got to the mountain that Sandy really had an opportunity to get to know him better. Norton was the only member of the expedition who was taller than Sandy. He stood a towering six feet four inches. He was slim, lithe and athletic. His face was handsome; he had a long nose, in which, Mallory claimed, he had a dint as a result of the sunburn he contracted in 1922. His efficient air hid a very generous and kind character and although Sandy was initially somewhat shy with him, he soon gained confidence and the two of them developed a good understanding. Norton could not resist pulling Sandy's leg, particularly about hygiene matters for which Sandy was a stickler but he was also quick to compliment him on his work on the oxygen apparatus and other mechanical matters.

Howard Somervell, also a veteran of 1922, was a missionary doctor working in Southern India. He spoke several Indian dialects fluently and was an accomplished watercolourist and amateur musician. On that trek, through his knowledge and love of music, he made a fine collection of Tibetan folk songs, which he later transcribed for Western instruments. He was a highly regarded Alpinist, recently having done a summer's climbing in the Alps with Beetham where they made some difficult ascents. Somervell was much thicker set than Norton physically and a few inches shorter. Finch had thought him too muscle-bound to perform well at altitude, but in this he was wrong. Somervell was extraordinarily strong and although he acclimatized slowly, once he did so he performed magnificently. He was much occupied in his role as expedition doctor during the 1924 march as the other medical officer, Hingston, was obliged to escort the general back to Darjeeling, only rejoining the expedition at Base Camp on 11 April.

Shebbeare, the transport officer, was a new recruit for the 1924 expedition and the man with whom Sandy found he had the most in common. Shebbeare worked for the Indian Forest Department and had experience of the local conditions and of working with the type of men that were to be the expedition porters. General Bruce was delighted to have someone of his experience and reputation as transport officer. He spoke very highly of him, in particular mentioning his sympathetic temperament which enabled him to get the best out of the men they had employed as porters. He had no previous experience of high altitude mountaineering but, as Bruce pointed out, that was not his job. In the event Shebbeare turned out to be an all-rounder and climbed as high as Camp III where he spent two days with Sandy helping him to make a rope ladder to ease the porters' passage up the formidable ice chimney between Camps III and IV on the North Col. He became the acknowledged 'King' of Camp II and Norton wrote of him in a dispatch to the *Times* dated 14 June 1924:

It was decided that Mr Shebbeare's knowledge of the language and of the psychology of the porters called for his presence on the lines of communication rather than at the Base Camp. Accordingly he was established as king of No. II. From that moment we at the higher camps never had to look over our shoulders or give a moment's anxious thought to our line of supply. Food for the Sahibs and porters, fuel and stores of all sorts, arrived smoothly as required, and, more important still, we knew that the comfort and health of the porters on the lines of communication were well cared for.

Like several of the others, Shebbeare kept an expedition diary. In 1939 he lent it to the Government press in Kuala Lumpur and thus fortunately it survived the Japanese invasion of Malaya in the Second World War, when his home and many of his other possessions were destroyed. When he was released from the POW camp at the end of the war he was able to retrieve the diary and some notes from the Head Lama of Rongbuk. He made a transcription in 1948, which includes the typewritten memoirs of the Rongbuk Lama. In the explanatory note at the front of the diary, Shebbeare rather plays down the relevance of his own writings, but it is a fascinating document and sheds much light on the march across Tibet and brings a deal of humour to the story. Sandy and Shebbeare worked closely together as mess secretary and transport officer and his gentle manner and practical approach put Sandy at his ease. I sense that he felt almost more comfortable with Shebbeare than anyone else on the expedition despite the fourteen-year age difference. Shebbeare had a keen wit and a wonderful eye for observing detail, not only about the wildlife, which was his chief interest on the march, but also about the other members of the expedition. Once, at Camp II, he sent a note up to III expressing concern as to the whereabouts of Beetham who had been due into II the previous evening. He had spent three hours out on the glacier with a lamp and concluded that Beetham must be dead. He sent a note up to Norton which read, 'If he left Camp III yesterday we'd better try to recover the body – if he didn't he's a bugger for not letting me know!'

Geoffrey Bruce was the general's nephew and another veteran of 1922. He had achieved a height record on that expedition with George Finch when the two of them reached 27,300 feet breathing supplemental oxygen and had been invited to join the 1924 expedition on account not only of his climbing achievements in 1922, but also on the grounds of his ability to get the Sherpas and porters to do what was required of them. He worked closely with Shebbeare during the march and frequently had to deal with truculent Dzong Pens and transport officials,[2] which he did in a calm but persuasive manner, always getting his own way in the end, but sometimes having to argue for hours with the locals. Shebbeare noted that the longest argument they ever had lasted for a full nine hours. Geoffrey Bruce was a close friend of Norton's and he helped him write the dispatches for the *Times*. In a private letter that

2 Tibet was divided up into districts and the Dzong Pen was the local headman or governor.

Norton wrote to members of the 1922 expedition after the deaths of Mallory and Sandy, Geoffrey Bruce allowed himself some asides which give an inkling of the repartee that went on between him and Norton whilst composing the dispatches. He makes interjections saying exactly what he thought Norton meant rather than the more tactful phrases that were finally written. At twenty-eight he was the closest in age to Sandy and right from the start the two had a good relationship and I sense that Geoffrey Bruce was the kind of man who Sandy would have been very glad to have as a friend in later life.

Hingston was the official expedition doctor and surgeon. He was also the expedition's naturalist. General Bruce was delighted with him and commented that he 'came bursting with energy and enthusiasm to test every member of the Expedition with every terror known to the RAF authorities.' He was of a cheerful disposition and had an 'unfailing humorous outlook'. He was not expected to climb high on the mountain but in the event he had to go up to Camp IV to rescue Norton when he was stricken with snowblindness after his summit attempt. Hingston had his work cut out during the expedition. His first casualty was General Bruce whom he escorted from Tuna to Gangtok before returning to join the expedition and by the time he finally arrived at Base Camp on 11 May there were several very sick men for him to attend to. Despite the problems he encountered in his professional capacity, Hingston seems to have thoroughly enjoyed the whole Everest experience. On the way back to Kampa Dzong from Gangtok he wrote to General Bruce giving descriptions of his enjoyment of the road through the forests and adding that he had captured 'no less than 300 different kind of bugs without even dismounting'. A *Times* journalist present at the Alpine Club and Royal Geographical Society meeting held at the Albert Hall in October 1924, described Hingston in his article the following day as 'the man who enjoyed it most'. As a naturalist, 'every stone in Tibet was to him a potential goldmine for under it might lurk something really fascinating – such as a tick'.

Capt. John Noel was the expedition's official cameraman. He was not part of the climbing party and worked independently from the rest of the expedition in that he ran his own outfit, organized his own porters, transport and runners, but he was a popular member of the team. He had accompanied the expedition in 1922 when he had set up a darkroom at Base Camp so that he could develop his photographs on site. In 1924 the whole photographic outfit was much more professional. Noel had approached the Everest Committee offering to buy the film and photographic rights for the whole expedition for a staggering sum of £8000, which, he and his backers believed, could be recuperated by future takings from the film he would be making. The Everest Committee needed to be asked only once. Such a large sum would in one fell swoop alleviate all their funding problems. Noel organized his team somewhat differently in 1924. There had been problems with developing photographs at Base Camp in 1922, since it had proven extremely difficult to keep the improvised darkroom tent dust free. This time he set up a darkroom in Darjeeling and had a series of runners between there and Base Camp taking films back for developing, thus enabling him to keep the *Times* supplied with photographs of the expedition as it progressed. Sandy, being a keen photographer, got on well with Noel. The two of them had similar interests in the technology of photography and Sandy more than once was called in to repair a broken piece of photographic equipment. Mallory was less than enthusiastic about the filming of the expedition but he liked Noel and wrote to Ruth from Darjeeling: 'Noel's movements are independent (i.e. he doesn't belong to one or other party); he is more than ever full of stunts; the latest is a Citroen tractor which somehow or another is to come into Tibet – a pure ad of course.'

Such was the makeup of the expedition, not forgetting Odell, Hazard and Beetham, that met on 23 March 1924. Everyone was full of optimism and the 1922 veterans each privately expressed the belief that they had the strongest possible team. Indeed Norton wrote later: 'I don't believe a stronger party will ever be got together for Everest.'

The day after they arrived in Darjeeling Bruce called a meeting to hand out duties for the trek. Hazard and Sandy were appointed as the two mess secretaries, and spent a good deal of time receiving instruction about how to fulfil their task, 'most unpleasant & difficult as I don't know a word of the language', Sandy observed. It was an obvious job to give Sandy, he being the youngest and least experienced member of the party, but it was the lowliest of all the jobs and brought him into contact with the porters with whom he foresaw much fun trying to talk in signs and pictures. He was allotted two porters of his own, neither of whom spoke a word of English.

The baggage was due to leave on the Monday after their arrival and Sandy struggled to pack all his kit and clothing into the limited amount of weight that he was allowed. He was carrying a tool kit that weighed as much as his tent and this meant that he had to restrict himself to fewer clothes and other items in order not to overburden the pack animal. Each team member was permitted a pair of mules to carry their baggage and each mule could be loaded with 160 pounds of kit but that had to include their own tent, which weighed sixty pounds. This left 260 pounds to be distributed between suit and ice axe cases and Sandy's very heavy tool kit and cameras. He gave himself quite a headache trying to arrange all his own affairs in time for their departure but eventually succeeded. He had another task to fulfil in Darjeeling which was to test the equipment that had been ordered in England. The first thing to command his attention was a new paraffin cooker, which he described as looking like an enormous brazing lamp. This, he concluded, 'seemed very satisfactory but rather heavy'. He then examined the ladder bridge, the primus stoves and the tool kit, the box for which had already almost fallen to pieces, he noticed to his disgust.

In addition to testing the stoves and packing and repacking his kit, Sandy visited Lady Lytton, the wife of the governor of Benghal, who happened to be Tony Knebworth's mother. He wrote to Lilian:

I've had one afternoon's delightful tennis with Lady Lytton & family who wanted to know all the news about her son Tony Knebworth otherwise Lord K – who was out at Mürren all the time with us – I tactfully kept off the subject of Oxford as I believe he has just been sent down from Magdalen for playing roulette! Lord Lytton (or whatever his title is) is Governor General of Bengal & in Calcutta at present but the rest of the family & all the ADC's at Government House are a very delightful lot.

Lady Hermione Lytton, Tony Knebworth's sister, was a girl of fifteen or sixteen in 1924 and was living at the time in Darjeeling. I wanted to know whether she had any memory of Sandy but she sent back a reply saying that while she had no clear recollection of him she did recall being very taken with Colonel Norton which is hardly surprising: he was very dashing. Sandy was so enjoying his time with the Lyttons that he left his final packing rather to the last minute on the Sunday and did not get it done until 1.30 a.m. on the Monday when the baggage was due to leave for Kalimpong.

On the Monday evening, the night before the expedition members left Darjeeling, Hingston carried out a series of medical experiments on the climbers to assess their physical and mental condition at 7000 feet. The tests were of necessity rudimentary as Hingston had no means to carry complicated apparatus on the trek. They were based on tests that had been carried out on RAF pilots and involved observations on alterations in breathing, circulation, muscular power and mental activity. Sandy could hold his breath at 7000 feet for twenty seconds longer than any of the others and his expiratory force matched that of Geoffrey Bruce and exceeded the others as well. When it came to blowing mercury up a tube and holding it he performed less well, only coming third. He made careful notes of his own performance and seemed satisfied with the results although he noted that he 'got the arithmetic right but slow for me'. Mallory consistently outperformed all the others in the mental activity tests and by ever-increasing margins as the altitude increased.

Just before they left on the Tuesday morning Sandy penned a quick note to his father asking him to send a letter to Spencer in London requesting reimbursement for the cost of the primus burners and the tool box 'which incidentally has nearly disintegrated already'. There had been some confusion over the address that had been given for post and he was anxious that his parents should use the correct address which was given as Mt Everest Expedition, c/o Post Master, Darjeeling, '& not Yatung Tibet as the Everest Committee informed us after we had sailed'. Keeping in touch meant much to the expedition members. Time and time again in their letters and diaries they refered to their delight or disappointment when the post bag arrived in camp.

With all arrangements in place Sandy told Lilian that the trek was due to start in earnest: 'We are splitting into 2 parties from Kalimpong to Phari as there are huts that will accommodate 6 Sahibs[3]; each a days march apart, between the two places; which will be comfier than tents.'

---

3 The title used by the porters when addressing the English expedition members.

From Darjeeling to Kalimpong it would be '7000 ft down & 4000 ft up – quite a good start for the 1st days work'. To his father he wrote, 'I believe its Sunday today. Do tell Grandfather that we have a Medical <u>Missionary</u> as well as a Doctor with us. We start about 6 a.m. tomorrow morning.'

7

Under the Finest Possible Auspices: The Trek Across Tibet

From the top of the pass for the first time the whole of the Everest system enters into close view. The five highest mountains in the world are there in one grand coup d'oeil, *west to east, Cho Uyo, Gyachungkang, Everest, Makalu and Kangchenjunga. Everest has pride of place in the centre immediately opposite, and is already displaying the great cloud pennon on its peak.*

E. F. Norton, published 17 May 1924 in the *Times*

In the 1920s the only way to get to Everest was to trek from Darjeeling. The Nepalese border being closed to foreigners, the only possible approach to the mountain was across the Tibetan plain, a march of some 350 miles. There were no proper roads so that the assistance of motorized vehicles was out of the question. Everything the expedition would need for the march in the way of equipment and, for the great part, food had to be carried by pack animal. Norton had arranged for a few luxuries for the party such as tins of quail in foie gras and four cases of Montebello Champagne. The route took the expedition from Darjeeling to Kalimpong, a hill station and the last town encountered before entering Sikkim; through the steaming valleys of Sikkim to the Jelap La pass (14,500 feet) which is the border between India and Tibet. From there the route leads down into the beautiful Chumbi Valley to Phari and thence onto the Tibetan plain, at a constant altitude of about 14,000 feet, with passes to be crossed at regular intervals, often three in a day at over 17,000 feet.

It was an enormous organizational feat and the experiences of the 1922 trek had led them somewhat to modify the march, allowing for more time to cross the plain, but in the main the 1924 expedition took

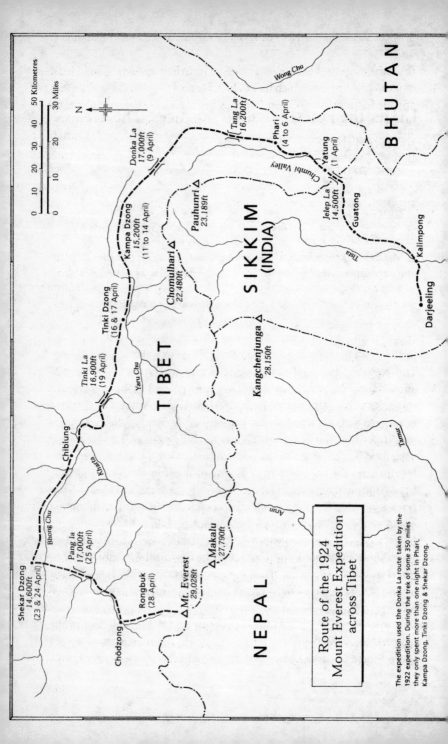

N

50 Kilometres
30 Miles

0   10   20   30   40

0   10   20   30

B H U T A N

Wong Chu

Tang La
16,200ft

Phari
(4 to 6 April)

Yatung
(1 April)

Chumbi Valley

Donka La
17,000ft
(9 April)

Jelep La
14,500ft

Guatong

Kampa Dzong
15,200ft
(11 to 14 April)

Pauhunri △
23,189ft

Chomulhari △
22,480ft

Tinki Dzong
(16 & 17 April)

Tista

Kalimpong

Tinki La
16,900ft
(19 April)

T I B E T

Yaru Chu

S I K K I M
(INDIA)

Darjeeling

Kangchenjunga △
28,150ft

Chiblung

Khara

Shekar Dzong
14,600ft
(23 & 24 April)

Bhong Chu

Pang la
17,000ft
(25 April)

Chödzong

Rongbuk
(28 April)

Everest △
29,028ft

Makalu △
27,790ft

Arun

Tamur

N E P A L

Route of the 1924
Mount Everest Expedition
across Tibet

The expedition used the Donka La route taken by the
1922 expedition. During the trek of some 350 miles
they only spent more than one night in Phari,
Kampa Dzong, Tinki Dzong & Shekar Dzong.

the same route as that of 1922. The expedition had some 3000 lb of food, tents and equipment which had to be transported on mules and ponies, and the two transport officers Geoffrey Bruce and Shebbeare took charge of the luggage train. It was they who had to negotiate the frequent changes of transport required *en route*. General Bruce was concerned that he should get all his men to the foot of Everest in the best health possible. He described this responsibility as almost like dealing with 'the crew of a university boat. They must be brought up to scratch without having suffered in any way from the arduous 300 mile journey across Tibet, or from degeneration in any form from the effects of a somewhat elevated route at a very early season of the year.'

With their porters employed and all their personal packing complete, the expedition was ready to leave Darjeeling on 26 March. They drove to 6th Mile Stone in Willis, or buses, from where they proceeded on foot to Tista Bridge. Sandy was absorbing the new sights and impressions that he encountered: 'Coming down from Darjeeling', he wrote in his diary that evening, 'we saw some most beautiful butterflies and got some wonderful wafts of perfume on a very hot breeze. At one point ... we came across a fine lizard sitting on a rock with its tail stuck straight up in the air.' From Tista they proceeded on foot and pony to Kalimpong. Sandy was amused that his pony did not even start at the sound of a huge tree being felled above them: 'a most impressive sight and a tremendous noise but curiously enough none of our ponies showed any sign of alarm.'

As far as I know Sandy had not had a great deal of experience of horse riding and it took him a while to get used to this mode of transport. There were several occasions when he was lucky to escape with nothing more serious than a scraped knee. As he was so tall and the ponies so small he found that the most expeditious way to stop them when they ran away with him was to put his feet onto the ground and, in effect, lift the animal into the air. This slightly unorthodox approach to horse-manship was evidently of amusement to him and the other expedition members and he related the story of such an incident in a letter to Geoffrey Milling: 'All our ponies work on the rocket principle – that's how they get along up the hills so well! They are tough little brutes, mine ran away with me up hill today, I had to put my feet down & lifted it off the ground to stop it.' To his mother he was rather more honest about the discomforts he faced when riding. It would appear that, like his father, he had somewhat delicate insides. He wrote to Lilian, 'the pony shakes my bladder up rather & tends to give me the old trouble but I think I ought to get hardened to that soon. For that reason I have been walking most of the way so far.' In fact, for a variety of reasons, he ended up walking a good two thirds of the entire march on foot. He eventually got the hang of his pony and had some lovely rides with Mallory and Hazard during the trek.

Sandy was keen to give Lilian the richest picture he could of the scenery and the sights he was encountering. He wrote to her whenever he could find a moment, which was not often and frequently under less than ideal circumstances and sometimes he had to break off mid-sentence: '– sorry if this writing has been rather shaky but my lad Tsutrum would insist that I had sweated in my stockings & they must be dried before the sun goes down so he has been taking off my shoes & stockings while I've been writing – well to continue ...' He went into great detail about all the arrangements for their overnight stays and was clearly impressed by the dak bungalows which were 'very well looked after ... this one has a lovely balcony with a superb view (if clear) & flower pots full of flowers all round & the whole place is most awfully clean'. He drew sketches in his diary and letters of many of the daks they stayed in, always making a note of the location of his own bedroom. His photography however he reserved for the scenery and the Tibetan people he met. He wrote to Lilian early on that he had kept a diary 'so far which is pretty good work for me! Please keep my letters to fill out my diary when I get home.' When he was in Spitsbergen he had kept a notebook and then written up his diary when he got back to Bergen after the expedition. He was clearly planning to do the same thing with the Everest expedition and had determined to write a somewhat fuller account on his return, hence the request to Lilian to keep his letters. His letters are fluent, descriptive and give a very clear picture of his state of mind as well as of the sights he saw and the experiences he enjoyed.

The expedition arrived in Kalimpong in the early afternoon and Sandy at once set to work on checking the oxygen stores, the stoves and the ladder bridge, all of which had arrived in advance of the party. Others were equally busy checking stores and adjusting to the thought of a five-week march where they normally would spend only a single night in any one location. Bruce had explained to the team that they would be split into two parties, walking one day apart, because the bungalows that they had arranged *en route* for Phari would not accommodate the whole expedition. After Phari they would all join up and continue together, sleeping in tents as they made their way over the Tibetan plateau. Sandy was in the second party, which as he had informed Lilian, comprised Mallory, Hingston, Shebbeare, Odell and Norton.

In keeping with the tradition he had established in 1922, General Bruce and the other members of the expedition visited Dr Graham's Home in Kalimpong where he instructed Nepalese children in the tradition of the Boy Scouts. Bruce bore a message from Sir R. S. Baden-Powell and made an inspection of the ranks of children, who were beautifully turned out in their scout uniforms, complete with badges but bare feet. This was one of Bruce's most pleasant duties as he reported with great pride and delight in his next *Times* dispatch: 'A parade of the Boy Scouts and Girl Guides at the Kalimpong Homes was extremely attractive, and we were all immensely struck with their very remarkable appearance and the general enthusiasm and happiness of everyone. We had a charming meeting with them all and a great send-off.' Duties thus dispensed, the first party set off from Kalimpong and over the border into Sikkim. On the frontier they encountered a border guard who clearly tickled Bruce's sense of humour: 'When we had finished the necessary official documents, "Right hand salute" roared the guard at himself and duly saluted with the right hand; "left turn" he bellowed, and turned to the left; "quick march" he shrieked, and straightway took himself off. He was a Gurkha, and all Gurkhas love drilling themselves if they cannot get anyone else to drill them.'

After the first party left for Pedong the second party was obliged to spend a further day in Kalimpong. From the outset, whenever there was a break, Sandy would turn his attention to the oxygen apparatus and anything else that required his engineering skills and ingenuity. I have a sense that this first day of forced inactivity was something of a burden to him, for as Norton and others socialized with the MacDonalds, Perries and Waights, all local worthies, he hid himself away in his room with the excuse that he had things to fix, such as his watch. He was not yet feeling confident in the company and he preferred to keep away from events which would bring him into contact with yet more strangers. He wrote three long letters to friends in England, including his old rowing partner Geoffrey Milling, and Audrey Pim, Evelyn's close friend from school.

Once he was on the march the next day Sandy's spirits improved and the irritation of his broken wrist-watch, which he had only made worse the previous afternoon, paled. The road from Kalimpong to Pedong was one of outstanding scenery although the views were somewhat obscured that year owing to the mist which appeared to be as a direct result of an unduly dry season and thus a great number of forest fires. Kangchenjunga, the great mountain that dominates Sikkim and whose name means 'Five Treasures of the Great Snows' was only dimly visible through the mist. He wrote to Milling:

It's perfectly wonderful being able to go about in a bush shirt & shorts all day & get every damn thing done for you & be able to ride when ever you get tired of walking & through the most pricelessly wonderful glades in the jungle. We are under 6,000 ft here so the forest is pretty thick still; the only pity is that the visibility has not been good just lately – not for distances over 2 miles or so, otherwise the scenery would be wonderful. This is a remarkable place: it's pitch dark now & it was bright sunlight when I started this letter – at least very nearly! ... I say old Man Odell is just the same as ever! He longs to have you here the other members are getting quite fed up with our side illusions to you & Spits. They get such a lot of them.

But Odell was not the only person Sandy was talking to. He had gained confidence in Mallory's presence and right from the beginning I sense that he took considerable pride and delight in the fact that Mallory often chose to ride or walk with him. He invariably notes this in his diary and even mentions it on a few occasions in his letters home. I know from the photographs of the trek that he and Odell frequently rode and walked together as well, but apart from a reference to Odell in this letter to Milling and the occasional reference to him in his diary, usually in connection with his health, the focus of his attention was Mallory. It was clear that if he were going to have any chance at getting himself onto a summit party Sandy would have consistently to impress Mallory and this he set out to do from the word go. If Odell had been a role model for him in Spitsbergen, how much greater a role model was Mallory on this expedition? With his knowledge of the mountain and his reputation as the best climber of his day and the man with the greatest chance to reach the summit, it is hardly surprising that Sandy switched his allegiance. Odell was never going to be in contention as a lead climber in the present company, and Sandy realized this immediately. Sandy had set his sights no lower than the summit of Everest before he even left England and he was going to make sure that he got his chance at the top when the time came. Some ambition for a twenty-two year old. Whether or not this was hurtful to Odell is difficult to say but he did observe that Sandy 'could not readily be drawn out to say much unless the environment was sympathetic. The high altitudes of Tibet perhaps a little emphasised this'. If there was a little friction it was never noticeable to the others and Odell and Sandy worked together for hours on end in respect of the oxygen apparatus and later, on the mountain, where they became a formidable relief team to climbers coming down from higher camps. Norton even referred to them as 'the well-known firm of Odell and Irvine'.

One of the particular delights on the first few days of the march through Sikkim were the bathes Mallory, Odell and Sandy took in the rivers along the route. 'I had 3 most delightful bathes yesterday & 2 today', he wrote to Lilian, adding that unfortunately he had still not succeeded in acquiring the swim suit he had hoped to buy in Port Said, 'though I manufactured quite a good one out of a belt & 2 handkerchiefs. It is a very bad thing indeed to be seen naked by any one in the country – just the opposite to what I expected.' The water was deliciously warm and they even succeeded in finding a pool deep enough for a shallow dive. Later they found a spot where the river ran fast over rocks in small rapids and they spent a happy hour or so sliding over the warm rocks and small waterfalls, although Sandy did this once too often and scratched his bottom. Mallory was enjoying the bathes as much as Sandy. All the anxiety and impatience he had felt up to this point seemed to have dissipated. He was on the way to Everest in good company and he was quite relaxed. He wrote to Ruth extolling the virtues of the bathing and added: 'We couldn't be a nicer party – at least I hope the others would say the same; we go along our untroubled way in the happiest fashion.' Everyone did indeed seem to be very happy. Shebbeare spent a great deal of time chasing and catching butterflies, Norton sketched and painted the scenery, Mallory read and planned with Norton the assault on the mountain, Odell was fully occupied with matters geological and Sandy was having a delightful time, watching and observing closely everything he saw in the villages they passed through, swimming whenever the occasion permitted and, in any spare time at the end of a march, fiddling with the oxygen apparatus. Despite his real enjoyment of the trek the apparatus was causing him some anxiety. He was appalled by how badly the cylinders leaked and how fragile they were. In the letter to Geoffrey Milling from Pedong he concluded: 'The oxygen has been already boggled! They unfortunately haven't taken my design but what they've sent is hopeless – breaks if you touch it – leaks & is ridiculously clumsy & heavy. Out of 90 cylinders 15 were empty & 24 badly leaked by the time they arrived at Calcutta even – Ye Gods! I broke one taking it out of its packing case!!' The anguish over the oxygen apparatus is a recurring theme in Sandy's diary and by the time he got to Base Camp he had completely lost his sense of humour. At this stage, however, he was still examining what Siebe Gorman had sent and discovering to his increasing disquiet the extent of the task that lay ahead of him.

The route through the forest from Pedong 'was very delightful through sunlit glades over roads of stone full of mica which looked like silver in the sun'. From Rangli the road began to rise and the bathing stopped, much to Sandy's regret. The route led up towards the first of the high passes the expedition would encounter and it was on this road through the forest that Sandy had his second incident with his pony. He was in the process of trying to overtake a mule loaded with cotton when it was nipped in the bottom by another mule from behind. The loaded mule did not take kindly to this aggressive nibble and leapt forward, dislodging a bale of cotton which knocked into Sandy's pony and sent them both tumbling down the hill from the narrow rocky path. Fortunately there was a ledge some ten feet below which broke the fall and the pony scrambled at the edge just long enough for him to jump clear before they both rolled down the hillside together. 'Fortunately the beast came off with only a slightly cut hock & I got away with a scraped knee.' In a similar incident some days later Odell did not come off so well and had his knee badly crushed in a fall from his pony. Riding seems to have been altogether one of the main hazards of the trip.

Another, unseen hazard was the stream water. They had been given a long lecture before they left Darjeeling on the dangers of drinking from the streams and rivers. One of the recurring themes of the previous two expeditions had been the debilitating gastric problems that had afflicted several members and which had contributed to the death of Kellas in 1921. General Bruce, mindful that he needed the very fittest and strongest team of climbers available when it came to making the assault on the mountain, asked Hingston to make every effort to keep the men as healthy as possible. Thus, when confronted with thirst and a fresh stream, they all felt a great deal of guilt as they broke the pledge and drank from the waters.

As the route rose out of the valleys they reached their first pass, above Sedongchen. At 5500 feet it was the same height as the peak Sandy climbed in Spitsbergen with Odell the previous summer. They stopped at the little tea house at the top of the pass and agreed that this march was the most beautiful one they had done up to now. The forests were of rhododendron, all mauves, pinks, cerise, cream and white with butterflies and birds darting in and out above their heads. The march passed through several villages with their mud-lined huts and rush roofs. Sandy thought the people to be very cheery and friendly, much more so than the folk in the Indian villages closer to Darjeeling. He couldn't resist a familiar comparison: 'some of the women look just like Aunt T.D. in spite of the rings in their noses', and the very pretty girls pleased him greatly as they knew 'how to turn themselves out to the best advantage'. As if to reassure his mother that it was not only the girls who interested him, he went on to describe in some detail his observations about the religion, which he found very romantic. 'Most of the houses have tall bamboo poles with a strip of flay all the way down with prayers written all the way down in their strange hieroglyphics. The idea is that the wind wafts the prayers off to their gods … I think it's a shame that missionaries come and put strange and far less romantic ideas into their heads.' Naïve and innocent as this remark might seem, I do not think it would have gone down particularly well at Park Road South, where several Irvine relatives had worked as missionaries in India. With the knowledge that he was several thousand miles away from home he probably felt comfortable making a gentle dig at his family's devout religious beliefs. This theme recurs later in the trek, when he arrived in Shekar Dzong.

Several of the villages had a form of merry-go-round which Sandy described as 'the predecessor to the great wheel in Blackpool' and on which he and Mallory were photographed by Odell. He made a sketch of it in a letter as it had clearly caught his eye, as had the Tibetan shrines which he also drew for his mother. 'They are rather curious things to meet in out of the way places.'

From the very beginning of the march Sandy's fair skin caused him great problems. He burned his elbows and knees badly in Sikkim but it was his face that was to cause him the greatest agony later on. By mid-April he had serious sunburn to his face and had lost several layers of skin around his nose and mouth. Most of the other members grew beards to protect their faces, but Sandy, for some reason, elected to keep himself free from facial hair. He was also painstaking about his daily washing and this did not go unremarked by the other members of the party. Norton, in a dispatch to the *Times*, went into some detail about the habits of the expedition members. 'The effect of the sun and wind is less felt than previously, thanks to the early issue of lanoline and vaseline, and to the cautious avoidance of the ultra-English vice of cold bathing in the open. Thus we have retained a high average proportion of skin on the nose, lips and finger-tips … In this respect a fair man offers the most vulnerable target, and the Mess Secretary seems to have hit on the expedient of growing a new face every second day, but then he is suspected of indulging in the said English vice, or why his frequent pilgrimages in the direction of a frozen stream, clad principally in a towel?'

The trek followed the route from Guatong to Langram where they encountered snow for the first time. 'It was very curious', Sandy wrote, 'to change from almost tropical climate to above the snow line in 3 hours.' The going was much rougher here than it had been up until now and several of the ponies slipped and fell. When they arrived in Langram Sandy settled down to another afternoon with the oxygen apparatus. More trouble. He found that all but one of the oxygen frames had been more or less damaged in transit and worked away well into the night repairing them with copper rivets and wire.

As the route gained height so the affects of altitude were beginning to be felt. On 1 April they crossed the Jelap La, at 14,500 feet, from Sikkim into Tibet. Sandy climbed 3000 feet in one morning and noted that he 'felt a slight headache towards the top, especially if my feet slipped & shook my head much. I felt quite tired in my knees & panted a good deal if I tried to go fast. At the top of the pass put the largest stone I could lift on the cairn from about 20 yards away, just to make sure that the altitude wasn't affecting me unduly! Anyway I was quite glad to sit down for a few minutes, the altitude being my record up to date, 14,500 ft.' He took photographs of the cairn with its prayer flags fluttering in the wind and continued down from the pass into Tibet on foot. He was interested in the different characteristics of this side of the pass, where the tree line was some 2500 feet higher than on the other side. They had come from a valley of lush vegetation into a dryer and cooler valley in the lee of the pass where the trees were now predominantly pine.

Norton was very pleased to record in his diary that he had felt absolutely no effects at all from the same altitude, observing that his performance to this height was considerably better than it had been in 1922. This concurs exactly with Hingston's later findings, that the climbers who had already been to altitude on previous occasions acclimatized far more quickly than those who had not. Whenever Sandy reached a new height record he was blighted with a headache. Odell, too, was suffering somewhat from the altitude, but he was also affected with a gastric complaint: 'mountain trots, I expect', Sandy noted somewhat disingenuously in his diary. A fall with his pony only added to his woes. It fell and landed heavily, crushing Odell's knee and leaving him stiff and sore for a few days. Mallory, however, was full of energy and bounding ahead of the others on the march. When Sandy was not keeping up with

Mallory he walked with Shebbeare. The two of them seemed to have a good understanding and Sandy described him as 'a very fine specimen of a man & most awfully wise. He impresses me more every day.'

They spent the night of 1 April in a 'no good' guest house where the first party had stayed the previous night and Geoffrey Bruce had left them a half bottle of whisky with a note saying that they had plenty with them. They were all delighted by the find and, with the prospect of five teetotal months ahead of them, spent quite some time discussing the best way to make the most of this unexpected gift. In the end they decided to take it in their tea and they all declared they'd loved it until Shebbeare tried a drop neat and discovered it was the dregs of the whisky bottle filled up with tea. It was only then that they recalled the date. 'We'll have to hush this up from the first party!' Sandy wrote. Being only a few days into their march and still full of the beer and the benevolence of civilization, they thought it quite a good April Fool's joke. 'I doubt if we should have thought it funny a few weeks later when we were beginning to feel the strain.' Shebbeare wrote, 'There were times later on when we ran short of sweet things (we were never short of food) when an irregularly broken stick of chocolate seemed a premeditated plot to defraud us of our share.'

The Chumbi valley, which leads down from the Jelap La, has a very different climate from that of the Sikkim side. Now they were walking in warm rather than hot sunshine and the whole area was dryer and the going on the roads much rougher. They arrived in Yatung where they joined the first party and were entertained by the son of the British trade agent, John MacDonald, who instructed them in Tibetan etiquette and table manners. 'The chief difference between Tibetan and English table manners (besides the use of chopsticks) is that the more noise you can make in dealing with such things as vermicelli soup the better from the Tibetan point of view,' Shebbeare recalled. Fully briefed, the party was given seats of honour and treated to a performance of Tibetan Devil Dancers. This weird and wonderful performance lasted for four and a half hours during which time they were plied with *rakshi* and *chang* by two very attractive girls, one Tibetan, one Chinese. *Rakshi* is distilled barley which the Tibetans claimed to be 100 per cent proof, while *chang* is their local beer which Sandy described as looking like 'very unfiltered barley water'. Tibetan hospitality brooks no refusal so the wise men among the party, including Shebbeare, kept strictly to the Chang and remained almost sober. Others, less experienced, were somewhat worse for wear the following morning. The dancing was extraordinary and they were all fascinated by the performance. Shebbeare described it most evocatively: 'The best of the performers seemed to be leaning inwards at quite 45°, spinning on their own axes as well as working round the ring and looking, in their long dokos, like milk churns being trundled along a platform.' Towards the evening Sandy ran back to his tent to put a colour film in his camera and photographed the dancers in the evening light. They were all in very good spirits by the time they left the performance and had to negotiate a single tree bridge above the foaming river Amo-Chu in order to get back to their camp. Some of the porters were in a bad state and had to be helped across the bridge. Fortunately no one ended up in the river.

The next morning one of the girls who had been serving drinks came over to the camp selling blankets and coloured garters. Sandy, clearly quite taken by her, bought three pairs of garters and took a colour photograph of her. That day the first party left with Norton, while the general, who was not feeling well, remained with the second party in Yatung. Sandy spent the day wrestling with the badly smashed-up oxygen carriers and taking a short walk with Mallory where they hoped to find some rocks to climb on. The cliffs were full of grass and gave no good holds so they had to give up and return to camp. That night two muleteers got very drunk and bit a Tibetan woman. Bruce fined the men and their punishment was to carry the treasury, which weighed 80 pounds, as far as Phari, a three-day march. In order to ensure that none of the porters was carrying a load lighter than 40 pounds the expedition had a set of brass scales where the loads would be checked regularly. Bruce was fair but tough with the men and this punishment meant they had to carry twice the normal weight.

The general's health was beginning to give some concern and there was a definite change in the atmosphere within the expedition at this point. All the contemporary records betray the concern they all felt at the prospect of Bruce possibly not being able to continue on the march. Hingston and MacDonald arranged for him to proceed at a lower altitude and the others made their way over the next pass, following the first party, to Gantza. There was relief that evening as the general was clearly feeling better and 'had some good stories for dinner'.

The march from Yatung to Phari took them as far as the Tibetan plain. They walked and rode through impressive gorges where the going was rough but the views spectacular. The trees were now predominantly birch and their trunks glowed gold in the sunshine. The great white pyramid of Chomolhari, the first major peak in Tibet from the Sikkim district, dominated the view. As they came out of the gorge onto the plain they saw three or four herds of Tibetan gazelle and kyang, or wild asses, grazing before them, some of them within 300 yards.

With the prospect of the long trek across the plains, Sandy became increasingly anxious about the question of his mount. His pony had been causing him some problems, not least as it was very frisky and ran away with him at every opportunity. MacDonald tried to sell him another pony but that one was equally 'full of oats'. The Tibetans frequently expressed concern that their little animals would not hold his weight but eventually he found one which seemed to fit the bill; however, it ran away with him when he challenged Mallory to a race. This caused the whole baggage train to stampede, which must have been a spectacular sight. In an effort to get the pony to stop he ended up pulling the saddle right over its head. 'I must get a crupper¹ fitted as I did that three times today', he wrote in his diary. In fact he did not have time to fashion himself a crupper because he was obliged to spend the afternoon testing and comparing the different cookers that were under consideration for the higher camps. He concluded that the meta cooker gave by far the best results. He had also been busy working on dymo torches and sewing the zip fasteners he had brought with him onto his sleeping bag. That evening they drank the health of the Oxford Boat Race crew in some of General Bruce's 140-year-old rum.

One of the most important aspects of the march for the party was the matter of post. Information from home was always received with great enthusiasm and on occasions when the post did not get through or an

---

1 A leather thong which fits under a pony's tail and is attached to the back of the saddle to stop it slipping forward.

expected letter did not arrive, it could cause great disappointment. Sandy had asked all his friends as well as his family to write to him on the expedition and on 30 March he received his first letters from home which had arrived via the SS *California*. He immediately sent off the three letters he had written to Milling, Audrey Pim and another friend from Oxford. Communication with home was as important to him as it was to the others, not least when the morning after they had drunk to the crew he received a cable telling him that Cambridge had won the 1924 Boat Race by four and a half lengths. I really get a sense of his frustration at not being able to ask hundreds of 'where', 'why', 'what on earth was going on' type of questions. He wrote in his diary: 'I still can't get over Oxford being beaten by 4 ½ lengths – I would like to have some details of the race.' A post mortem of Oxford's defeat not being possible, he had nevertheless given vent to his surprise at dinner that evening and the other members of the second party were very sympathetic. Bruce wrote in his dispatch to the *Times* from Phari: 'Unfortunately we have to condole with our representative of the Oxford eight on his crew's defeat in the Boat Race, although it is perfectly clear to us why the race was won by the Light Blues. All are confident of the result of the next race.'

In his job as mess secretary, Sandy was trying his very best to communicate with the porters. As Norton pointed out, the lack of Hindustani did present several problems when he was trying to demonstrate the more intricate workings of a cooker. 'Mr Irvine, for instance, knows the Hindustani for jam already, and the resultant permutations and combinations are somewhat quaint and usually end in the summoning of Captain Bruce or Mr Shebbeare to get to the bottom of the matter. It is curious that some of the least qualified for interpreting are the most persistent in their efforts.' Sandy's efforts at communication, however, were sometimes well rewarded and he did succeed in greatly speeding up the process of erecting the mess tent. He spent an entire morning on the problem, 'drilling coolies to pitch it quickly – finally I made a rectangle of chord [sic] with diagonal marks all along rope for positions of pegs. If this doesn't get too tangled it should enable all pegs to be put in the right places straight away & tent pitched quickly.' Once again a simple solution proved to be extremely effective and he noted with satisfaction the next evening, 'The mess tent was pitched perfectly after our drill yesterday.' As an encore he finished putting the zip fasteners on his sleeping bag.

The second party caught up with the first in Phari on 5 April where they encountered their first severe setbacks. The members of the 1922 expedition had had little positive to say about Phari. It had been bitterly cold and the town unbearably dirty. General Bruce thought it somewhat improved since 1922 but Sandy was pretty taken aback by the squalor and wrote in his diary: 'I was very much impressed by the dirtiness of the whole place & also the smell. As each batch of Yaks left a crowd of natives rushed after to collect any Yak dung that might be forthcoming; this they put in the baggy part of their coats or carried it in their skirts ... The whole of the camp site (the only level bit near water) is about 6" deep in sling. Is suppose it's very wholesome really!' He was not the only person who had something to say about Phari. Shebbeare was equally scathing: 'Phari is supposed to be the dirtiest place in the world & I should think it is.' The alleys were 'in places, almost knee deep in filth. The houses are dark, smokey rabbit warrens and the people are black with grime.'

There were endless transport problems in Phari. Each region in Tibet was under separate jurisdiction and the provision of transport and food had to be negotiated with the Dzong Pen, the man who governed the region. It was to the Dzong Pen that the transport officers Geoffrey Bruce and Shebbeare would go with the expedition leader, in this case Norton who took over from the general half way through the negotiations, to work out a deal for the loan of transport animals. There was invariably a certain amount of haggling, even though the arrangements had been worked out in advance. In Phari the negotiations plumbed new depths and it took a great deal of patience and determination on the part of Shebbeare and Geoffrey Bruce to get the Dzong Pen and his men to agree to the rate they wished to pay. A rate, the general had pointed out to the Dzong Pen before he left, that had already been agreed in Lhasa. Norton was deeply frustrated. 'The anticipated transport trouble materialised with a vengeance. The Phari Dzong Pen & Gembus [men] obstructing in every way.' Shebbeare, who had spent nearly three days negotiating the loan of 300 transport animals, was even more outspoken in his diary. 'With a few honourable exceptions we found the Dzong Pens shifty customers, ready to promise anything, and their gembus useless parasites probably too extortionate to have any control. The Phari Dzong Pen & his hangers on were the worst we met, living on the trade route this might have been expected on the analogy of the inhabitants of sea ports.' It took Shebbeare and Geoffrey Bruce nine solid hours to get all the loads on the move.

Not only were they having to contend with grim conditions and truculent Dzong Pens, but the general's health was showing no signs of improvement. In addition, Mallory was suffering from severe stomach pains which Somervell suspected might be appendicitis and Beetham had contracted a bad bout of dysentery. It was a watershed for the expedition in terms of the health of the party. Hingston elected to escort the general via a different route to see whether the effect of a lower altitude and slightly warmer conditions would improve his condition. This left Norton in temporary charge of the expedition and Somervell as the only remaining medical officer tending to Mallory and Beetham.

While the negotiations were taking place Sandy was busy working away, his tent having taken on somewhat the appearance of a workshop. 'My tool box has been worth its weight in gold already' he told Lilian, 'every one is bringing things to be done. There's not another tool of any kind except 1 doz screw drivers – not even a hammer on the whole expedition, so its lucky I got them to give me a free hand in getting tools'. By the time the expedition had been on the road for two weeks, Sandy had repaired his own watch, Mallory's camp bed, Beetham's camera, had fitted crampons to Mallory's boots, and designed tin shades for the lamps (the cardboard ones were prone to catch fire very easily). He was still trying to salvage what remained of the broken oxygen frames and it became clear to him soon after Phari that he would have no option but completely to rebuild what Siebe Gorman had sent.

From Phari the expedition moved up onto the Tibetan plain where they encountered cold and wind of exceptional ferocity. Norton had commented in 1922 on the single most memorable characteristic of the Tibetan plain: 'It is hardly necessary to note the wind – that well known feature of Tibet. Morning usually breaks still & sun is so hot one can strip & wash in frozen stream & have breakfast in the open. By about 9

the wind (generally S.W.) is blowing bitterly keen off the snow mountains & increases in force until it begins to die down again at sunset when
night is generally still. This wind, as I said before, is like a toothache – one
can't forget it', and he didn't like it any better in 1924.

The Tibetan plain is one of the highest land plateaux on earth. It lies
at about 14,000 feet with passes of 17,000 to 18,000 feet a regular feature.
Its vastness is almost impossible to comprehend with horizons tens of
miles away in every direction. Although there is practically no vegetation
on the plateau, the colours of the sand and rock, the hues created by the
light, the sky and the clouds produce the most beautiful panorama of
browns, purples and blues. On the plains they saw herds of kyang and
Tibetan gazelle 'looking as sleek and round as if their chosen habitat
were the finest pasture in Asia'. To the south they could see the snow
capped peaks of Pau Hunri, Kangchenjunga and Chomulhari. Ahead of
them the great gravel plain, windswept with sand blowing around in
great dust devils, held little appeal. Norton described it as the 'very
abomination of desolation'. There was little respite from the wind and
the temperature at night plummeted to thirty-four degrees of frost, that
is −2° F or −20° C. Sandy wrote to his mother, 'for the last 5 days we've
been travelling over absolute sand & stone desert not a sign of vegetation
or shelter (varying from 15,500 to 17,800 ft) with a burning dry sun &
half a gale blowing; the coldest wind I've ever known, 22, 28, 34, 20° of
frost 4 nights running with this wind is enough to chill anyone'. At Phari
he had made a further effort to buy a pony but had thought the one on
offer was too expensive and frisky. He was therefore allocated a mule, a
decision he regretted somewhat as it was extraordinarily uncomfortable
to ride which meant he was forced to make the march over the plateau
on foot.

On this part of the trek the new mess tent, designed by Norton, came
into its own and was a great comfort to the party. It was commented on
and admired by everybody. Mallory was as impressed as anyone and
wrote to Ruth: 'The mess-tent also is a great improvement on last
year's: there is ample head-room, and the mess-servants can pass round
without hitting one on the head with the dishes; the tables are wooden
(three-ply wood varnished), and it is supposed that messes will be wiped
off without difficulty; and they fit conveniently round the poles.' The

tent was taken down every morning before breakfast, which was usually taken in the open before the wind got up, and packed onto the back of two mules, christened Jack and Jill, and dispatched with the earliest loads. This way it was amongst the first to arrive at the next camp and could be pitched quickly, using Sandy's template, giving the party somewhere to escape from the wind after their day's trek. It was crossing the passes on the plateau that they encountered the first serious altitude and Sandy made particular note of his performance both in his diary and in his letter home from Kampa Dzong. To Lilian he wrote:

The altitude has had no very ill effect yet provided I go slowly I find I go up hill at about 17000 at about 2 miles per hr & breathing-in on every left foot. On the level at about 3 m.p.h. I breathe every other left foot & down hill every 3rd. I can hurry up hill for about 30 seconds, but have to pant tremendously after that. Lifting heavy boxes & driving in refractory tent pegs are much the most exhausting pastimes!

In his diary entry for that evening he noted that there had been a biting head wind amounting to almost half a gale which he found very tiring when he was trying to climb to 17,000 feet. As soon as they reached the top of the first pass they saw another, equally high about five miles away so they dropped down about 1,000 feet and found a sheltered corner which was quite warm in the sun.

We had tiffin of 2 biscuits & a few raisins here, and most of us went to sleep for a bit. After an hour or so we started up the 2nd pass & found the top was not the top & after another hour or so we reached the top under awful wind conditions only to find another pass about 5 miles further on. All 3 passes were just under 17,000 ft. I noticed that I was breathing in every time I put my right foot down going uphill, every other time on the level & every third time when going downhill gently.

Mallory was less affected by the altitude than any of them and stormed up and down the passes, much to Sandy's frustration as he was unable to keep up. Norton, who had initially been very pleased with his performance, had to admit that he was unable to keep up with Mallory either.

If he were to arrive in camp early of an afternoon, Sandy always made a point of helping the porters to put up the mess tent and his own Whymper tent, assistance which earned their respect and affection. He was impressed with the porters' ability to walk sometimes fifteen or sixteen miles in a day and then buckle down in camp to produce dinner for the expedition and themselves.

They were beginning to encounter some very cold nights as they camped on the plateau. On 8 April they had 28 degrees of frost, or a temperature of 2° F (−18°C) and there was a wind of 30 m.p.h. blowing. That day Sandy celebrated his twenty-second birthday in Lung-Gye-Dok and they made of fuss of him with a particularly good meal that evening. The following night as they were sitting in the mess tent 'with twelve people and two gas lamps' both Norton and Sandy recorded in their diaries that the temperature in the tent was 25° F (7 degrees of frost) and 10° F outside the tent. The cold was to become a familiar and recurring feature from now onwards. The clothing they had been advised to purchase in London was soon to be put to the test. Sandy wrote: 'All today I kept quite warm by wearing thick woollen under-clothes, flannel shirt, wind-proof coat, fleece lining, leather waist-coat and 3-ply burberry. But', he added, 'found the weight of the clothes made me quite exhausted getting onto my mule at the top of the pass.' He must have been wearing about twenty pounds of clothes.

From the plateau they descended to Kampa Dzong where they encountered warm sun and no wind, a welcome change for them all after four days of being blown about like leaves. It was here that his birthday telegram from the family caught up with him. The trek had taken its toll on the equipment and the 'Irvine workshop' was bustling with activity as soon as the party settled in camp. Mallory's bed, Beetham's camera and Odell's camera tripod were the first articles to be mended with the use of Sandy's brazing lamp. In the process he suc-ceeded in tearing his windproof trousers, much to his frustration. The day after their arrival he and Odell spent the day working on the oxygen apparatus. They weighed oxygen bottles at random and were dismayed to find some of them empty and others only half full. The apparatus they tested leaked badly but after a lot of hard work they did succeed in reducing the leak somewhat. It was at this point that Sandy realized nothing short of a complete redesign would have any hope of working. He would have to recreate what he had worked on in Oxford and Birkenhead before he left for India. With Odell's encouragement he set about designing Mark I, which was soon replaced with Marks II, III and eventually IV and V. His aim was to do away with the clumsy tubing, valves and flowmeters, to lighten the apparatus and to make it more reliable. He inverted the cylinders, as he had done in his Oxford laboratory, and began to fashion the simplified set he hoped would be less prone to leaks and failures. It was a start but his workshop was limited and he was constantly irritated by the conditions he was trying to work under and the few tools he had to hand. Despite his frustration with the apparatus, he was very happy to be in Kampa Dzong where he was able to have a hot bath. 'My arms & knees have recovered from the tropical sun down in the valleys', he wrote to Lilian, 'but this sun & wind has removed most of the skin from my nose & mouth which is most painful. It is a wonderful change to get here only 14,500 so hot you can bathe in the stream coming straight off the snow & no wind at all.'

The camp was sited in a delightful, sheltered spot below the magnificent fortress of Kampa Dzong which Sandy sketched for the benefit of his mother, likening it to a familiar Cheshire landmark: 'the Dzong is a fort standing on a rock about 500 ft straight above us very like Beeston Castle, but of course a different style, very tall and rectangular'. For a day or so the atmosphere in the camp was relaxed but then came the stunning news that the general, who had hoped to join them in Kampa Dzong, having taken a lower route via Tuna, was too ill to continue. Hingston had diagnosed a severe recurrence of malaria which the general had contracted some months earlier tiger hunting in India. It was announced that he was to be taken back to Darjeeling on a stretcher, with Hingston in attendance. This was a most terrible blow to the expedition. Norton, the general's deputy, was now appointed the leader of the expedition. It was a responsibility that he had in part anticipated as the general's health had not been good for the best part of a week.

Mallory, in the meantime, had recovered from his stomach complaint and the logical thing to do, in the light of Norton's change of role, was to appoint Mallory as leader of the climbing party. This they did and Mallory, understandably, was delighted and told Ruth the following day: 'Norton takes command. He has appointed me second-in-command in his place and also leader of the climbers altogether. I'm bound to say I feel some little satisfaction in the latter position.' It was absolutely the right thing to happen and it meant that Mallory, who was already totally preoccupied with his plans for the assault on the mountain, could discuss them with fresh enthusiasm and greater authority – as if anyone had ever doubted it! – and he set to work immediately on formulating a plan of attack. The ripples resulting from the general's departure were felt right down the line of the expedition. The porters had had great affection for Bruce and held him in high regard. Norton wrote of the his departure sympathetically and with a genuine note of sadness:

Yesterday we received the severest blow in the news that our leader, General Bruce, had been forced to return to Phari en route for Yatung and Darjeeling, owing to severe malaria. There is every reason to fear that his absence will be permanent. To all who know what the personality of General Bruce meant to the British members, to the Himalayan staff, to the Tibetan officials, and to the others with whom the expedition comes in contact, the news speaks for itself. General Bruce creates a unique atmosphere, and his place cannot be filled adequately, while from the point of view of practical efficiency his knowledge of the people and of the conditions of the country, and the light-hearted method he had of sweeping away all difficulties, makes his absence a handicap of which we shall continue to feel to the end.

He went on to explain the arrangements for getting Bruce back to Darjeeling, accompanied by Hingston, adding with some humour: 'We can ill spare our medico and naturalist in either capacity though to some of us the gap caused by his absence is compensated to some extent by relief from the various tortures in the shape of altitude tests to which he periodically subjects us – breath-holding, blowing mercury up a tube, and, worst of all, the sums whereby he unerringly detects a steady decay of our intellects as the altitude increases.'

Norton proved to be a superb substitute for General Bruce and he had the unconditional support of both the expedition members and the porters. He was very much liked by everybody and had already shown, in the build-up and preparation, that he was a natural leader. Nevertheless, he felt the pressure of taking over the leadership to be a great responsibility and was very fortunate to have in Geoffrey Bruce an excellent right-hand man.

Mallory wasted no time in his new role as climbing leader and had a long discussion with Norton the following afternoon, after which the plan was explained to all the members of the climbing party at dinner. Two men, not using supplemental oxygen, would establish a camp at 26,500 feet and sleep there. The following day, if health and conditions permitted, they should make a summit bid. In the event of this not being possible they should stay at Camp V and melt snow for the next party to arrive. The second party, comprising three climbers using oxygen, would get to camp V to receive the first party who may or may not be returning from the summit, and climb themselves to the summit the next day. Such was the plan that was to be worked on between now and arrival in Base Camp. Sandy was in no position to comment but he knew that he would be a contender for the oxygen summit party, if he performed well at altitude, because of his work on the oxygen apparatus. He had good reason to feel optimistic on all counts. He was proving to be very fit and acclimatizing faster than the other new members and his work on the equipment could not fail to be appreciated by all. The afternoon before they left Kampa Dzong they had a demonstration of the oxygen apparatus, 'How to test for leaks'. 'We found the leaks alright but couldn't cure them', Sandy noted rather forlornly in his diary that night.

As they prepared to leave the comfort of Kampa Dzong after two days of rest and planning Sandy signed off his letter to Lilian: 'Everything smells or tastes (or both) of yak dung – generally the smoke of – which is most unpleasant but I'm getting used to it. I think its worst when my man comes in to wake me in the mornings after sleeping over a sling fire! Am enjoying this trek tremendously.'

Beetham's condition was sufficiently improved that Somervell felt confident that he could continue on the trek. They left Kampa Dzong early on the morning of 15 April with much more satisfactory transport arrangements than they had had from Phari, although Sandy observed the loads had not been as well strapped on to the yaks, 'for one saw on average 2 loads per mile on the ground'. Once again spirits were high, the rest at Kampa having benefited them all considerably. They walked and rode across an immense sandy plain criss-crossed with pockets of quicksand which they learnt to avoid after MacDonald and his mount had fallen into one spot leaving a big hole behind them as they extricated themselves. Sandy rode with Hazard, cantering for mile after mile across the sand dunes. 'At one point my hat blew off and Hazard and I had a great hunt after it at full gallop trying to spike it with our walking sticks. The ponies seemed to enjoy it quite as much as we did.' The immense size of the plain could be judged by the fact that there was a horizon in every direction between themselves and the nearest mountains in the distance. The sight of this deeply impressed Sandy who described it in his diary as magnificent, an unusual use of a superlative from him. They spent two days covering this part of the plain and his diary is full of his impressions of it. 'The last 4–5 miles of our trek today was through enormous sand hills, some perfectly uniform blown sand, some held together with star grass and some covered with stone and rock, obviously sandstone in the process of weathering. Over one of the last hills we came in full view of a priceless blue lake about 5 miles long and covered with thousands of duck, geese and all kinds of birds.' I have the strong impression that this was the area in Tibet which most appealed to Sandy, as he mentions it in his letter to his mother from Tinki Dzong in equally glowing terms.

As they came in to Tinki they were met by Shebbeare and a number of Tibetans on horseback whom he introduced as the Tinki cavalry. They all rode together into the village where the party was plied with chang, later celebrating Somervell's thirty-fourth birthday with a big plum pudding. 'We burnt absolute alcohol on the plum pudding as it was easier to get at than the brandy!' Sandy noted: 'I also took it in my coffee, but it tasted like chloroform and left me very thirsty.' The following morning, a rest day, found him struggling again in his tent-cum-workshop. He'd already spent the previous afternoon mending Geoffrey Bruce's office table and developing photographs with Beetham. On this day he discovered, to his great frustration, that Siebe Gorman had misinformed him about the make of screw they had used on the oxygen apparatus. This was a significant blow and he was very angry as there was nothing he could do but to press on and try to make something 'out of the present box of tricks'. He wrote to Lilian:

I have my work cut out with the Oxygen! Every apparatus tested yet leaks more gas than one breathes. None were tested before leaving England. 34 Cylinders out of 90 had to be refilled at Calcutta because they had leaked. So far we have tested 16 & found 6 empty. I am at present completely redesigning the apparatus & trying to make up a serviceable design before we reach the base camp. Before I left England I rang up Siebe Gorman to know what threads they used on the Ox. apparatus, they said Standard Whitworth so I got a set of taps & dies to suit. Today I used them for the first time & found that the Ox app. had B.A. threads throughout & <u>not</u> Whitworth. With my limited workshop it makes things rather difficult.

In the past writers have pointed to Sandy's cheerful outlook, his easy-going nature and his enviable reputation for good humour. I find myself wondering whether it has almost made him seem as if he were too good-natured and thus lacking in spirit. But there was an altogether different side to Sandy, one that harboured the energy, the drive, the 'fire in his belly', as one his rowing friends put it, and that would occasionally burst out in an explosion of temper and fury.

Just after Tinki his fiery temper got the better of him. His troubles finding an adequate pony for his size and ability had been solved when he chanced upon a good little mare in Kampa Dzong. Four days later, as he was walking far ahead of the party he met the owner of the mare who demanded he change it for a different animal. He was incandescent with rage: 'I told him to go to the devil and went on, but looking round found Tsuchin calmly changing my saddle. I went back and cursed them violently and came away with my original pony. I couldn't understand the fellow's argument but I gather he was the pony's owner and as it is a mare did not want to risk it being used too heavily.' The owner of the mare caved in at the sight of a sunburned six-foot Hercules bellowing incomprehensibly at him and Sandy kept the pony for the rest of the trek. He really did not take kindly to anybody interfering with what he regarded as his personal affairs, especially after he had taken so long to resolve the riding problem anyway.

Clearly invigorated after his altercation with the Tibetan, he stormed over the next 17,500-foot pass feeling very fit, 'my breathing was not nearly so fierce as before and I could move quite fast without breathing more than once to a complete step'. Atop all the passes are cairns, or piles of stones, placed there by the Tibetans who believe that the passes are inhabited by spirits. In order to appease the spirits the travellers place stones for them, often carved with elaborate prayers and decorated with prayer flags flapping noisily in the wind, attached to bamboo sticks or canes. Respectful of their customs, Sandy had early on made a note in his diary of the Tibetan prayer he should offer when placing a stone on the cairn. Reaching the top, he placed his stone on the cairn, said the prayer and sat down to rest and wait for the others to catch him up. 'Just before I reached the top of the pass I looked back over to see a wonderful glimpse between two steep mountains of a deep blue lake with four humpy rocks some 3–400 ft high formed by curves of a vertical strata giving the appearance of four great dinosaurs with their rocky spines, all following each other. The border of the lake was white with salt giving an idea of surf on its shores.' Hazard arrived a few minutes later and insisted on running all the way down the other side, some four or five miles, where they had tiffin and lay down for a sleep in the sun. Mallory, Odell and Norton had also used the 17,500-foot Bahman Dople pass to test their acclimatization and Norton was a little aggrieved that he was unable to keep up with them right to the top. They too ran down the other side where they joined Hazard and Sandy.

That evening they heard a rumour that the general was better and that he and Hingston were hoping to join them further along the march. This rumour turned out to be untrue and Karma Paul, one of the expedition interpreters, caught up with them and gave them details of the general's trip back to Darjeeling on a stretcher, 'evidently his appearance having been the source of rumour last night amongst the last yak men to leave Tinki' Sandy observed. As they set off from Chiblung for Jikyop the landscape changed again. The sand was white with salt and heavy as they walked down a waterlogged gorge, heavy going for the yaks but evocative for the men who caught the smell of seaweed in their nostrils and it carried their thoughts far away from Tibet. In a brief, nostalgic moment Sandy wondered how his family were spending Easter back home.

Two days later he and Mallory climbed a small hill behind their camp at Jikyop and gained their first, clear view of Everest. They examined the south and east side of the final pyramid very carefully through binoculars, discussing possible routes and sites for camps. It was a thrilling moment for Sandy and although they were still some sixty miles from it 'the whole mountain, or what of it we could see, gave the impression of tremendous bulk'. It was from here that he took the photograph of Everest that he sent back to Evelyn. That afternoon he was back struggling with the oxygen apparatus with renewed vigour. He had already dismissed two designs and was on to Mark III when he was called to dinner where the climbers were allotted to their summit parties. He noted in his diary:

Odell and Geoff (Bruce) to pitch Camp V
Norton and Somervell – 1st non-ox climb
Mallory and Self – 1st ox climb
Odell, Geoff, Hazard and Beetham – reserve
I'm awfully glad that I'm with Mallory in the first lot, but I wish ever so much that it was a non-ox attempt.

The die had been cast and Sandy's hopes fulfilled. He must have felt confident of his ability to perform on the mountain if he considered he would be happier climbing without oxygen, or perhaps it was just that he knew what the others perhaps did not, that the 'infernal' apparatus was hideously unreliable and could not be guaranteed to work, even with his major rebuilds. On the other hand he told Odell later that if the mountain was worth climbing it was worth doing without the use of adventitious aids. After dinner Sandy returned to his tent and worked until late into the night, while the others were sleeping, on Mark IV. 'Only defect, no pressure gauge.' To Lilian he wrote the next day:

I have provisionally been chosen to do the first Oxygen climb with Mallory. Norton & Somervell doing Non Ox. on same day. It will be great fun if we all 4 get to the top at the same time! I say provisionally because I don't know that I will be fit at 26,500 ft yet (our kicking off camp). The Non Ox start a day earlier from the North Col stopping at 25,500 & 27,300 while we stop only at 26,500. This gives 3 camps as refuges on the way down in case of exhaustion or bad weather. The weather has behaved in a most peculiar manner so far – no one knows if it is a good sign or not.

He added, 'It will be a great triumph if my impromptu ox.ap. gets to the top, I hope it does … If we reach the top it will be probably May 17th.' This date was immediately entered into Willie Irvine's 1924 pocket diary and later revised, on the basis of the *Times* dispatches, to 23 May 1924 when Willie noted 'Top of the Hill ACI'.

The following afternoon, immediately after arriving in camp, he took to his tent surrounded, as usual, by his tools. With a brief interruption for dinner and a drink of whisky he worked again until after midnight. His diary entry is extremely succinct for 22 April but he notes with some satisfaction, '3 chota pegs^{2} of Scotch put new inspiration into me at dinner tonight. Have just completed and designed Mark V ox.ap. Very tired.' Such labour on behalf of the expedition was surely beyond the call of duty but it was not in his character to give up until he had finally solved a problem, however much of his time and energy it took up. I suspect on this occasion that his election to the oxygen climbing party put as much inspiration into him as the three measures of Scotch.

The successful completion of Mark V and a musical accompaniment at breakfast the following morning left Sandy feeling very cheerful for the march to Shekar Dzong. 'The tunes were quite the pleasantest I've heard yet, and they kept time with their little diabolo shaped drums very well. After breakfast the local George Roby gave a performance for Noel's cinema.' This beggar musician, with his gnarled hands and toothless smile, posed for a photograph for Sandy and the result is a delightful portrait of the cheerful old man. Sandy took a number of photographs on trek of the Tibetans and was particularly interested in the dress the women wore. He made a beautiful study of one woman, a curvaceous middle-aged lady in full costume and with a magnificent

2 The Hindi for a small drink.

head-dress which he described, in his usual somewhat irreverent manner, to one of his Oxford tutors, Geoffrey Mure: 'I like the Tibetan women's permanent head dress – a great kind of frame – specially constructed so that they only ever lie on their backs! The men must be weaklings if they can't look after their own interest without such artificial devices!'

The trek to Shekar Dzong was short and uneventful. They arrived below the village at midday to find that a camping place in a walled garden had been acquired for them by MacDonald. That afternoon, whilst busy working on the oxygen apparatus, Sandy realized he had become something of a local attraction and found himself surrounded by Tibetans gawking at him. He jumped up and chased them 'with a loudly hissing cylinder of oxygen. I've never seen men run so fast – they must have thought it was the devil coming out!' Thereafter Norton arranged for a sentry at the entrance to the garden to ensure the privacy of the party from prying locals, which could at times become a considerable burden.

The latest oxygen apparatus design was tested on the rocks below the Dzong by Mallory, Somervell, Odell and Sandy, and seemed to be an improvement on previous trials. 'They all seemed very pleased with it and there is nothing to go wrong and nothing to hamper climbing or to break if you slip', Sandy wrote to Lilian. Norton reported on the trials in his dispatch to the *Times*:

After the usual checking of stores and routine work, we finished with a trial trip of the oxygen apparatus on the steep rocks of a fine pyramid, on which stands the Dzong and the monastery. This was intended to test the relative merits of the apparatus as originally constructed and sent from England and an adaptation designed by the fertile genius of Mr. Irvine. The adaptation, besides eliminating certain leaks and mechanical defects which had developed during the transit from home, lightens and simplifies the apparatus, and, most important of all, does away with the vulnerable portions carried on the climber's chest, and so frees him to tackle rocks with less Agag-like delicacy than formerly. Even so, at the elevation of Shekar Dzong (14,500 ft) we found the rocks were much more easily climbed without the apparatus.

The fortress of Shekar was prized by Tibetan travellers of the past as a sort of wonder of the world. The Dzong, as the fort is called, is a large secular building that towers above the monastery of Shekar and is joined to it by a perilously steep wall. The buildings were destroyed during the Cultural Revolution, but in 1924 they were still standing and their magnificence did not fail to impress expedition members. From the very top of the Dzong it was possible to gain a view of Everest, rising inexorably above the neighbouring peaks. Here the Tibetans brought incense and other offerings to Chomolungma, as 'she stretches out her white arms on both sides, a goddess in the form of stone and ice'. Sandy and MacDonald spent the following morning climbing to the top of the fortress to get a view of the mountain. After that they visited the monastery and presented the Chief Lama with two polished half-oxygen cylinders. 'They made two fine gongs of different tones. We also told him there was a devil inside whose breath would kindle a spark – we showed him on incense.' Despite the introduction of a devil into his monastery, the Chief Lama made them very welcome and allowed them to spend as much time as they wanted in the temple. Sandy's interest in the temple was genuine and he was deeply impressed by the statues, the hangings and the devotional offerings. He was also amused by the meeting of different cultures, as he related to Lilian a few days later.

Grandfather will never own me as a grandson again because I bowed down before a colossal Buddha about 20 ft high with an altar covered with most brilliant jewels. I had to make great pretence to worship in order to get a photograph from a camera concealed in my coat as I had to give a 70 sec. exposure in the very dim light of the holy of holies – my devotions had to be very prolonged!! Some of the hangings in the temple were perfectly beautiful & the ornaments & offering bowls spotlessly clean – the only clean things in the whole of Tibet. I enjoyed myself enormously in the monastery at Shekar. I think they rather regarded us as Buddha or devils.

The photographs he took did indeed come out and they were among the collection sent back to Evelyn and which came to light in May 2000.

After visiting the temple he spent a long time watching some novices in the monastery turning a prayer wheel. His absence from camp had been noticed and after he had been 'missing' for over two hours Somervell and Noel went off to see if they could find him. They spotted him standing some distance away, with his hands in his pockets, shoulders hunched, studying the monks at the prayer wheel with great concentration. 'What is Irvine doing?' asked Noel. 'I expect he's trying to work out how to mechanize it for them,' was Somervell's response.

From Shekar Dzong they had a five-day trek to the site of their Base Camp at the foot of Everest. This final leg of the march was a struggle for Sandy. The wind was vicious and carried tiny stones and sand from the plain which cut his badly sunburned face and caused him considerable pain. In addition, he had been feeling unwell since leaving Shekar Dzong. He complained of feeling 'seedy' which is the description he often used when he was not 100 per cent fit. On this occasion he attributed it mostly to the fact that he'd been up until midnight or 2 a.m. most nights working on the oxygen apparatus and then rising each morning at 6.30 a.m. and trekking twelve to fifteen miles each day, mostly on foot. When he was not feeling well his temper was short and his diary entries betrayed his frustrations: 'my blasted pony trod on my walking stick and broke it' he wrote two days after leaving Shekar. Despite this, he still kept up his usual cheerful outward manner and no one appeared to be aware of anything untoward. When he arrived in camp in Tashi Dzong he put himself straight to bed in his tent, only to be woken an hour later by Mallory with a box of crampons. 'I spent until dinner time fitting crampons to Mallory and my boots and trying to fix them without having a strap across the toes which is likely to stop the circulation. Inside feels all wrong but still have a good appetite.' Like his father, Sandy had learned how to dose himself up with a variety of medicaments to cure his problems. This time he took four castor oil tablets but noted they had the opposite of the desired effect.

The next day he was feeling no better as they trekked from Chödzong to Rongbuk. The monastery at Rongbuk was the last outpost of civilization before they reached Everest Base Camp. The monastery, or the ruins of it today, to be precise, stands half way down the Rongbuk valley, about eleven miles from the site of the 1924 base camp. The valley is some eighteen miles long and rising only 5000 feet is overwhelmed at its head by the mass of Everest, dominating the view with its huge bulk and dramatic pyramid, from which, so often, there flows a stream of spindrift. The name Rongbuk means 'Monastery of the Snows'. Long before the first European expeditions came to the Himalaya, the great peaks were places of pilgrimage. It would never have occurred to the Tibetans to climb the mountain, for they represented the domain of the gods. But pilgrims came to worship Chomolungma and meditate at Rongbuk. The monks were supplied with food by the pilgrims, gifts of flour, yak butter, warm materials and other presents and the monastery was often bustling with life despite its remoteness.

When the expedition arrived at Rongbuk on 28 April the Holy Lama, ngag-dwang-batem-hdsin-norbu, was unable to see them as he was ill. This was something of a disappointment as they had hoped to be able to receive a blessing from the Lama before they began their approach to the mountain. Such a blessing was held in particularly high regard by the porters who understood that the Lama would be able to pray for their safety from the demons of the mountain. He became a friend to all the Everest expeditions of the 1920s and 1930s and this was in no small part due to his meeting with General Bruce in 1922, with whom he established an excellent rapport. Bruce had explained to the Lama that 'his climbers were from a British mountain-worshipping sect on a pilgrimage to the highest mountain in the world'. He had sought to convey to him that the motives the expedition had for climbing the mountain were not in any way for material gain but were entirely spiritual. As the Lama was indisposed Norton had to content himself with making gifts and exchanging greetings with the other monks and promising to return if the Holy Lama, when better, would grant them an audience and bless the expedition. The Lama let it be known that he would give them an audience on 15 May.

Norton was very pleased to see at Rongbuk the Shika, or head man, from Kharta with whom he and others on the 1922 expedition had formed good relations. The Shika was there paying his respects to the Head Lama and Norton was able to tell him that they had already sent greetings and presents from Shekar Dzong three days earlier. The Shika, in return, promised to send them a consignment of fresh green vegetables and luxuries. This was very welcome news to Norton and the others for such things were otherwise unobtainable in this inhospitable district.

As Norton was paying his respects at the monastery and arranging for the audience with the Holy Lama, Sandy was once again huddled in his tent mending things. This time it was Beetham's camera, Mallory's saddle and his own sleeping bag. His health and mood did not improve the next day when they finally arrived at the place below the mountain where they were to put up their Base Camp – their 'refuge' for the next two months. 'Bloody morning, light driving snow, very cold and felt rather rotten ... Walked all the way from Rongbuk monastery to the base camp 1¾ hours over frozen river and very rough terrain. The Base Camp looked a very uninviting place.'

8

Trust in God and Keep Your Powder Dry

Irvine is the star of the new members. He is a very fine fellow, has been doing excellently up to date & should prove a splendid companion on the mountain. I should think the Birkenhead News ought to have something to say if he and I reach the top together.

G. L. Mallory to his mother, 26 May 1924

Situated eleven miles from the Rongbuk monastery, at the foot of the Rongbuk glacier, Everest Base Camp was a bleak place. No sign of vegetation, dominated by the bulk of Everest and frequently in shadow, its rocky, rough terrain was uninviting at best. It was, however, to be home to the expedition party for the next six weeks and it became a veritable little village of tents with comings and goings of porters, tradesmen, interpreters, messengers and the all-important postal service.

Norton described the approach in a *Times* dispatch on the day they arrived. 'Today, April 29, finds us again in the 1922 Base Camp and a cold welcome we have received. We walked over five rough miles of tumbled moraine and a frozen watercourse to the camp just under the snout of the Rongbuk glacier, in the teeth of a bitter wind. Here, indeed, it is winter.' Despite the inhospitable conditions they encountered and the ever-present wind that whistled down the Rongbuk valley off the glacier in the afternoons leaving the temperature at Base Camp well below freezing, there was a feeling of great optimism in camp. Everyone was busy with his allotted task of sorting, checking, repairing the stores. Mallory and Beetham were in charge of the high altitude Alpine equipment to be sent to the upper camps; Shebbeare and Hazard were occupied with labelling the boxes of stores which had been dumped unceremoniously off the transport animals the day before; Somervell was busy with the medical and scientific stores and Sandy and Odell were locked in their usual, daily battle with the oxygen apparatus. And a battle it had indeed become. Working at Base Camp was hard work and the climbers all felt the lack of oxygen at 17,800 feet. Even taking off their boots and climbing into their sleeping bags left them breathless. Sandy wrote in his diary: 'felt rather exhausted with the altitude. A simply perfect day, everyone working like mad sorting stores. I spent an hour or so on Beetham's camera and the whole of the rest of the damn day on oxygen apparatus.' The next day he was hard at it again: 'completed the repair of Beetham's camera and spent the whole of the day struggling with the infernal apparatus.' By 6.30 p.m. that day he had his first perfect set which he put outside his tent to see if the solder would crystallize in the freezing air. The struggle was made all the more difficult by the fact that he was having to work inside his tent with the doors closed. 'Another full day at the ox app with an incredible number of reverses. Sweating in the HP tubes[1] is a difficult job at the best of times, but cramped in a tent (too windy outside) it was a perfect devil – on every possible occasion the solder would flow and break the HP tube which meant reheating at the risk of the pressure gauge and blowing the tube clear. By 6pm tonight I had 6 done and all sound except one which leaked in the HP tube itself.' I sense from these three diary entries that he had lapsed into a state of rising panic about the oxygen apparatus. The conditions under which he was working were far from ideal and his tool kit was at best basic. Furthermore he knew that the oxygen apparatus would be required soon and should be ready to be carried up to the higher camps quickly. He was also aware that work was taking him out of the picture as far as the other climbers were concerned and was clearly worried that if he did not complete the work he would get behind in the climbing schedule.

Each camp had its own diary in which the climbers all made entries about a variety of matters, from the state of stores to accounts of their climbing experiences. In the Base Camp diary there was the plan of campaign neatly written out so that each climber knew exactly where he was expected to be at any one time and, more importantly, where on

1 High Pressure tubes.

the mountain his colleagues were to be. From the outset the two climbing teams, Norton and Somervell, and Mallory and Sandy, were scheduled to make their acclimatization trips prior to the summit assault together. Sandy and Mallory were to be the first team to set off and occupy the higher camps where they would be overtaken on 15 May by Norton and Somervell who would be setting up two camps (V and VII) on 15 and 16 May. The other two would be resting on the 15 at Camp IV and pushing to an intermediate camp, No. VI, on the 16, so that both would be making the summit attempt on the 17, but from different camps. This would give them three camps to retreat to on the way down if necessary and provide oxygen support if the non-oxygen party, Norton and Somervell, got into difficulties.

May 2 was Sandy's last day in Base Camp and he spent it working flat out on the apparatus. In his lengthy diary entry for that day he goes into great detail about the repairs, alterations, modifications he made, but I sense a great feeling of relief that, in the end, he had been able to make it work to his satisfaction. As an encore that afternoon he repaired a roarer cooker which had been brought to his workshop tent two days earlier and shortened Mallory's crampons by half an inch: 'in so doing I spiked one hand and burnt the other in 2 places so was glad Nima didn't understand my French accent! I reduced the tool box as much as I dared to send up to Camp III'. He was ready on time, scheduled to leave the following day with Mallory, Odell and Hazard to climb past Camps I and II to III. 'I hope to put up a good show when the altitude gets a bit trying. I should acclimatize well at III the time we will spend there.'

Geoffrey Bruce was the man charged by Norton with the responsibility of stocking the first two camps above Base Camp, Camp I at the foot of the East Rongbuk glacier, at 17,800 feet, three miles from Base and Camp II, three miles further up the glacier at 19,800 feet. These camps were to be set up by the Gurkha NCOs in order to conserve, as far as possible, the energy of the climbers by keeping them at Base Camp and not requiring them to haul loads at this stage. The actual portering to Camps I and II was done by 150 Tibetans whom Bruce had recruited in Shekar Dzong with permission from the Dzong Pen. The condition of their employment was that they would be given some rations and

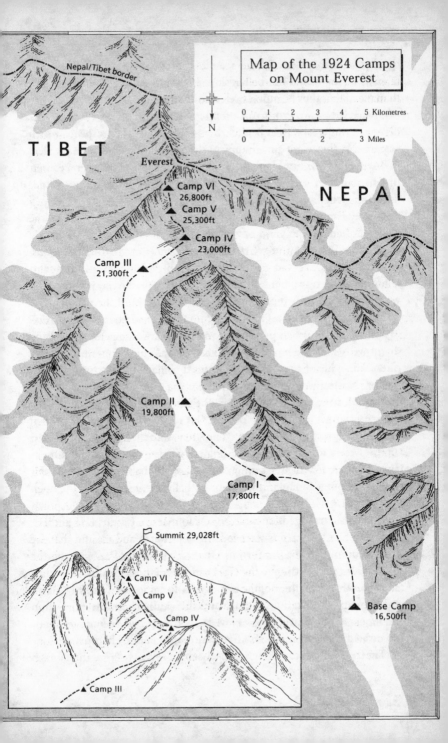

Map of the 1924 Camps
on Mount Everest

N

0 1 2 3 4 5 Kilometres
0   1   2   3 Miles

Nepal/Tibet border

TIBET

NEPAL

Everest

Camp VI
26,800ft

Camp V
25,300ft

Camp IV
23,000ft

Camp III
21,300ft

Camp II
19,800ft

Camp I
17,800ft

Base Camp
16,500ft

Summit 29,028ft

Camp VI

Camp V

Camp IV

Camp III

paid four *tankas* a day (about 1 shilling, nowadays worth about £1.50) and that they would not be employed on snow or ice. The Dzong Pen had asked that they be quickly released after their work was done as they were needed to sow crops and attend to their fields on their return. The Tibetans undertook to look after themselves in all other respects, which meant that they were quite happy to sleep out in the open at 18,000 feet with neither tents nor blankets. 'Had they been of a less hardy race, their maintenance in such country would have been well nigh impossible,' Geoffrey Bruce admitted later.

Bruce arranged for loads of up to 40 lb to be handed out to the Tibetan men, women and boys who had been employed to carry. He made an effort to ensure that the women and boys had lighter loads, but to no avail. 'I had to resort to the only plan that ensures swift allotment and complete satisfaction in Tibet. Tibetans all wear prettily woven garters of distinct colouring round the tops of their boots, and immediately recognize their own colours. The best method of distributing loads consists in collecting a garter from each person, shuffling them well, and throwing one on to each load. The owner of the garter then claims his or her load, and carries it all day without further complaint.' Norton was amazed that the porters were adopting a pace that he would imagine a fit climber in the Alps would only manage if he were carrying a load of 25 lb or less. Not only were these men, women and boys rugged, often barefooted but they were cheerful as they walked up the valley towards the East Rongbuk glacier, singing and joking as they went. A few of the women were carrying babies on top of their loads and one woman and her baby actually spent a night in the open at Camp II.

Bruce had arranged for three NCOs to manage Camps I, II and III, ensuring that the porters were fed and kept warm and fit, and that the loads, coming up the 'line', to use the military phrase adopted by the expedition, were getting to the right camps. All the high altitude equipment destined for the higher camps was to be left at Camp II. With this superb organization in place and the weather fair, the expedition members felt quite rightly that a very good start had been made. They celebrated that evening with a five-course dinner and champagne.

The instructions to the NCOs had been for seventy-five of the Tibetan porters to return to Base Camp for further loads and for the other seventy-five to stay at Camp I in preparation for load carrying to Camp II the following day. They were greeted with the news the next morning that fifty-two of the Tibetans who had been meant to stay at Camp I had disappeared in the night. 'This was a very serious matter', Bruce wrote, 'for everything depended on these men, and a transport strike at this juncture would effectively cripple the whole programme.'

Norton, Shebbeare and Bruce hot-footed it up to Camp I to see what was going on and to ascertain the whereabouts of the fifty-two defectors. As they arrived, a convoy of Tibetans came down from Camp II, full of good cheer. They were told that there would be more rations and higher wages if they carried more loads from I to II and this they did in great heart. Order was restored but the fifty-two men were not to be found. The performances of the women really impressed Bruce and he could not resist noting in his account of the stocking of the lower camps, that one woman had carried her two-year-old child on top of her 40 lb load from 17,500 feet to 19,800 feet, deposited the load and carried the child back down again. She had declared herself ready to repeat the process. Another older woman had performed a little step dance for them, having returned from carrying her load, and before she had her food. With these willing helpers, and a little additional help from the porters they had brought from India, Bruce felt happy that they would be able to keep to the original schedule. His confidence was well placed and on the evening of 2 May he received a message from the NCOs at Camps I and II that the work had been completed, all the loads had arrived and were safely stored and the Tibetans could be paid off.

The next job was to establish and stock Camp III and for this the expedition would use their own porters. It was now time to start the process of acclimatization at higher altitude for the climbers, hence the departure on 3 May from Base Camp of Sandy, Mallory, Odell and Hazard. Before they left, Somervell took specimens of their blood for a haemoglobin test. 'Mine came out by far the greatest percentage of red corpuscles, and Odell next, showing very good acclimatization', Sandy noted with some pride, adding, 'hope this is a really good sign.' It was planned for Mallory and Sandy to remain at Camp III for acclimatization whilst Odell and Hazard had been briefed to push on to establish the North Col Camp or Camp IV at 23,000 feet. The four climbers left Base Camp after an early lunch, arriving in Camp I in exactly two hours. An hour or so before they left they had sent off fifteen porters carrying all the kit including the oxygen apparatus. 'I'm glad that I didn't have to carry any of their loads 100 yards', Sandy observed in his diary that evening. In fact the climbers overtook most of the porters on the way up to Camp I and Sandy overheard a good deal of grumbling about the heavy loads. They encountered very unpleasant conditions at Camp I, which was generally held to be the most comfortable of all the camps, catching any sun going. They spent a draughty, cold night and headed the following morning up to Camp II.

The going from I to II was very rough. Mallory and I kept to the lateral moraine as long as possible. After crossing onto the glacier just opposite a side glacier we found a lovely frozen lake surrounded by seracs where we rested for about half an hour – photographing and studying the map. When we moved on a devil must have got into Mallory for he ran down all the little bits of downhill and paced all out up the moraine. It was as bad as a boat race trying to keep up with him, in spite of my colossal red corpuscles.

In Camps I and II the porters slept in stone shelters they called *sangars*, with a tarpaulin or fly sheet over the top. At Camp I a *sangar* was also used as the mess tent. When Mallory and Sandy arrived at Camp II they could see that the porters had lost heart and were not willing to prepare their own accommodation. After cups of tea and a brief rest, Sandy and Mallory put up two Whymper tents for themselves, Odell and Hazard, who were coming up behind them, and then set to work collecting boulders in order to make a two-room *sangar* for the porters. 'I worked for about 2 ½ hours shifting colossal boulders – trying to set an example to the coolies which was quite successful as they all started to work with quite a heart singing and shouting,' Sandy wrote. The effort was too much and his nose began to bleed after the strenuous work, so he took a well-deserved break while Mallory and Odell went out up the glacier to prospect a route up to Camp III. That evening they had dinner in Captain Noel's tent, who was also on his way up to Camp III with his cameras and assistants. Noel's movements on the mountain were independent from the rest of the expedition but he was always a popular figure in camp. His plan was to establish himself and his team at Camp IV and to film the summit attempt from there. Sandy was feeling positive, despite the rather worrying weather they were experiencing. Whenever he felt confident he made observations about his surroundings, whereas when he was anxious he tended to worry about his own physical condition and the nuts and bolts of the organization. In Camp II on 4 May he was full of optimism. The schedule worked out on the march had so far been kept to with barely a hitch and he was off up to Camp III in the morning, to an altitude 2500 feet higher than he had ever been before. That evening when they went to bed at 7.30 Sandy observed that a certain amount of snow had fallen: 'The great ice cliff behind the camp looked very fine in what little evening sun we got between the rather stormy looking clouds.' Sandy was clearly pleased with his performance to date, despite the nose bleed he had suffered earlier in the day, now recognizable as a sign of the effect of altitude.

It was a very cold night at Camp II, with the temperature dropping below 1° F (−19° C) and they awoke to powder snow on the glacier the next morning. After slightly revising the loads and deciding which boxes to send up to Camp III, they set off mid-morning in intermittent sunshine and driving snow. 'We left camp at 11 a.m. and had a very heavy day, starting up the glacier for 1½ miles and we dropped down into a trough about 100 ft tall amongst the most fantastic shaped ice seracs. Here we waited a long while to collect all or rather most of the coolies, which we roped up, myself with 6, Odell with 6 and Hazard on a long rope with 11, Mallory going alone, sometimes in front and sometimes behind. I led all the way up the gorge – found it very laborious going.' He was forced to stop every five minutes for a rest while the porters caught their breath. He found this very frustrating and soon realized that the man behind him on the rope was 'an awful dud, continually grumbling and stopping, so in fury I changed loads with him. It was not unduly heavy but awkward to carry. Fortunately for me Mallory insisted on me not carrying it any further, so we put the man off the rope and told him the ice devils would get him and proceeded as before.' All the porters were feeling the altitude and their heavy loads further aggravated their condition. Although the acclimatization issue was well recognized in the 1920s, the problems relating to altitude sickness were not so well understood. Sandy was as tough as Mallory on the men and insisted on setting an example to exhort them to increase their effort. What neither of them understood was that the men were not being lazy; they were genuinely suffering from altitude sickness. The result was that of the twenty-odd men they got to Camp III only four were not sick the following day.

They finally reached Camp III at 6 p.m., cold, exhausted and hungry. The food supplies at the camp were not as well organized as they should have been and the climbers were without soup that night, and therefore vital liquid. Added to that the jam and cheese were frozen solid. 'One course of mutton and veg, the first morsel since breakfast, and two cups of cool coffee left me very thirsty and hungry', Sandy complained. At that height the human body requires an enormous amount of liquid each day, somewhere in the vicinity of six litres as it is now understood. In 1924 this was not appreciated and Sandy's lack of liquid intake had a very big bearing on his performance over the following days. That night he slept for the first time at 21,300 feet. 'I slept like a log despite the stones we lay on until midnight, after which I couldn't get comfy. The sleeping bag grew to half its normal size, all my clothes felt uncomfy and I kept turning over into patches of frozen breath. From 5 am I slept soundly till 9.'

Mallory was so concerned by the lack of food and drink at Camp III that he decided to descend to Camp II to supervise the stores coming up the line. He got up at 6:20 a.m., 'energetic beggar', Sandy observed, and set off down the glacier. Breakfast was an even more measly affair than dinner the night before. They ate a sausage each and had half a tin of condensed milk per man. To their distress most of the porters were too ill to get up, due, they believed, to sleeping with the tents tightly closed. Mallory returned around lunchtime and reported on the state of the stores. Later that afternoon Sandy, Odell and the four porters who were able and willing to work set off down the glacier to collect the loads dumped by the porters from Camp II some three-quarters of a mile short of Camp III. 'We got 6 loads up, I led the pack with a Whymper tent so that none of the porters dared to complain of their loads or the pace I was setting.' This was exactly the scenario Geoffrey

Bruce had been at great pains to avoid. He and Norton knew full well that the only hope they had of getting to the summit of Everest was with wholly fit climbers and a strong team of porters to support them and carry loads high. Here were three of the key climbers squandering their energies carrying loads between camps that should, by right, have already been in Camp III. The picture was bleak.

That night they had temperatures at Camp III of −21° F, −30° C, and the next morning the porters were in a very much worse state. Several of them were vomiting, a clear sign of severe altitude sickness, and were quite unable to go on. Mallory knew that there was no point in keeping them at Camp III so he escorted them part of the way down to Camp II. Sandy too was suffering from the altitude: he had developed the characteristic headache which is the blight of so many climbers past and present. Hazard went down the glacier to oversee other loads coming up from Camp II. Sandy and Odell remained in camp but by 3.30 p.m. they elected to descend to meet Mallory and Hazard as only four of Noel's porters had reached them since the morning. They found Mallory, Hazard and eight worn-out porters about three-quarters of a mile below camp. 'The porters were in a very exhausted condition. I carried their loads in turn to rest them, but they were almost too exhausted to walk without loads. At last we got them into camp and distributed the eight sleeping bags I was carrying and got a primus going in one of their tents.' Sandy was frustrated by the situation he found himself in but he had neither the experience nor the knowledge to do very much about it, so he followed his instincts and tried to make a bad situation as good as possible for the porters. Meanwhile, Mallory was exhausted and off his food. He'd had a lousy day of it, they all conceded.

The next day things had not improved much. Sandy was suffering from a splitting headache so he was detailed by Mallory to stay in camp and do various jobs there. Odell and Hazard set out for the North Col to reconnoitre the route and find a possible camp site; Mallory hurried off down the glacier to Camp II to try again to organize the loads. Sandy's job was to rearrange the camp to accommodate more men. The only help he could enlist was from Karmi, the indefatigable cook, who was of great assistance. Together they got the primuses going for each party that arrived from Camp II and distributed sleeping bags to the porters in the hope that this would stop them from going sick so often. That afternoon Somervell arrived from II while Hazard and Odell came in from above Camp III. They had been driven back from the North Col by the wind and bad weather. That evening Sandy got the roarer cooker to work and they had a better meal, prepared for them by Karmi.

The situation at Camp II was little better than that in Camp III. Norton had asked Geoffrey Bruce to follow him up the glacier, a day behind, and to inspect the camps and ensure the NCOs understood exactly what was expected of them. The plan was for Bruce to arrive at Camp III by May 11 and from there be ready to go on to Camp IV on the North Col and then on to establish Camp V. When he arrived at Camp II on 8 May he expected to meet only the cook and a couple of porters, instead of which he found it fully occupied. Norton was there as well and it soon became clear that there had been some kind of major breakdown in the line. Of greatest concern to both men was the fact that the porters were miserable, demoralized and lacking in their usual courage and high spirits. With double the number of men in Camp II it was necessary to break open the stores of food and tents intended for the higher camps in order to meet this emergency. Some of the porters had struggled down from Camp III where they had spent two days holed up in their tents with a blanket between them and only a handful of barley to eat. This was a grave situation and Norton was deeply concerned. All he knew was that Mallory, Odell, Hazard and Sandy were up at Camp III in goodness only knew what conditions and that he had on his hands a large number of sick and dispirited porters. Mallory arrived the following morning and amplified the porters' story, telling Norton of the high winds and low temperature they had suffered on the night of 7 May.

The situation called for a radical reorganization and Norton immediately came up with a plan. He would send Somervell, who was a favourite with the men, up to Camp III with as many porters as he could muster. Shebbeare, who was currently in charge of Base Camp, would be brought up to run Camp II and Hazard would be sent down to replace Shebbeare in Base, as Norton was unwilling to leave the camp without a sahib in charge as all their money, stores and remaining equipment was housed there. For the remainder of the day Norton,

Bruce and Mallory made attempts to cheer up the porters and render Camp II more habitable. It was a great load off Mallory's mind when he was able to discuss with Norton the problems he had encountered at III and he wrote to Ruth of his feelings that day 'A great day of relief this with the responsibility shared or handed over.'

The following morning with snow falling thickly around them, the three climbers, with twenty-six porters in tow, including the twelve reserve porters who had been assigned to Bruce and were therefore fit and willing, set off for Camp III. Half-way up the trough they met Hazard who told them of his and Odell's reconnaissance of the North Col, or as far as it had gone, and painted a very bleak picture of Camp III to them. 'We gathered from him that Camp III was an exceedingly unpleasant place. With the wind and snow increasing every moment it was obviously going to be even worse than he painted it, but it was little use trying to talk in half a gale, so we bade him farewell and pushed on as rapidly as possible.'

Matters in Camp III were indeed bleak. 'Perfectly bloody day – nothing else will describe it. Wind and driven snow,' wrote Sandy, who spent the morning in his tent trying to repair a cooker which had not been functioning well in the cold. It was a fruitless task and left him with very near frostbite in his fingers. Odell and Somervell considered the weather too inclement for a further foray towards the North Col so they remained in Camp where they were all joined by Bruce, Norton, Mallory and a few porters at lunchtime. The porters in Camp III were in a worse state than ever and would make no effort to look after themselves, despite the fact that Sandy busily prepared their primus stoves, pushing them into their tents so that they could cook some food for themselves. Bruce's reserve porters were, however, much fitter, and they set about helping their friends and proving themselves to be invaluable in raising spirits among the porters' ranks. Meanwhile the climbers all lay down in their tents as the wind got up and the blizzard intensified. That night there was little sleep for anyone. 'Had a terrible night with wind and snow. I don't know how the tent stood it', Sandy wrote, 'very little sleep and about 2" of snow over everything in the tent. Had a lot of rheumatism in the night and an awful headache this morning.' Bruce had an equally miserable time: 'snow drifted into our tents covering everything to a depth of an inch or two. The discomfort of that night was acute. At every slightest movement of the body a miniature avalanche of snow would drop inside one's sleeping bag and melt there into a cold wet patch.'

In the morning Norton, realising what a toll the six nights at Camp III had taken on Mallory and Sandy, decided that in order to conserve fuel and to give the two a respite they should descend to Camp II. 'These two had been in the thick of it from the start, never sparing themselves for a moment. Irvine's capacity for work was immense. After the most gruelling day on the glacier, he would settle down with his tools inside a tent, improving the oxygen apparatus, or mending stoves, regardless of time or temperature, long after the rest of us were inside our sleeping-bags.'

Sandy was suffering not only from an altitude-induced headache but from severe dehydration. He had neither eaten nor, more importantly, drunk sufficient quantities for several days and the result was that when he and Mallory set off down the glacier towards Camp II he was very close to collapse. 'Must have been touched by the sun or something, for I have found it difficult to keep up with George and the rough ice shook my head terribly. Just at the top of the Trough I became completely exhausted panting about twice to every step and staggering badly at times. George trying a new route took us through a narrow crack between seracs which made me still more exhausted.' To Evelyn he confided, 'it was all I could do with George's praises & curses to get down to II alive with piles of snow on my head. However I think a lot if it was lack of food & drink as the fuel question made snow meltings very few & far between. After about 6 cups of tea at II & a couple of glasses of glacier water I quite recovered.' Feeling considerably revived by the liquid and food, he was delighted to find six letters waiting for him in camp. He retired to his tent and read the letters until it was too dark to see.

Camp III was still being battered by wind and snow. Norton, Somervell and seventeen porters succeeded in bringing up to the camp the remainder of the loads that had been dumped on the glacier by the exhausted men four days previously. Bruce was deeply shocked by the state of the porters when they returned and it became obvious to Norton, as the storm continued to rage, that there was no other course open but to retreat. The temperature at night plummeted again to −21° F (−30° C) and sleep was impossible. The next morning Camp III was evacuated, the tents were collapsed and Norton and Somervell made lists of what was left in the camp. The porters took a great deal of persuasion to leave their tents and it was only due to Bruce's cajoling and convincing them of the delights of Base Camp that they emerged and set off down the glacier.

As they headed down to Camp II they were met by Sandy who, completely recovered from his dehydration and exhaustion of the day before, 'sped up towards Camp III to hurry Somervell'. One of the porters, Tamding, had fallen on the ice and broken his leg. He was in great pain and Somervell's help was required to set the leg. Tamding had been his servant during the journey across Tibet and *en route* Somervell had noticed that one or two articles of his underwear had gone missing, never to be traced. On inspecting the fractured leg Somervell was somewhat bemused to discover that the missing garments had been 'borrowed' by Tamding. A makeshift stretcher had been arranged, using a carrier and a Whymper fly, and the sick man was carried down to Camp II by two porters. When Sandy got to Camp I he found another porter, Manbahadur, lying out in the cold making no attempt to keep himself warm. Sandy was horrified. 'The 3 coolies that had carried him down from II took absolutely damn all notice of him. I'm afraid both feet are lost from frostbite', he wrote in his diary.

He finally got down to Base Camp on the afternoon of 11 May to discover that Hingston had arrived from Darjeeling. That night they all relaxed and after a very good dinner Sandy wrote an assessment of his fellow climbers:

George and I and Noel came to the base camp to find Hingston just arrived and very cheery having left the General quite fit again. We had a very amusing dinner with a couple of bottles of champagne. A very dirty and bedraggled company. Hingston clean shaven and proper sitting opposite Shebbeare with a face like a villain and a balaclava inside out on the back of his head. Hazard in flying helmet with a bristly chin sticking out farther than ever. Beetham sat silent most of the time, round and black like a mixture of Judas Iscariot and an apple dumpling.

George sitting on a very low rookie chair could hardly be seen above the table except for a cloth hat pinned up on one side with a huge safety pin and covered with candle grease. Noel as usual leaning back with his chin down and cloth hat over his eyes, grinning to himself. Everyone very happy to be back in a Christian mess hut eating decent food.

Relieved though they might have been to be back in the comfort of Base Camp, sleeping in luxurious camp beds and breathing the thick air of 16,500 feet (which had left them breathless two weeks previously), there were still men higher up the mountain and all was not well. Sandy had written a bald assessment of the situation to Evelyn that afternoon: 'One has I think pneumonia, one has lost both feet from frost bite & one has a broken leg.'

Hingston's return on 11 May was auspicious and he wasted no time in assessing the health of the men. The climbers were all basically fit but when Hingston made an inspection of the porters who had come off the glacier he was very concerned by the condition of all of them in general, and one or two individual men in particular gave him very great cause for worry. There was Manbahadur, the cobbler: he was in a very bad state and Hingston judged that he would probably lose both feet above the ankles if he lived. Meanwhile Bruce and Norton had met up with Somervell in Camp I where they found him with his hands full tending to the casualties. The worst case was one of the Gurkha NCOs, Shamsher, who appeared to have a blood clot on the brain. He was probably suffering from what is now known as HACE – high altitude cerebral edema, an extremely dangerous condition when fluid leaks from the cerebral blood vessels causing swelling of the brain. As pressure builds up inside the skull, mental and motor skills deteriorate rapidly and unless the victim is quickly brought down to a lower altitude the risk is of slipping into a coma and dying.

By the time Somervell saw Shamsher he was already unconscious. He left him in the care of two NCOs and descended to Base Camp. Hingston and Bruce went up to Camp I to see Shamsher who, they hoped, would have improved with the rest and care he was receiving at Camp I. They were disturbed to hear that his condition had deteriorated overnight and Hingston immediately ordered his evacuation to a lower altitude.

Despite their best attempts to carry him carefully to Base Camp, Shamsher died about a mile from the camp without ever regaining consciousness. He was buried in a sheltered spot outside Base Camp.

End of Round One, as Norton put it. The setbacks they had suffered on the mountain had been a very great disappointment to them and Shamsher's death a profound shock, but they were far from defeated. A few days' rest in Base Camp was the first consideration, during which the weather, it was hoped, might improve. For the first time since he left Darjeeling Sandy wrote in his diary that he'd done more or less nothing. 'Restful day in camp. Mountain looked pretty beastly and clouds to north looked very threatening. Did nothing much all day.'

The following two days were also quiet, although Sandy was busy once again in his workshop tent. He spent the first morning making Noel a candlestick out of a broken reducing valve and the following day worked 'practically the whole day up till 10 p.m. taking cinema motors to pieces and making gadgets for Noel's camera.' In between he gave the cooks for the higher camps instruction on how to use the primus stoves. This must have been quite amusing, bearing in mind his inability to speak a word of their language. The training took place at the request of Norton and Geoffrey Bruce who spent the days after the retreat planning their next attack. One of the few advantages of the adverse conditions they had suffered was that they had been able to assess the performance of the porters and were now in a position to select the six strongest men who would become leaders. They allowed them, as far as possible, to pick their own teams, thus encouraging an *esprit de corps* and a little friendly rivalry. In reallocating the porters they were very careful to ensure that each party had at least two men who knew their way around the primus stoves and the use of meta fuel (solidified spirit). There was a huge amount of organization to be completed before another attack on the mountain could be considered. Although the camps had been stocked as far as III, careful lists needed to be made to ensure the right quantity of food, fuel and equipment was in place. Lists had been made by the departing climbers as to what was where, so Bruce spent a whole day collating these and marrying the new schedule with Mallory's revised summit campaign.

Mallory had returned to Base Camp on 11 May and confided at the end of a long letter to Ruth, in which he'd described their climb and retreat in great detail, 'I felt that I was going through a real hard time in a way I never did in '22. Meanwhile our retreat has meant a big waste of time.' Part of the problem had been that when Mallory had arrived at Camp III he had not found the situation that he had anticipated. The Gurkha NCO had not taken the control Bruce and Norton expected of him and Mallory found himself having to fulfil the role he felt least comfortable with, that of camp organiser. Sandy, Odell and Hazard were of little use to him other than in support as none of them had been up to III before, and, more importantly, had had no experience of an expedition on this scale. Had he had Bruce or Norton there with him it is likely that the problems that arose in the line of supplies could have been dealt with in another way. But the lost days were what really bothered Mallory. The later the summit day, the more likely they would be to encounter the onset of the monsoon. He revised his climbing schedule with a new summit day of 28 May and agreed the proposal with Bruce and Norton. The climbing parties were to remain as before: Norton and Somervell without oxygen, Mallory and Sandy with.

One of the single most important aspects of the whole summit attempt was the morale of the porters. It had been that which had most deeply concerned Bruce on his arrival in Camp II and it was Norton's foremost thought now. If their morale and courage could be restored there would be hope for a renewed assault. He sent Karma Paul, the interpreter, down to Rongbuk Monastery to enquire as to whether the Chief Lama would grant them an audience. Norton knew that this would mean a very great deal to the porters who held the Lama in the highest regard. He agreed and on 15 May the whole party of climbers and porters made their way down to the monastery for the ceremony. Norton had arranged for each of the porters to be given some rice and a few coins to use as an offering to the Lama, while he had with him a gift of a painting on silk of the Potola Palace[2] and a wrist-watch.

Sandy's account of the visit is a slightly tongue in cheek version of the blessing but it is at least factually accurate, bearing in mind the pepper

2 Palace of the Dalai Lama, the Spiritual Leader of Tibet.

pot to which he refers was a prayer wheel and the iron bedstead the Lama's throne.

After sitting for an hour and a half eating meat and macaroni with chop sticks (well-chewed ends), drinking Tibetan tea and eating radish with very strong pepper in an ante-chamber, we were ushered into the presence of the Lama who sat on a red throne on an iron bedstead just inside a kind of veranda ... we sat on beautifully upholstered benches on either side of an alcove in the roof. Noel had his camera about 30 ft away on the edge of the roof. After being blessed and having our heads touched with a white metal pepper-pot (at least it looked like that) we sat down while the whole damn lot of coolies came in turn doing 3 salams – head right onto the ground and then presented their caddas and offerings and were similarly blessed. Next bowls of rice were brought and the Lama addressed the coolies in a few well-chosen words and then said a prayer or prayers – it all sounded the same, ending on a wonderfully deep note.

Shebbeare also noted the ceremony in his diary and commented on the Lama's address, 'which as interpreted by Karma Paul afterwards, was very much what the Archbishop of Canterbury would have said in similar circumstances; if the spirits were willing we should succeed, the sahibs must not plan anything that would endanger human life and the porters must obey the sahibs'.

The effect of the Holy Lama's blessing was dazzling. The porters returned to Base Camp in fresh heart and with renewed vigour and determination. 'Nothing could have been more satisfactory', concluded Bruce. 'The reverence with which the men entered and left the presence of the great Lama was eloquent proof of his influence over them.'

The Lama's blessing may well have made a good impression on Sandy but the food he'd eaten at the monastery had not, and he had a disagreeable few days when he was troubled with diarrhoea which left him at times feeling rather rotten. He was in good spirits, however, and wrote in his diary the next morning: 'Perfect morning – evidently the direct result of the Lama's prayers. After a conference about our future plans I gave the coolie cooks another lesson in Primus stoves. Lots of odd jobs kept us busy all day. Lots of carrying frames, etc, to be repaired before they go up the glacier again. Hingston performed his awful tests on us after tea.' The results of these tests had Sandy still looking fit. He was able to hold his breath for thirty seconds (as opposed to 120 in Darjeeling), with only Somervell markedly stronger at forty-one seconds. His expiratory force was the same as Norton and he was strongest in the endurance test, when they had to blow mercury up a tube and hold it there. In the mental arithmetic tests Mallory was spectacularly quicker than any of them, so his faculties appear to have been little affected by the altitude to date.

The greatest anxiety for the climbers now was the weather. The onset of the monsoon over the Himalaya would, they all understood clearly, make an assault on the summit quite impossible. They were receiving information on its progress from Mallory's sister, who lived in Colombo, Ceylon, where the monsoon typically arrived three weeks earlier than in the Himalaya, and from the meteorological department in Simla. Owing to the slowness of the postal service the most important information on the monsoon only arrived with them at Base Camp after the final descent on 11 June. They knew, however, that in 1922 the monsoon had broken on 1 June and they also knew that it was generally preceded by a fortnight of warm, clear weather. It was this period on which they were pinning their hopes of a successful attempt on the summit.

On 17 May, originally planned as their summit day, Norton, Somervell, Mallory and Odell set off for Camp I and Sandy followed them the following day in the company of Hazard and Noel. Geoffrey Bruce, Hingston and Beetham remained at Base Camp, Beetham having been struck by a bad attack of sciatica, adding insult to injury to the poor man. Sandy was not feeling as fit as he had been and noted in his diary at Camp I, 'have had diarrhoea for 3 days and feel rather rotten with it. However am trying the effect of lead and opium. It looked a very dirty day on the mountain this afternoon.' After a very warm and comfortable night at Camp I he was feeling considerably better and set a record time between Camps I and II, arriving at II in one and three-quarter hours. 'Rested in Camp II till 4:30 then as no other sahibs had arrived I strolled up the glacier and met Shebbeare at the entrance of the trough – very tired. I took his rucksack full of crampons and we both returned by easy stages to Camp II.' The next morning he and Hazard made their way up to Camp III as planned. They sorted porters on their way up, helping them to exchange loads and ensuring that as much of the food, fuel and equipment as possible got into camp. When they arrived they discovered Somervell suffering badly from the effects of sunstroke, with a high fever. Sandy, as usual, found that various repair jobs had been left for him in camp, so he spent the early afternoon mending the primus stoves which were malfunctioning in the cold. He also effected repairs to various tent poles which had suffered in the last winds. After these jobs were completed he set out towards the North Col to meet Norton, Mallory and Odell who had been up to establish Camp IV, but he was not properly dressed for the cold on the glacier and had to return to Camp III before he met up with them. 'They had a pretty exciting time coming down. Norton glissading out of control and George going down a crevasse unseen and unheard by the rest. All were very tired when they got in.'

This bald statement hides the truth behind a dramatic story. Norton, Odell, Mallory and a porter named Lhakpa Tsering had made their way up from Camp III that morning, equipped with Alpine rope and pickets. Their intention was to fix ropes in all the most difficult places on the climb up to the North Col where they would then establish Camp IV, the true jumping-off point for any summit attempt. As Norton explained in his chapter entitled 'The North Col' in the expedition book *The Fight for Everest*, the nature of the slopes above Camp III changes every year, for they cross the path of a glacier which, after all, is a frozen river that moves, albeit slowly but inexorably down the mountain. In 1924 the approach to the North Col had changed considerably from that in 1922. They were confronted by an enormous crevasse which they would have to cross before gaining access to the slopes below the North Col. Mallory lead the route through the crevasse and up a steep, icy snow chimney which Norton described as 'the deuce'. 'It was very narrow, its sides were smooth blue ice and it was floored – if the term floor can be applied to a surface that mounts almost vertically – with soft snow which seemed merely to conceal a bottomless crack and offered little or no foothold. The climb was something of a gymnastic exercise, and one is little fitted for gymnastics above 22,000 ft.' The 200-foot chimney took an hour to climb and the exertion was utterly exhausting. Above the chimney were steep slopes of snow and ice where the climbers fixed ropes using pickets and tying on, where possible, to natural features such as a large serac, or block of ice, which would act as a good anchor. The system of fixing ropes is adopted now as it was then, and it offers some protection over highly exposed, steep ground, such as that which they now encountered. One Himalayan climbing guide told me that nowadays he and his team of Sherpas fix 6,000 metres of rope on the route up to the summit from the north side of Everest. In 1924 they succeeded in fixing less than 1,000 metres. A well-recognized technique in the 1920s was step cutting, at which Mallory was an acknowledged master. He cut broad, deep steps up the steepest sections of the slopes above the chimney in order that the porters might use them when they carried their loads up to the North Col. Step cutting is exhausting work, especially at altitude, but vital for the sake of the porters who were less at home on the steep ice and snow than the British climbers.

They arrived at the place where they had pitched their tents in 1922, only to discover that the shelf was somewhat smaller this year, forming a 'hog-backed ridge of untrodden, glistening snow barely affording level space for our proposed row of little 6-foot-square tents'. Well pleased with their efforts thus far, Mallory and Odell set off to prospect the route up towards the summit. The terrain between the camp site and the North Col itself was heavily crevassed and made crossing it extremely hard work. Odell succeeded in finding a bridge across the most serious crevasse, which meant that access to the col was easier than it had been in 1922. Nevertheless, Mallory, who had borne the brunt of the heavy work that morning on the way up, was played out and as the four of them turned to make for Camp III at 3.45 there were a number of incidents on the descent each one of which might well have proven fatal. The first slip was by Lhakpa who, having tied himself on to Odell's rope with an inadequate reef knot, slipped and fell, saved only from a disastrous tumble into oblivion by a soft patch of snow which arrested his fall. It was a very sobering moment for him and he was extremely afraid. Mallory, by his own admission severely exhausted, fell into a crevasse:

The snow gave way and in I went with the snow tumbling all round me, down, luckily, only about 10 feet before I fetched up half blind and breathless to find myself most precariously supported only by my ice axe somehow caught across the crevasse and still held in my right hand – and below was a very unpleasant black hole. I had some nasty moments before I got comfortably wedged and began to yell for help up through the round hole I had come through where the blue sky showed – this because I was afraid my operations to extricate myself would bring down a lot more snow and perhaps precipitate me into the bargain. However, I soon grew tired of shouting – they hadn't seen me from above – and bringing the snow down a little at a time I made a hole out towards the side (the crevasse ran down a slope) after some climbing, and extricated myself – but was then on the wrong side of the crevasse, so that eventually I had to cut across a nasty slope of very hard ice and farther down some mixed unpleasant snow before I was out of the wood. The others were down by a better line ten minutes before me. That cutting against time at the end after such a day just about brought me to my limit.

They arrived back in camp exhausted in the late afternoon. Next day while Mallory, Norton and Odell were recovering from their ordeal Sandy set out with Somervell and Hazard to take twelve porters and several loads up to the North Col. The weather was diabolical, 'snow falling steadily, no signs of improvement. Conditions and going were perfectly bloody.' When they reached the ice chimney in the big crevasse it became clear that the porters would not be able to climb it with the loads on their backs, so Sandy and Somervell scrambled up to the ledge above it and spent two and three-quarter utterly exhausting hours hauling the loads up the 200-foot chimney. Hazard stood at the bottom with the porters and oversaw the loading of the rope. It was a gargantuan task and left all three men very weary. When finally all the loads had been safely winched up and the porters and Hazard had climbed the chimney, Sandy and Somervell set off towards the North Col camp, fixing ropes in all the most exposed places. As there was insufficient accommodation for everyone at Camp IV, they left Hazard and the porters on the North Col and returned to III 'at the double as the mist and snow were thickening and the hour late'. Sandy had a nasty slip on the way down but was none the worse for it. The visibility on the glacier was less than 100 yards and they arrived at dusk at Camp III 'very tired and thirsty'. Sandy's first impression of the North Col had not been a favourable one. He wrote a few days later to his mother, 'I've been up to the North Col in a blizzard and never want to do it again.'

The day after his foray up to the North Col Sandy remained in Camp III mending the broken primus stoves. Late that afternoon he learned from Norton that six oxygen appliances would be required early the following morning. They would be taken to Camp IV in preparation for a summit attempt on or around 28 May. This was news indeed for Sandy and he stayed up until midnight working away at the sets, desperate to have them ready and fully functioning. The following morning he was up early again working feverishly until Odell and Geoffrey Bruce left Camp III. The late night, early morning and extreme cold had taken their toll on Sandy and he was 'feeling seedy'.

One of the most unpleasant aspects of life at Camp III was the cold. Everybody complained of it in their letters and diaries. Norton described it as a truly horrid spot. It was sited on the moraine on the edge of the East Rongbuk glacier so that the ground underfoot was of rough stones. In 1922 these stones had been warmed by the sun and there was a gentle trickle of drinking water available. In 1924 the stones were always covered in fresh snow and deadeningly cold. Every drop of water they required had to be melted over the primus stoves and the aching cold of the ground left their feet numb. Before turning in to their tents at night they had to make an effort to warm them up: 'as the moraine was too rough and the glacier too glassy to admit of a tramp, we used to carry out that military manoeuvre known as "double mark time" on a flat stone, sometimes for ten minutes', wrote Norton, 'and even then, perhaps without much effect.' The night of 22 May was the coldest night recorded to date at Camp III, −24° F or −30° C. Sandy's feet were so uncomfortably cold that he had to get up four times in the night to attempt to warm them, in vain. The low temperatures they were experiencing were nothing in comparison to what the Arctic and Antarctic explorers had had to put up with. The very great difference, however, is that at altitude the intense cold is a very serious matter. The body has much less strength to fight it, the lack of oxygen greatly exacerbates the feeling of cold and the risk of frostbite is very real. Few of the men at Camp III got any sleep at all that night. 'The eiderdown sleeping bag is a wonderful invention,' wrote Norton in his dispatch to the *Times* the next day, 'but it has its limitations.'

Odell and Bruce only got half-way up to Camp IV when they decided that the snow was too unstable and it would be dangerous to proceed. Meanwhile Hazard, who had been up at the North Col for two days in miserable conditions and who was expecting to be relieved by Odell and Bruce, headed down from Camp IV with eleven porters, leaving Phu, the cook, in Camp. Hazard and his men were spotted descending the ice chimney by Bruce and Odell and this further confirmed their view that to proceed would have been a mistake. What they did not know at that stage was that Hazard was accompanied by only eight of his twelve men, the other four being marooned in Camp IV. It appeared that Hazard had gone first across the dangerous traverse, rendered infinitely more so by the new, deep snow, and eight men had followed him, crossing one at a time, but the remaining four had lost their nerve as they saw the snow slipping below their feet and had been afraid to go further. They had turned back to Camp IV and hidden in their tents. This was an extremely serious situation and Norton was truly afraid that they might lose the men if he did not mount a rescue. Not only were they stranded with very little food, but they were also 'prey to the superstitious terrors to which those of their race are always prone on the big snow mountains'. Hazard reported that at least two of them were suffering from frostbite and that one of the food loads had been dropped down the mountain, so that their rations were woefully inadequate. Norton surveyed his troops and concluded, 'the whole party at Camp III was already in a bad way. Mallory and Somervell were both suffering from very bad high-altitude throats. Odell had had hardly any sleep for several nights; Irvine had diarrhoea and Hazard had just had a very trying three days. The porters were for the most part quite unfit, morally and physically, for further efforts at present.' Norton called a conference and discussed the situation with the climbers. Sandy wrote in his diary that evening, 'Norton decided that we must again retreat. Norton, Somervell, George and I are due to get off early and fetch the 4 down from the col.' In the event, Sandy felt too ill to join in the rescue the following day but he clearly felt guilty at not being able to accompany them: 'A lot of snow fell in the night so the col will be very dangerous. I hope they get on alright.' It was probably no bad thing that Sandy did not accompany them. Under those circumstances and in such appalling conditions Norton, Somervell and Mallory were absolutely reliant on their mountaineering knowledge and skills. They trusted each other completely and had, after all, the experience of climbing high together in 1922. Sandy's inexperience might have hampered rather than helped their rescue, although his brute strength and courage were sorely missed. As the three climbers left Camp III for the North Col, Norton ordered Hazard and Sandy to evacuate camp leaving only Odell and Noel *in situ* should there be casualties to assist down the glacier.

Norton realized that in using three of the strongest climbers, who might well be expected under different circumstances to be resting up before their summit bid, he would be jeopardizing their future attempts by attempting such a dramatic and exhausting rescue. But they had no option. 'Personally', Norton wrote later, 'my one fixed determination had all along been that we must on no account have any casualties among our porters this year, and here we were, faced with the very real possibility of losing four men; for it must be admitted that our chances of rescuing the marooned porters did not appear rosy at this time.'

What followed that day was one of the most dramatic rescues on Everest to date. Norton and Somervell, encouraged and at times chided by Mallory, made their way up the steep snow slopes and into the chimney from where they negotiated the snow traverse. From there they could see Phu standing on the edge of the shelf. After some communication problems they managed to establish that all four men could descend under their own power although one man, Namgya, had very badly frostbitten hands. This was a huge relief. Norton acknowledged that despite the fact that they had come prepared with a stretcher they could never have negotiated the steep descent carrying a man. The traverse was in a very dangerous, unstable condition and Somervell insisted that he should be the one to cross it to the porters, while Mallory and Norton belayed him on the rope. He moved slowly, diagonally upwards across the traverse, pausing occasionally to cough painfully. After one of the coughing fits, Norton saw him rest his head on his arm in exhaustion, the slope so steep, he recalled, that 'the mental picture I have of him as he did this shows him standing almost upright in his steps with his elbow resting on the snow level with his shoulder.' Eventually Somervell reached the end of the 200-foot rope, still some ten yards short of the ridge where the men were huddled together. After a brief consultation at the tops of their voices he persuaded the men to take a chance over the first ten yards to the safety of the rope. The first two men did this and passed along the rope to Mallory and Norton. The last two made the mistake of leaving together with the result that a big patch of snow below them gave way and sent them flying down the slope on their backs. 'For one paralysing second I foresaw the apparently inevitable tragedy, with the two figures shooting into space over the edge of the blue ice cliff, 200 feet below.' By a miracle their fall was broken by the depth of the new snow but they were out of reach of the rope and too petrified to move. In a moment Somervell realized that the only option was to unrope himself, and pull them to safety. He held the very end of the rope in his hand, leaned forward, arms outstretched and grabbed the porters by the scruff of the neck, pulling them towards him, to 'apparently gather them to his bosom in a paternal manner worthy of Abraham' as Mallory observed. They stumbled along the rope to the spot where Mallory, Norton and the other two were standing, while Somervell roped up again and made his way back to the same spot giving 'a fine object lesson in mountain craft ... balanced and erect, crossing the ruined track without a slip or mistake'. The team made their way down the ice chimney and across the snow slopes to the safety of the glacier where they were met, three-quarters of a mile outside camp, by Odell and Noel with hot soup. The relief they all felt at the successful outcome of the rescue was tempered by the extreme discomfort at having to spend a further night in Camp III. The following morning a bedraggled and exhausted party limped into Camp II.

Sandy, accompanied by Bruce, had made his way down to Camp II whilst the rescue above him was under way. He was feeling extremely unwell and the castor oil he had dosed himself up with had had little effect. He struggled into Camp II where he flopped into a tent, unable to get down to Camp I. Later that day, he and Bruce received a note from a porter informing him of the successful retrieval of the porters and he wrote in his diary, 'A note came through to say that they had nearly lost two men from slipping off the N.C. but in the end had arrived at Camp III safely at 8 pm very tired and Somervell obviously knocked up. Noel had come to meet them on the glacier with a huge thermos of soup.'

By the time Norton and his men arrived into Camp II that afternoon Sandy was up and about, feeling much better. He, Mallory, Bruce and Shebbeare walked down to the relative comfort of Camp I. Sandy was trying some rubber-soled boots. He had only come down twice on the surface of the glacier, which was at its most slippery stage, and was pleased with the performance of the boots. Shebbeare, particularly, was amused by Sandy's seemingly incessant desire to try out new things. The warmth and lower altitude did them all a great deal of good but their mood was subdued when they received news from Base Camp that Manbahadur, the cobbler with the frostbitten feet, had died.

The next morning Sandy and Shebbeare scrambled up some rocks above the camp searching for the hermit's cell that was reputed to be there, but failed to find it. On their return they met Norton and Somervell who had arrived from Camp II and Hingston who joined them shortly afterwards from Base. The meeting that followed lasted two hours and was inconclusive. A second set-back so late in the season was considered by all to be a very grave disappointment. The onset of the monsoon, they felt sure, was imminent but they could not bear to give up now and clung to the belief that Norton held, namely that there would have to be two weeks of good weather before the monsoon proper would begin. Bruce, Norton and Shebbeare put their heads together and concluded that out of the fifty-five porters they had started with, only fifteen were fit to go up the mountain again. Such a drastic reduction in porter numbers meant that a revised summit plan had to be considered and to Sandy's great disappointment it did not include him in either of the first parties. Bruce's plan, which was eventually adopted, was to drop the oxygen attempt as the apparatus was heavy and required many more porters than were available. There would therefore be two attempts, a day apart, both without oxygen. Mallory doubted that he personally would be strong enough to climb high again, but he had more experience than anyone else so he agreed to make the choice of the two climbing parties. As Geoffrey Bruce was the only really fit man among them he chose him to be his partner and Somervell and Norton to make up the second party. Sandy wrote to Lilian that evening, 'We have now reorganised our plans and I hope to be in the 1st or 2nd party. Geoff is considered the fittest & I'm next but neither being experienced climbers we can't make a single party between us. So George Mallory & Geoff; & Norton and Somervell will probably make the 1st two parties, Odell and I have to be reserve.'

This letter, which belongs to the find of May 2000, points up something I had not really understood before. When Hingston declared Geoff Bruce to be the fittest man and Sandy the second fittest, that meant that he deemed the others, Norton, Somervell, Mallory etc., to be less fit still. This puts paid to many of the arguments proposed in the more recent past that Mallory's choice of Sandy as his partner for the final climb was a spur-of-the-moment decision. Ever since Sandy and Mallory first met the idea of the two of them being members of the same summit party had been clear in Mallory's mind. Now, faced with a non-oxygen attempt and the declaration by Hingston that Bruce was the fittest of the climbers, Mallory had no option but to drop Sandy and climb with Bruce although I do not believe this was his preferred option. When Norton invited Mallory to choose the make-up of the second climbing party, there was again little choice. Norton and Somervell had climbed together in 1922, Mallory knew they were strong enough to go high without oxygen, whereas Sandy was still untried above the North Col, and thus this decision was more or less taken out of his hands.

It must have been a very bitter moment for Sandy as he saw the chance of his summit attempt slipping away. He put a brave face on things however and added in his letter, 'Afraid there's not time for more as the post is just going and I have to go up to Camp II to make a rope ladder for them!' This rope ladder appears to have been entirely Sandy's idea. As usual, his fertile and inventive mind had been working all the while and it struck him that if it were fixed in the ice chimney above Camp III it would greatly help the porters carrying loads up to the North Col. On 28 May he set off up to Camp II, recording a fast time of 1 hour 35 minutes. He brought with him a dozen large tent pegs and 'spent all afternoon making the ladder. Every third rung was wood, the rest rope, the splicing of which was very hard on the hands.' The following day Odell and Shebbeare helped him and by evening they were able to show Norton, Somervell, Bruce and Mallory a 60-foot masterpiece. Norton was impressed, especially after it had been installed and proved such a useful aid. 'Like all the work of the well-known firm of "Odell and Irvine" this proved a most complete success.'

On 30 May Sandy and Mallory set off for Camp III with the other climbers. The two made good progress and arrived well ahead of the rest. Although to the others he appeared his usual cheerful self, inside Sandy was boiling with frustration. Being assessed by Hingston to be second fittest after Geoffrey Bruce and yet left out of the summit teams was something Sandy felt deeply. 'Feel very fit tonight. I wish I was in the first party instead of a bloody reserve.' But despite his inner feelings he kept his composure and even made a gift to Bruce of a lightweight rucksack he had fashioned out of one of the oxygen carriers, although when he had found time to manufacture that I cannot imagine.

On 31 May the four climbers, the reserve party and fifteen porters, the so-called Tigers, made their way up to the North Col. After fixing the rope ladder in the chimney, which took some time, they finally arrived at Camp IV where Sandy instantly set about preparing a meal of cocoa, pea soup and tongue. Sandy and Odell had been appointed by Norton as the official support team. This was the first time in the history of Everest that a team had been put in place with the single task of feeding and assisting the climbing party, welcoming them home after the climb and tending to their every need as required. This the two men did, by all accounts, with great dedication and their hard work was much appreciated. Norton wrote about it in a *Times* dispatch:

Since 1922 we have recognized the necessity of this *rôle*, picturing the comfort to a returning party of weary climbers such support might afford. The most optimistic imaginations fell short of the reality, as produced by that 'well-known firm.' For over a week those two have lived on the North Col (23,000 ft), and have cooked every meal – and only those who have done it can appreciate the recurring hatefulness of this operation. They have gone out day and night to escort and succour returning parties of porters and climbers over the intricate approaches to the camp, carrying lamps, drinks, and even oxygen to restore the exhausted. They have run the camp and tended the sick. Whether we reach the top or not, no members of the climbing party can pull more weight in the team than these two by their unostentatious, unselfish, gruelling work.

Again, Sandy's diary gives a brief and graphic account of his task: 'Up at 4:30 a.m. to cook breakfast for the climbers. Very cold and disagreeable job. Thank God my profession is not a cook!'

When Sandy spoke his mind in his diary he was generally feeling fit and well, and at this stage he had recovered from his gastric complaints and was as strong as any climber can be at that altitude. As he watched Bruce and Mallory leave the Col he was consumed with feelings of frustration and disappointment. But he didn't show it, and he soon got back to the task of caring for the incoming climbers, this time Norton and Somervell who had climbed up from Camp III.

Mallory and Bruce succeeded in establishing Camp V about 200 feet higher than the 1922 site, but the wind got up considerably and it took the heart out of the porters. In addition, Bruce had strained his heart retrieving a rucksack which had been left below the camp. They spent the night at Camp V but were unable, the next morning, to persuade the porters to carry loads higher in order to establish Camp VI. The wind was still raging and despite Bruce's best endeavours nothing could be done to alter the porters' attitude. Mallory decided that they had no option but to retreat, a bitter decision for him. He told Odell when he arrived in Camp IV that he was upset by the porters' refusal to go on. Despite this comment, it would appear that at some stage before he came back down from Camp V, Mallory had already resolved to make an attempt with oxygen, returning to his initial climbing plan. This I believe he felt was going to be his only chance of success. Another height record was not something Mallory was prepared to settle for, even without gas. He wanted to give himself the best chance he could at the summit and the attempt with Bruce had not represented that. If he returned to England with Everest unclimbed he would have to face once again the decision as to whether he should put himself forward for a further attempt, thus inflicting another separation on Ruth and the children. While he still had energy and the weather remained fair he would have felt he had no option but to try again.

On 2 June Sandy was up again in the small hours, this time preparing breakfast for Norton and Somervell. They left for their summit attempt at 6 a.m. with two porters. One of Mallory's porters came into Camp IV at about 10 a.m. 'very done in'. He reported that the others were pushing on. An hour later Sandy looked up again and spotted the first party, Mallory, Bruce and the remaining porters, returning. He was surprised. He set two primus stoves going for drinks and soup and, picking up a rope, set out to meet them at the Col. The porters were exhausted and had been unable to tolerate the wind at Camp V. Geoffrey Bruce, having strained his heart, was keen to get down to a lower altitude as soon as possible. Mallory was tired but preoccupied. Before he retired to his tent Mallory confided in Sandy his idea for another attempt, this time with oxygen and this time with Sandy. This was exactly what Sandy wanted to hear. He hotfooted it straight down to Camp III with Hazard and Geoffrey Bruce and began to prepare the apparatus. He confided in Odell that he was delighted at the turn of events and Odell remarked later that he had exhibited real boyish enthusiasm at the thought of getting the chance he had seen slipping away from him over the last few days. His excitement was palpable tempered only by the appalling sunburn he had suffered through the wind and sun at Camp IV. 'My face was badly cut by the sun and wind on the Col and my lips are cracked to bits which makes eating very unpleasant.'

His fair skin had given him trouble throughout the expedition and he had written home about it on several occasions. The great discomfort he was now suffering was exacerbated by the use of the oxygen mask. Years later Odell told Bill Summers that in order to derive maximum benefit from the oxygen, Sandy had been forced to clamp the mask onto the scar which had developed above his nose and in the soft tissue around his mouth and that every time he removed it, the frozen material would remove another layer of skin from his face. The pain must have been excruciating and it makes one wince to think of it. Despite this he was still in optimistic mood and spent the whole of the afternoon of 3 June getting the two sets ready and ensuring that the porters were able to carry the maximum number of cylinders up to Camp V. Mallory too had descended to Camp III to discover from Bruce how many porters could be mustered and to discuss his plans for the assault with Sandy.

That evening they heard a rumour that Norton and Somervell had returned to the North Col.

This turned out to be untrue and he wrote in his diary for 4 June, 'Mallory and I prepared for our oxygen attempt but shortly after breakfast a porter came down to say that N and S had established Camp VI at 27,000 ft and stayed the night there. Great was the excitement in the Camp.' Noel had his telephoto lens trained on the summit all day but could see no sign of the climbers. Finally, shortly before midday, Mallory and Sandy 'put the worst aspect on things and decided to go up the NC and be ready to fetch sick men down or make an oxygen attempt ourselves a day later.' As they climbed they breathed oxygen, using 1.5 litres per minute, and Sandy was pleased to note that it slowed his breathing down at least three times. 'George and I both arrived at the camp very surprisingly fresh.' Odell, at Camp IV, had been scanning the mountain all morning with binoculars but had seen no trace of Norton and Somervell. Mallory took over the watch and believed that he could see downward tracks some 700 feet below the summit. Sandy could hardly contain his feelings and dashed to his diary to note, 'I hope they've got to the top, but by God I'd like to have a whack at it myself.'

Norton and Somervell left Camp VI early on the morning of 4 June but encountered their first set-back almost immediately. One of the thermos flasks they had prepared the night before had leaked in the sleeping bag. Mindful of the need for liquid higher up they were forced to delay their start and melt more snow for the thermos. They finally left at 6.40 a.m. and trudged slowly up the steep, rocky shoulder slanting towards the summit. As the sun began to warm them they encountered the Yellow Band, a seam of yellow sandstone that crossed the whole north face of the mountain. It consisted of sloping slabs and ledges where the footholds were difficult and the ever-present threat of a tumble would take them 7000 feet onto the Rongbuk Glacier below. They had reached an altitude of about 27,500 feet. Here they noted a big change in their breathing. A little lower down they had been taking three or four breaths to each complete step; at this altitude their pace slowed dramatically as they were gasping eight or even nine breaths per step. Norton set himself the target of walking twenty paces and then resting but noted that his ability fell woefully short of his expectation and he managed only about thirteen before having to pause. They found themselves having to stop every twenty yards or so for a rest and Somervell understood that they had reached the limit of their endurance. At a height of 28,000 feet he sat down: he could go no further. His breathing was laboured and greatly hurt his throat which was already raw after weeks of suffering from a high altitude cough. Norton agreed to go on, but his progress was painfully slow and Somervell watched him labouring for an hour, gaining little height. The going was even more treacherous than before and when Norton eventually reached the couloir which he hoped would lead him to the base of the summit pyramid he found it full of waist-deep snow and overshadowed by fearsomely steep rock beyond. Since about 27,500 feet he had been experiencing difficulty with his eyesight. He was seeing double and had some trouble in placing his feet. He and Somervell had put this down to the altitude, despite the fact that Norton secretly wondered whether it was the onset of snowblindness. He had not been wearing goggles for the climb as the rims interfered with his vision and there was only relatively little snow at this height. His hunch of course was right and when he found himself on the steep slabs below the north ridge he was barely able to see the tiny footholds. In addition, these slabs were covered with powdery snow, which rendered them treacherously slippery and the snow masked what few footholds there were. 'It was not exactly difficult going, but it was a dangerous place for a single unroped climber, as one slip would have sent me in all probability to the bottom of the mountain.' There were a further 200 feet of this going before he reached the relative safety of the summit pyramid and he calculated that in the time left to him he would be unable to climb the 800 or 900 feet to the summit and return safely. At 28,126 feet he turned his back on the summit and climbed cautiously down towards Somervell.

Somervell had not benefited from his rest. His breathing was still desperately laboured and his throat perfect agony. They made their way painfully slowly down past Camp VI where they collected their belongings and collapsed the tents. They reached the level of Camp V by sunset when Norton glissaded on down, only noticing a brief while later that Somervell was not with him. He waited for half an hour and eventually saw him emerge from the rocks above him. By now it was dark. Somervell had been forced to stop frequently on the descent as the coughing fits were racking his entire body. He finally sat down in the snow. He was unable to breathe, his throat was almost completely blocked and he was sure he would die. In desperation he performed a number of compressions to his chest and succeeded in dislodging the blockage. A huge wave of coughing overtook him and he spat out the obstruction in his throat and a good deal of blood. He had in fact removed part of the mucous membrane of his larynx which had been damaged by frostbite. He stood up, able to breathe more freely than he had done for days and resumed his descent, although the pain in his throat was unspeakable.

As they approached the North Col, Norton began to holler and shout and was finally heard by Mallory who, with Odell, came rushing up to meet them carrying an oxygen apparatus. They derived no benefit from the artificial air and were far more desperate for liquid than anything else. 'Mallory and Odell were kindness itself, and they kept congratulating us on having reached what we estimated as a height of 28,000 ft, though we ourselves felt nothing but disappointment at our failure.' As the two weary climbers were escorted back into camp at 9:30 p.m. Sandy was busy preparing hot tea and soup for them. When Norton lay in his tent after supper, Mallory talked him through his plans for a further summit attempt with oxygen. Norton 'entirely agreed with this decision and was full of admiration for the indomitable spirit of the man – such was his will power and nervous energy – he still seemed entirely adequate to the task.' He was not happy, however, with Mallory's choice of partner and argued that Odell had far more mountaineering experience, was now fully acclimatized and fitter. Mallory was emphatic. He would take Sandy, he told Norton, as Odell was sceptical about the oxygen apparatus and Mallory needed to be with someone who was not only *au fait* with it, but who believed in it. Norton did not stand in Mallory's way, 'it was obviously no time for me to interfere.' In any case he was suffering from a severe attack of snow-blindness, the pain of which is intense, but he later confided in Noel that he thought Mallory's decision was risky.

As final plans were being made the following day Norton was lying in his tent, the tent covered in sleeping bags, coping with his condition.

He occasionally crawled to the edge of the tent to offer help in encouraging the porters, but he had a very hard day of it. In fact it was trying conditions for all of them with freezing air temperature and the heat in the sun being somewhere about 120° F (38° C) with a very strong reflection off the snow.

Sandy spent the last day in Camp IV with Odell putting finishing touches to the oxygen sets. They talked a little about his delight at the prospect of having his chance to climb for the summit before turning in. The last entry in Sandy's diary reads, 'My face is perfect agony. Have prepared two oxygen apparatus for our start tomorrow morning.'

The diary breaks off at this point.

9

Going Strong for the Top

'It is 50 to 1 against but we'll have a whack yet and do ourselves proud'
G. L. Mallory to Ruth Mallory, 27 May 1924

Sandy and Mallory left Camp IV at 7.30 a.m. on 6 June 1924. Odell and Hazard were up early preparing a breakfast for them of fried sardines, biscuits and ample hot tea and chocolate. Odell was not a little indignant that, despite being pleased the breakfast had been fixed, they did little justice to the meal. Out of excitement or restlessness, he concluded. Their packs, which included the modified oxygen apparatus with two cylinders each, some food rations and a few other small items, weighed some 25 lb. It may sound like a heavy load, which indeed it was, but it was considerably less than the 35 lb the load would have weighed with the apparatus of the original design. Sandy's assiduous work had not been in vain. They were accompanied by eight porters who had in their packs bedding, provisions and the additional oxygen cylinders. The porters were not using oxygen.

They looked in on Norton who was lying in his sleeping bag still suffering badly from snowblindness. 'My last impression of my friends,' he wrote later, 'was a handshake and a word of blessing, for it was only in my imagination that I could see the little party winding its way amid the snow humps and ice crevasses leading to the Col.'

Odell took out his camera just as they were preparing to leave and snapped a shot of the two men, Sandy with his hands in his pockets, head bowed, waiting patiently, while Mallory fiddled with his oxygen apparatus. Little did Odell know that this would be the very last photograph taken of Mallory and Sandy alive. He watched them as they climbed the Col and disappeared out of sight amidst the broken ice masses.

The weather that morning was brilliantly sunny although later in the afternoon cloud gathered and it began to snow a little in the evening. They made good progress from the Col up to Camp V at 25,600 feet and at five o'clock that evening four of Mallory's porters returned with a note for Odell to say that there was no wind and that things were looking hopeful. The following morning Odell and his porter, Nema, headed up to Camp V in support. Owing to the limited size of the camp, – two tents, one for the climbers and one for the four porters – Odell had to restrict his support activity to one camp below the high camp occupied by Mallory and Sandy. Not long after their arrival the four porters who had carried loads to Camp VI arrived in V with a note from Mallory which read:

Dear Odell,

We're awfully sorry to have left things in such a mess – our Unna cooker rolled down the slope at the last moment. Be sure of getting back to IV to-morrow in time to evacuate before dark, as I hope to. In the tent I must have left a compass – for the Lord's sake rescue it; we are without. To here on 90 atmospheres[1] for the two days – so we'll probably go on two cylinders – but it's a bloody load for climbing. Perfect weather for the job!

Yours ever G. Mallory.

Odell, it must be said, was sceptical about the benefit of oxygen. He had tried a set on more than one occasion and claimed to have derived no benefit from it. He carried a set up to V, even though it had no mouth-piece as Sandy had taken it with him as a spare. He thought he might find a mouthpiece in Camp V. Interestingly, when Norton and Somervell had been offered oxygen from this same set on their return from the summit attempt they had derived no obvious benefit either. This led them all to conclude that oxygen was of no great help. How can it then be that Sandy could claim his breathing was slowed down by three times when he used oxygen and Mallory elected to use it for his final climb, despite it being a 'bloody load'? I suggest that Odell was attempting to

---

1 This refers to the pressure and thus the amount of oxygen they had been using. For full supply the pressure stood at 120 atmospheres.

use a rogue set, an apparatus Sandy knew to be faulty, otherwise he would not have taken the mouthpiece from it.

After Odell had received the note, he searched the tent and found Mallory's compass. His man Nema was suffering badly from the altitude at Camp V so Odell sent him back down to IV with Mallory and Sandy's four porters. He was not entirely sorry to be on his own. He would be able, he wrote later, to spend more time on the ascent to Camp VI examining the geological aspects of the upper mountain. He sat outside his tent on the evening of 7 June looking across to the impressive and 'savagely wild jumble of peaks towering above the upper Rongbuk glacier ... culminating in the mighty Cho-uyo and Gyachung Kang, bathed in pinks and yellows of the most exquisite tints.' Opposite him were the cliffs of Everest's north peak and as he surveyed them he considered 'with what hopeful feeling and exultant cheer Mallory and Irvine would take their last look around before closing up their tiny tent at VI that night.' Odell had shared a tent with Sandy several times on the mountain and more than once Sandy had told him how desperately he wanted to have a 'go' at the summit. He also told Odell that despite his work on the oxygen apparatus and his complete understanding of its functions, he would rather get to the base of the final pyramid without it rather than to the top with it. Mallory's experience of his attempt with Bruce, however, had convinced him that the top would not be reached without oxygen and Sandy immediately accepted that view, forgoing any personal preference in the matter, as Odell put it. In fact, Odell recalled him welcoming the chance to have a crack at the summit with almost boyish enthusiasm. Sandy, 'though through youth without the same intensity of mountain spell that was upon Mallory, yet was every bit, if not more, obsessed to go "all out" on what was certainly to him the greatest course for "pairs" he would ever be destined to "row".'

No one knows for certain what Mallory and Sandy did on the afternoon of 7 June after their arrival at Camp VI. In the past Mallory had tended to arrive in camp and then go for a walk, prospecting his route for the next, upward leg, as Norton had done the afternoon he and Somervell got into VI. Mallory had done this on his first arrival at Camp IV earlier in May, so it is probable that he spent that afternoon considering their possible route for the following day. It is known that

Mallory favoured the 'ridge route', or 'skyline' as he called it. This was a very exposed ridge but it was always his preferred option. The route favoured by Norton was across the face of the upper mountain and up the couloir to the base of the summit pyramid.

Nowadays climbers tend to follow 'skyline' or Mallory's route, and when I talked to the Himalayan guide Russell Brice we discussed which route he thought Mallory would have taken. He has summited twice, both times from the north side, but this record hides the fact that he frequently climbs above 28,000 feet from where, at a camp some 1000 vertical feet below the summit, he keeps track of his guides and clients. His knowledge of the north-east ridge route of Everest is unrivalled. Given the distance from the 1924 Camp VI and the fact that Mallory and Sandy were route-finding, which is by its nature slower than following a known route, he felt it unlikely that they had made it. He also pointed to the old chestnut, the Second Step, a vertical slab of rock, some fifteen feet high. 'No one can agree whether they could have climbed it or not,' he said, 'hey, not even the guys from 1999 were agreed.'

More interesting, however, than whether or not Brice thought Mallory and Sandy could have free-climbed the Second Step is his contention that the distance from Camp VI to the summit is so great that he had introduced a further camp, Camp VII. He recalls that the elite climber Ed Viesturs has climbed to the summit and back from roughly the site of the 1924 Camp VI but he points out that Viesturs is in a class of his own when it comes to performance at high altitude. 'It's just too far,' Brice considered, 'with route finding and all that, I just don't think they could have made it.' Then he stopped and composed his thoughts again: 'Of course, that's assuming that Mallory and Irvine took the same route that we take up the ridge nowadays.' This was too much for my son, Simon, who had been sitting patiently listening to the conversation, nodding his head at references he recognised. 'Why don't you try a different route?' he enquired. 'Well, Simon,' Brice replied, 'I guess we're just too lazy to try a different route!' It was a good point though. The fundamental difference between now and then is that climbers are using a known route. Sandy and Mallory were pioneering the path to the summit and there is no certainty that they did not find a way around the difficult obstacle of the Second Step which may or may not exist. No one knows. Nowadays climbers take the ridge route and use the Chinese ladder and the thought of setting out to try to find a different route is not on the agenda of most modern Everesters. 'In that harsh environment experience counts,' Brice concluded. No climber with any sense is going to question that.

In 1924, however, the route was still to be established. Mallory sent down a note to Captain Noel telling him to look out for them on skyline at about 8 a.m., but that was before the afternoon of 7 June. 'Dear Noel, We'll probably start early to-morrow (8th) in order to have clear weather. It won't be too early to start looking out for us either crossing the rockband under the pyramid or going up skyline at 8 p.m.' It has been universally accepted that by 8 p.m. Mallory in fact meant 8 a.m. and some have used it to indicate that he was suffering from the well-recognized malfunction of his cognitive powers as climbers do at altitude. I find that a little difficult to accept in the light of the way he consistently outperformed the other climbers when Hingston conducted his 'mental' agility tests on them. If Mallory was indeed out on a reconnaissance mission the afternoon of 7 June it is likely that Sandy was busy preparing their meal, the Thermoses for the following day and making last-minute checks on the oxygen apparatus. He had few tools with him for the final climb, but he had a pair of pliers and a spanner although he couldn't have done a lot with those.

That evening, after supper, Sandy asked Mallory to help him make one last check on the oxygen cylinders. While Sandy measured their individual oxygen contents, Mallory scribbled down the numbers of the cylinders and the pressures on the back of an envelope. In all they checked five of the cylinders in their cache at Camp VI; four had a bottle pressure of 110 and the fifth of 100. The envelope with these scribbles was found on Mallory's body in May 1999 and it was a few months before the relevance of the notations was understood.[2]

On the morning of 8 June Sandy was detailed to make their breakfast while Mallory got himself ready for the climb. At what time they set off

2 Jochen Hemmleb, the Everest researcher and member of the 1999 expedition, realized in August 1999 the significance of the notes on the envelope and expands on this at length in his book on the find, *Ghosts of Everest*. He argues that they could have been climbing with three and not two oxygen cylinders as previously believed, which would have given them more 'air' and thus time for the final ascent.

has always been a point of debate. Norton and Somervell had aimed to leave at 6 a.m. but were delayed by the leaking thermos. Mallory was known to like early starts and in the Alps he frequently set out before dawn on his climbs. In April he had written to Ruth: 'We shall be starting by moonlight if the morning is calm and should have the mountain climbed if we're lucky before the wind is dangerous.' The morning of 8 June dawned bright and clear so it could well be that he and Sandy left Camp VI before daybreak as Mallory had proposed. Certainly if Mallory had suggested an early start he would have found no opposition from his young companion. After all, Sandy's greatest ambition, the single driving force in his life now, was to get to the summit and he would have agreed to anything that would have given them the best chance. They closed up the tent and headed off towards the north-east ridge, each man cocooned in a private world of hissing oxygen. To communicate other than by hand signals they had to remove their masks and this Sandy would have avoided on account of his sunburned face.

Odell awoke early on the morning of 8 June and, after two hours of preparations, breakfast and tidying the tent he set off up towards Camp VI, full of optimism for the climbers above him and enjoying the glorious weather. He was deeply fascinated by the geological finds he was making and was concentrating hard on the ground beneath his feet. At a height of some 26,000 feet he climbed a 100-foot crag that he admitted, could have been circumnavigated but which he elected to climb as much as anything else to test his fitness. When he reached the top of the crag, pleased with his performance and triumphant to have found the first fossil on Everest, he looked up towards the highest reaches of the mountain. As he did so the cloud, which had been building since the late morning, parted, affording him a view of the north-east ridge and the summit. What he saw, or what he claims to have seen, has been so minutely scrutinized that in the end Odell changed his story; however, in his expedition diary he recorded the following: 'At 12.50 saw M & I on ridge nearing base of final pyramid.'

Moments after he saw them the cloud closed in and the whole vision vanished from his view. The diary entry goes on: 'Had a little rock climbing at 26,000, at 2 on reaching tent at 27,000 waited more than an hour.' Odell checked the tent and saw that Sandy had left it strewn with bits of oxygen apparatus. There were also a mixed assortment of spare clothes and some scraps of food and their sleeping bags. He was amused by the sight of the tent which reminded him of all the workshop tents Sandy had made wholly his own during the trek. 'He loved to dwell amongst, nay, revelled in, pieces of apparatus and a litter of tools and was never happier than when up against some mechanical difficulty! And here to 27,000 feet he had been faithful to himself and carried his usual traits.' He examined the tent for a note which might give some indication of the hour they left for the top or whether they had suffered any delay. There was nothing to be found. Meanwhile the weather had deteriorated. There was a blizzard blowing and he was concerned that the two men would have difficulty locating the tent under such conditions. He went out to whistle and holler with the idea of giving them direction. He climbed about 200 feet above the camp but the ferocity of the storm forced him to take refuge behind a rock from the driving sleet. In an endeavour to forget the cold he examined the rocks around him in case some point of geological interest could be found. Soon his accustomed enthusiasm for this pursuit waned and within an hour he turned back for Camp VI. He grasped that even if Mallory and Sandy were returning they would not be within hearing distance. As he reached camp the storm blew over and the upper mountain was bathed in sunshine, the snow which had fallen was evaporating rapidly. He waited for a time but, mindful of the fact that the camp was too small to house three men and also that Mallory had particularly requested him to return to the North Col, he set off back down the mountain. It had been Mallory's intention, he believed, to get down to the North Col himself that night and even to Camp III if time and energy allowed as they were all aware of the possibility of the monsoon breaking at any moment. He placed the compass in a conspicuous position close to the tent door and, having partaken of a little meal, left ample provisions for the returning climbers, shut the tent up and set off back towards the North Col.

As Odell made his way down by the extreme crest of the north ridge he halted every now and again to scan the rocks above him for any sign of movement of the climbers. It was a hopeless task as they would be almost invisible against the rocks and slabs. Only if they'd been making their way over one of the patches of snow or were silhouetted on the crest of the north-east arête might he have caught a glimpse of them. He saw nothing. Arriving on a level with Camp V at about 6.15 p.m., some one and three quarter hours after he left VI, he decided that he was making such good progress that he would head straight down the North Col to Camp IV. He noted that the upward time between Camps IV and V was generally about three and a half hours whereas his return time was closer to thirty-five minutes. Descending at high altitudes, he concluded, was little more tiring than at any other moderate altitude.

Odell arrived at Camp IV at 6.45 p.m. where he was welcomed by Hazard who supplied him with large quantities of soup and tea. Together they scanned the mountain for any sight of light from a torch or distress flare but nothing was to be seen. It was a clear night with a moon that they hoped would help the returning climbers to find their camps. In his tent that night Odell reflected on the last two days. 'And what a two days had it been – days replete with a gamut of impressions that neither the effects of high altitude, whatever this might be, nor the grim events of the two days that were to follow could efface from one's memory.' So great had his enjoyment been of the romantic, aesthetic and scientific experiences that he was able quite to put out of his mind the great hardship of climbing upwards at altitude. His thoughts, too, were focused on Mallory and Sandy, 'that resolute pair who might at any instant appear returning with news of final conquest'.

The next morning they scanned the upper mountain and the two camps for any sign of life or movement but nothing was seen. At midday Odell decided that he would search both camps himself and before he left he arranged a code of blanket signals with Hazard so that they could communicate to some extent if necessary. This was a fixed arrangement of sleeping bags which would be laid out against the snow in the daylight. At night they would use a code of simple flash signals including, if required, the International Alpine Distress Signal. As Odell and his two porters left the North Col they encountered the evil cross-wind that had so taken the heart out of the first attempt of Mallory and Bruce ten days earlier. They reached Camp V in three and a quarter hours but the porters were faltering. Odell was disappointed to see that the Camp had not been touched or occupied. He had hardly expected to find Mallory

A Tibetan beggar musician, photographed by Sandy en route for Shekar Dzong, captioned by him 'The George Roby of Tibet'

View of Shekar Dzong taken by Sandy. This and the photograph below were developed in Tibet and returned to Evelyn with the following captions: 'Shekar on left, Shekar Monastery on right, Old Dzong Pen's abode in centre. Shekar Dzong on summit (ruins). Tibetan unemployed watching the last remains of Camp being removed'

'Looking from the Temple through the heavy wooden doorway to the Holy of Holies. The big Buddha cannot be seen as it stands about 20 feet above and behind. Taken while worshipping at the prayer rail about 5 steps below the altar in the pitch dark Temple! Don't tell grandfather!!'

'Everest from the first pass after Shekar', photograph taken by Sandy on 21 April 1924 and sent to Evelyn

1924 Mount Everest Expedition Members. Standing: Sandy Irvine, George Leigh Mallory, Edward Norton (leader), Noel Odell, John MacDonald (trade agent). Sitting: Edward Shebbeare, Geoffrey Bruce, Howard Somervell, Benthley Beetham

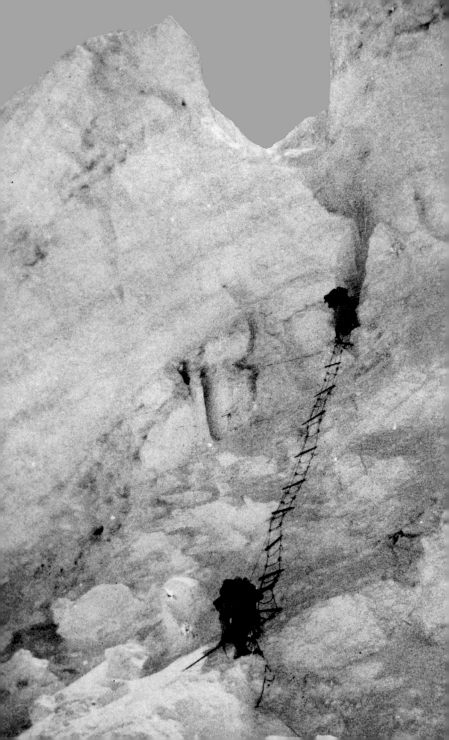

Climbers and porters in the trough. Those in the foreground were on Sandy's rope, the tiny figures in the background amongst the towering seracs were with Hazard. Photograph by Sandy

Left The Rope Ladder. Constructed by Sandy out of Alpine rope and tent pegs and erected in the ice chimney above Camp III to ease the porters' route up to the North Col. Photograph by Howard Somervell

Sandy and Mallory leaving Camp IV on 6 June 1924. Photograph by Noel Odell

SUMMIT
29,000 ft.

MALLORY and IRVINE
LAST SEEN HERE
28,400 ft.

HIGHEST BIVOUAC
N.E. SHOULDER
27,000 ft.

ODELL AT
WINDYRIDGE
CAMP

Photograph of the North East Ridge with markings to indicate the last sighting of Sandy and Mallory

The Blanket Signal which meant to those watching below 'No trace can be found, Given up hope, Awaiting orders'

Sandy's personal effects returned from Camp III by Odell including the pressure kettle he had specially designed, his passport, the wallet with the Llanfairfechan press cutting, a leather patch from his rucksack, the label from his spare ice axe and his address book

and Sandy there as any movement would have been visible from Camp IV but how desperately did he wish that a trace of them would be found. 'And now one's sole hopes rested on Camp VI, though in the absence of any signal from here earlier in the day, the prospects could not but be black.' In view of the lateness of the hour and the fact that his two porters were unwilling to go any higher, a search of Camp VI would have to be delayed until the following day. He passed a very uncomfortable night in the bitter cold, unable to sleep despite two sleeping bags and wearing every stitch of clothing he possessed. The wind threatened to uproot the tents and he had to go out from the safety of his tent to put more rocks on the guy ropes of the porters' tent. As he lay in his tent Odell fiddled with the oxygen apparatus lying there and determined to take it up to Camp VI with him the next day.

As day dawned on 10 June the wind was as ferocious as ever and the two porters were even more miserable. Odell sent them back down to Camp IV and prepared himself for the upward slog to Camp VI. 'Very bitter N. wind of great force all day', he wrote in his diary, 'climbed up slowly to W. of VI & finally reached tent.' He was climbing using the same oxygen set he had used before and although he admitted it did allay the tiredness in his legs somewhat, he was not convinced that it gave him any real assistance. The wind forced him regularly to take shelter behind rocks all the way up the ridge and when he finally arrived in Camp VI he found the tent closed up, exactly as he had left it two days earlier. Bitterly disappointed, he noted 'no signs of M & I around'. He set out along the probable route that Sandy and Mallory had taken to make what search he could in the limited time available. His spirits were low. 'This upper part of Everest must be indeed the remotest and least hospitable spot on earth, but at no time more emphatically and impressively so than when a gale races over its cruel face. And how and when more cruel could it ever seem than when balking one's every step to find one's friends?' After two hours of struggling in the bitter wind, aware of the futility of his search, yet almost unable to turn his back on the mountain, he reluctantly gave up. At that moment, the awful truth dawned on him: his friends were nowhere to be seen and nowhere to be found. That sense of anguish is as strong today as it was in 1924. Whenever I read his account of that final search I sense the desperate feeling of fading hope as he comes to understand that the chances of finding them alive are all but gone. A lull in the wind allowed him to make the signal of sleeping bags in the snow as arranged with Hazard. A simple T-shape meant 'No trace can be found, Given up hope, Awaiting orders'. Hazard received the signal 4000 feet below at the North Col but Odell was unable to read the answering signal in the poor light. What was there to read? He had sent down the mountain the worst piece of news conceivable and the only thought in his mind now was to get down safely in order to tell the others of his fruitless and hopeless search. Hazard relayed the message from Camp IV to the anxious climbers waiting at Camp III by laying out blankets in the form of a cross. Captain Noel spotted the sign through his telescope and when Geoffrey Bruce asked him what he could see, Noel was unable to reply. He simply passed the telescope over to him. 'We each looked through the telescope,' Noel recalled later, 'and tried to make the signal different, but we couldn't.'

Odell returned to the tent where he collected Mallory's compass and Sandy's modified oxygen apparatus. His last entry in his diary for that day reads: 'Left some provisions in tent, closed it up & came down ridge in violent wind & didn't call at V.' It cannot have been an easy decision to leave Camp VI; it meant turning his back on Sandy and Mallory forever. As he turned to look at the summit above him he sensed it seemed to look down with cold indifference on him, 'mere puny man, and howl derision in wind-gusts at my petition to yield up its secret – this mystery of my friends. What right had we to venture thus far into the holy presence of the Supreme Goddess, or, much more, sling at her our blasphemous challenges to "sting her very nose-tip"?'

And yet as he stood and gazed at the mountain, he was aware of the allure of its towering presence and he felt certain that 'no mere mountaineer alone could but be fascinated, that he who approaches close must ever be led on ... It seemed that my friends must have been thus enchanted also for why else would they tarry?' Such a beguiling presence, such a deadly vision. The mountain was destined to keep its secret for over seventy years.

Finally he accepted that the other climbers in the camps below would be anxious for news of his discoveries, if there were any, and he knew in his heart of hearts that Sandy and Mallory could not have survived another night in the open above 27,000 feet.

His climb down in the teeth of the gale, struggling with the heavy oxygen apparatus, took all his effort and concentration. Frequently he had to stop in the lee of rocks to protect himself from the wind and check for symptoms of frostbite, but eventually he was spotted by Hazard who sent his porter out to welcome him with hot tea while Hazard brewed soup in camp. On his arrival Odell was relieved to find a note from Norton and to discover that he had anticipated his wishes by abandoning the search and not putting any further lives at risk, namely his own, seeing as the monsoon was expected to break at any moment.

Odell had spent a staggering eleven days above 23,000 feet and had climbed twice to above 27,000 feet without oxygen. It was one of the many extraordinary feats of strength demonstrated on the 1924 expedition and was all the more remarkable for the fact that he climbed entirely alone on both occasions to and from Camp VI, the place he described as the most inhospitable on earth. His slow acclimatization was thorough and complete, otherwise how could he ever have coped at those altitudes when others could not? Odell's loyalty to the memory of his two friends has always deeply impressed me and it is a mark of the extraordinary man he was that he put himself through such torture in the vain hope that he might find them alive, or at least find out what had happened to them. Whenever I read his story of the last climb I always hold out a lingering hope that perhaps this time the story will be different, perhaps this time there will be a sign of them, that they don't just disappear into the mists and into legend.

The following morning Odell, Hazard and the three porters gathered together all they could carry from the tents, including Mallory and Sandy's personal belongings, Captain Noel's cine-camera which Sandy had thought he might take on his summit attempt, left the tents standing and made their way down to Camp III for the last time. There they found Shebbeare and Hingston who were preparing to evacuate that camp, the others already on their way to Camp II and Base. While Odell and Hazard had been in support and searching from IV, other members of the expedition had been waiting anxiously at III. 'During the next four days', Norton wrote, 'we were to pass through every successive stage of suspense and anxiety from high hope to hopelessness, and the memory of them is such that Camp III must remain to all of us the most ╵ateful place in the world.'

By 12 June all the remaining expedition members were gathered in Base Camp where they were greeted by spring. Alpine flowers were dotted here and there amongst the stones and the relative comforts of the mess tent, camp beds, decent food and a bath were much appreciated by all the men. 'Had lovely night in camp bed & 1st bath for a month', Odell wrote in his diary on 13 June. But despite the spring flowers and the comforts of Base Camp they were a sad little party. They accepted the loss of the two men 'in that rational spirit which all of our generation had learnt in the Great War ... but the tragedy was very near; our friends' vacant tents and vacant places at table were a constant reminder to us.' Norton admitted that he felt the loss of Mallory very deeply. They had climbed together both in 1922 and 1924, shared tents, planned and campaigned their assaults on the mountain; 'the sense of loss was acute and personal'. Odell was similarly affected by the loss of Sandy. Moreover he felt responsible that he had persuaded Sandy to come out to Everest, to pit his strength against the mountain and, tragically, in this, his greatest race, to fail. To Odell fell the unenviable task of sorting through his belongings, deciding what should be burned and what could usefully be sent back to his family in England. He carried out the same process with Mallory's affairs and finally, on Saturday 14 June, Ember Day, he labelled the cases and burnt the rest of the kit along with several old boxes and stores which they would not be transporting back to Darjeeling. Amongst the possessions he kept for Sandy's family were some very personal items, his passport, his wallet, the patch from his rucksack which bore his name. There was also a pressure kettle which Sandy had taken to Everest in the hope that it would boil water more efficiently at altitude than a normal one. Sandy's eccentricities were encapsulated in the small package of articles that were returned to England. It was to be as fitting an epitaph as much of what was later written about his great exploits. Like several other people, Odell had seen beyond the brave young hero and had come to have deep affection for the heart of this extraordinary young man. When all the items Odell returned were unearthed this year I had a great sense of that affection. It was deeply moving and it brought me closer to an understanding of what Sandy meant to other people.

There was never any question of a further attempt for the summit that year. The monsoon would be breaking within the next few days and besides, Hingston had made a medical assessment of all the men and declared that any further exposure to high altitude might result in some permanent damage. All the climbers showed some dilation of the heart, they were all debilitated and much 'wasted', having lost as much as 28 lbs in some cases.

Norton called a meeting to discuss the tragedy and to consider the facts. It was then that the debate began as to what had happened to Mallory and Sandy on 8 June. Odell was convinced, despite Mallory's insistence that he would take no risks on the final climb, that he had been overcome by his obsession for victory. He felt equally strongly about Sandy's desire for success. 'Sandy I know was willing, nay, determined, to expend his last ounce of energy, to "go all out", as he put it, in an utmost effort to reach the top: for had not his whole training in another hardy pursuit been to inculcate the faculty of supreme final effort?' Basing this judgement on his own experience of climbing in the Alps or other places, where good sense dictates that a turn-around is in order but the desire to climb in a race with darkness or in the teeth of a gale is overwhelming, he concluded, 'who of us ... could hold back when such a victory, such a triumph of human endeavour, was within our grasp?' He held the belief that they had probably succeeded in reaching the summit and that they had been benighted on the mountain and died of exposure. This view was quite at odds with that held by Norton and the others who were all convinced that they had fallen to their deaths in a simple mountaineering accident. Norton put the odds at their having made it at 50/50. Whilst Odell held that men with the skill and determination of Mallory and Sandy could never have fallen, Norton argued most convincingly that, in his experience, the snow-covered slabs on which they were climbing would have been treacherous and even the most experienced mountaineer might slip. He was also certain that, had the men been benighted on the mountain, the party at the North Col would have seen some kind of light signal from the torches or flares that he believed strongly they were carrying. An elaborate code of light signals had been worked out between the climbers and as 8 June had been a clear, dark night he was certain a light would have been visible. This argument convinced all the expedition members except Odell who remained a dissenting voice until the end of his life. What Odell had was a real knowledge of the two men, of their desires and their weaknesses. He understood their only too human condition and this, more than anything else, convinced him that they had not given up their goal without a fight.

Norton allotted tasks to all the remaining members of the expedition as they planned their return to Darjeeling. Odell was occupied with sorting through, and packing, Mallory and Sandy's belongings. Somervell and Beetham were commissioned to construct a monument to the twelve men who had lost their lives in the three British Everest expeditions. It was a big undertaking and Beetham, with a gang of assistants cut simple inscriptions into large flat slabs of blue slaty rock that left a white surface when chipped. Somervell, with all the porters who could be spared from other duties, constructed a solid square plinth of big rocks, three feet high and some fifteen feet square. Onto this plinth he set a cone of glacier-worn rocks and the inscribed slates were incorporated into the side of the monument which overlooked Base Camp. The whole cairn stood ten feet high and the inscription read: 'In memory of three Everest Expeditions. 1921 Kellas, 1922 Lhakpa, Narbu, Pasang, Pemba, Sange, Temba, Antarge, 1924 Mallory, Irvine, Shamsher, Manbahadur.' As this work was being carried out, the transport officers made preparations for the return journey, Hazard undertook to make a diversion from the trek to carry out the remaining survey work, the mapping of the West Rongbuk Glacier, and Norton wrote letters to Ruth Mallory and Willie Irvine, giving them as much detail as he could about the accident, and a moving dispatch to the *Times*. He had already sent a wire to the Mount Everest Committee, coded so that other news agencies would not pick up the story before the families had been informed. It read: 'OBTERRAS LONDON – MALLORY IRVINE NOVE REMAINDER ALCEDO – NORTON RONGBUK'. The news reached London on the afternoon of Thursday 19 June 1924, by which time the expedition members were already in Tagang, four days into their trek. Norton's letter to Willie Irvine, written in his meticulous handwriting, was among the find in May 2000:

Mt Everest Expedition
Rongbuk Base Camp.
13–6–24.

Dear Mr Irvine.

Unless the steps I have taken have miscarried you will long before this have received the news of your son's death – I hope first from the Mt. Everest Committee & then with full details in two successive communiqués to the *Times.*

I could not anticipate the latter method of communicating the news in full by a letter as the *Times* have a special relay post across Tibet & then wire their communiqués home by press code.

As to the facts & circumstances I fear I can add but little to what you will have heard from the above sources & a letter you will get from Odell –

Everything points to the probability of a sudden death – a slip by one or other – a purely mountaineering accident. Personally I cannot suggest any hypothesis to cover the idea of a lingering death from exposure, nor is there any reason to suppose that the cause might have been due to a defect in the oxygen apparatus for Odell's experience proves that for people as fully acclimatised to altitude as was your son oxygen may be entirely dispensed with as soon as the descent is begun.

Whether the party reached the top or not must always remain a mystery – I put it myself at a very even chance. They were unaccountably late at the point where they were last seen by Odell – but not too late to reach the top in time to return safely – They were reported as 'going strong' – on the particular ground in question a slip was more likely to occur descending than ascending for they had apparently surmounted the most serious obstacle in the ascent.

The pair of course hold the world's altitude record.

There must be so many points that you want to know; I shall be only too delighted to answer any by letter or to come & see you on my return to England – probably in October – The nearest I can give you as an address is c/o Cox & Co. Bombay until say Sept. 7th & then Uplands, Fareham, Hants –

I wish I could in any way help you in your great grief or adequately express my sympathy.

In the sort of experience I have shared with your son one gets to know people better in 6 weeks than often in 6 years of easy home life – so both from my own knowledge of him & from much that Odell has told me I can guess what your son was to you.

To me the whole thing is very bitter; my fixed determination was to bring off success if possible – but, success or failure, above all things to avoid casualties – & I thought it could be done; I was determined that such splendid lives as those we have lost were infinitely too high a price to pay for success.

Much that your son was to us I have already written of in various communiqués to the *Times* – From the word go he was a complete & absolute success in every way. He was spoken of by General Bruce in an early communiqué as our 'experiment' – I can assure you that his experimental stage was a short one as he almost at once became almost indispensable – It was not only that we leant on him for every conceivable mechanical requirement – it was more that we found we could trust his capacity, ingenuity & astonishingly ready good nature to be equal to any call. One of the wonderful things about him was how, though nearly 20 years younger than some of us, he took his place automatically without a hint of the gaucherie of youth, from the very start, as one of the most popular members of our mess.

The really trying times that we had throughout May at Camp III & the week he put in at Camp IV in June (of which I spoke in the last Communiqué before I knew of his death) were the real test of his true metal – for such times inevitably betray a man's weak points – & he proved conclusively & at once that he was good all through – I can hardly bear to think of him now as I last saw him (I was snowblind the following morning & never really saw him again) on the N. Col – looking after us on our return from our climb – cooking for us, waiting on us, washing up the dishes, undoing our boots paddling about in the snow, panting for breath (like the rest of us) & this at the end of a week of such work all performed with the most perfect good nature & cheerfulness.

Physically of course he was splendid – as strong as a horse – I saw him two or three times carry for some faltering porter heavier loads than any European has ever carried here before.

He did the quickest time ever done between some of the stages up the glacier – one of his feats was to haul, with Somervell, a dozen or so porters' loads up 150 feet of ice cliff on the way to the N. Col.

As for his capacity as a mountaineer the fact that he was selected by Mallory to accompany him in the last & final attempt on the mountain speaks for itself.

I hope you will express my deep sympathy & regret to Mrs. Irvine & to your sons & daughter – Please write to me if I can give you any information or help you in any way – otherwise do not trouble to answer this letter.

Yours sincerely

E. F. Norton

10

In the Shadow of the Peak

Your son was evidently <u>the best</u> of all the new recruits: so it is fit that he should fight to a finish along side of Mallory – the most tried and the most famous of all the Everest fighters. None of us climbers will ever think of Mt. Everest without remembering these two names.

T. Longstaff to W. F. Irvine, 21 June 1924

On Friday 20 June 1924, Lilian and the two youngest children were at their holiday cottage, Ffordd Ddwr in the tiny village of Llandyrnog, below the shadow of Moel Famau. Willie was at home and had planned to go to Ffordd Ddwr for the weekend with Evelyn, who was due up from Oxford that afternoon. She had almost finished her exams and was intending to spend a part of the summer at home. Kenneth was at Oxford taking his exams for entry into Magdalen College and Hugh was in Manchester where he worked as a solicitor.

On Friday evening, just after 7 p.m., a telegram arrived from Arthur Hinks, secretary to the Mount Everest Committee. It read: '*Committee deeply regret receive bad news Everest Expedition today Norton cables your Son and Mallory killed last climb remainder return safe President and Committee offer heartfelt sympathy Hinks*'. That was it. There was no other information. The last *Times* dispatch had been published on 16 June and told of the heroic rescue by Mallory, Norton and Somervell of the four porters at Camp IV. In that article, written on 26 May, Norton had spoken of the terrible cold and snow they had been enduring at Camp III and of Sandy and Somervell's hauling the porters' loads up the ice chimney to the North Col. He had written that they had hoped to retreat in preparation for a final assault and that Sandy Irvine, as usual, had been busy working on the oxygen apparatus. Sandy's letter to Lilian of the same date had not even arrived in England. And now the news came that he was dead. Willie immediately telephoned Lilian in Llandyrnog and then his father, James Irvine, who was staying in the Lake District, to tell them the news.

For a few hours, the tragedy was an entirely personal one but they knew that as soon as the news broke it would be in all the newspapers. It was decided that Lilian should remain in Wales with the younger children whilst Willie coped with what they rightly suspected would be an avalanche of letters and press enquiries. Willie certainly had been aware of the dangers Sandy was facing when he went to climb Everest and he had followed closely the story of the expedition, its difficulties, its dramas, all of which had been played out on a public stage. But I think nothing prepares you for the shock of the death of one of your children and he must have been heartbroken. He did not show it.

The following morning the story was all over the press but Willie got up and went to work as usual. Walking across the park to the station he met an acquaintance, a Mr Angus, whom he knew slightly. They fell into step and chatted about inconsequential matters until they arrived at the station to take their respective trains. Angus got into his office to be confronted with the newspaper headlines detailing the deaths of Sandy and Mallory. He was deeply shocked and could scarcely believe that he had 'prattled away' to Willie 'who never for an instant disclosed what must have been a terrible sorrow'.

Evelyn was taking her final exams on the Saturday morning. After breakfast a group of Sandy's friends, including A. T. Wilder, turned up at her boarding house in Oxford and hustled her, in a familiar cloak-and-dagger operation into the back of a cab, the windows of which were blacked out. The spirit of the 'kidnapping' convinced her that it was another of their pranks and she went into the exams unaware of the news which was breaking around her. It was only after she emerged from the room that she encountered those same friends from whom she now learned of the news of Sandy's death. They put her onto a train for Birkenhead where she joined her father that evening.

On the Sunday Lilian attended the local church in Llandyrnog where the family was already well known and liked, Sandy having already featured twice in the parish magazine. Pink Willie led a service in which prayers were offered in his memory and in support of the family. This was a great comfort to them all, especially Lilian, who had always sought advice and solace in her trust in God. Pink Willie had known Sandy who, with the family, had attended services in the beautiful fifteenth-century church, and was as moved as the rest of his congregation by the news of the tragedy. He wrote later in the parish magazine, 'The death of Mr A. C. Irvine, Plas Ffordd Ddwr Cottage, the youngest member of the Mount Everest Expedition, has brought great grief to us all, and our deepest sympathy goes out to Mr and Mrs Irvine and family. It is reported that Mr A. C. Irvine and Mr Mallory were last seen at 11 o'clock on June 8th (Whit Sunday) at a height of 28,000 ft and "going strong for the top". They have given their lives but they have not lost them. May they rest in peace.'

Willie and Evelyn attended matins at St Mark's in Birkenhead, which was full to capacity with people shocked and grieved by the news of the loss of two Birkenhead men. Many of them knew the family well and had known Sandy since he was a little boy. The Mayor of Birkenhead ordered the flag on the Town Hall to be flown half-mast from Saturday at 1 p.m. and all day Sunday. That afternoon they were joined by Dick Summers who had read of the tragedy in the newspaper in his hotel room in London. He was due to take part in time trials that day, but he cancelled and drove straight to Birkenhead to be with Evelyn.

As the news of the Everest disaster broke, the press erupted. They had only the telegram sent by Norton to the Mount Everest Committee and Norton's earlier dispatches on which to base their articles. The lack of information led to wild speculation and dramatic headlines: 'The Battle with Everest: The Mountain's Heavy Toll', 'Victors of Everest', 'Triumph Frustrated by Death: Two Lives Lost', 'Did Everest Climbers Reach the Top?' In newspaper terms it was a marvellous story and the press certainly made the most of it. Everyone who had an opinion expressed it, the papers full of arguments for and against their having achieved the summit. Had the oxygen given out? Did you in fact need oxygen to climb Everest? Did they fall, were they benighted?

Then there were the eulogies. People wrote of Sandy's courage, his strength, his rowing prowess, his work with the oxygen apparatus and, above all, of his cheerful disposition. They spoke of his youth and of what might have become of him had he lived. A *Times* journalist concluded: 'In accepting the offer to go to Tibet he, too, knew that he was facing inevitable risks, and for those who knew and loved him his untimely death, at so early and age, is a peculiarly tragic ending to the great adventure in which he engaged.'

On 5 July the *Times* published Norton's dispatch containing the details of the last climb which he had sent on 11 June 1924. It had been composed while he was still snowblind at Camp III on 8 June, dictated to Geoffrey Bruce, detailing the story of his and Somervell's climb. Once he had arrived in Base Camp he penned a footnote to his dispatch which stated: 'With the deepest regret I add these few lines continuing the above dispatch. Mallory and Irvine perished on the mountain beyond all doubt.' He described briefly the facts of the disappearance as he understood them, but had not at this point met up with Odell who was still on his way down from Camp III. He described the two men as having been seen 'going strong for the top' by Odell at about 11 a.m. This was the first concrete evidence about the accident and was only revised when Odell wrote up his own story three days later.

Norton continued to send home dispatches to the *Times* in which he was able to deal in much greater detail with individual aspects of the expedition. In one article he dealt solely with the difficulties of climbing at altitude, writing eloquently of the great effort required at high altitude merely putting on his boots or making a cup of tea. In another he considered the possibility that Everest would one day be climbed, concluding, 'The conquest of Everest is almost certainly assured. Sooner or later some climber as brave and skilful as the men of the Third Expedition, and with fortune better than theirs, will penetrate the last fastnessess of the highest mountain on earth, and gaze from its utmost peak on the wondrous world beneath him.' And in a third piece Geoffrey Bruce assessed the contribution made by the porters. As these appeared, further articles flowed from the pens of Longstaff, General Bruce and Younghusband, amongst many others, paying tribute not only to Sandy and Mallory, but to the other members of the expedition. Longstaff described the expedition of 1922 as a picnic in comparison to 1924.

It was Odell's story, however, that really captured people's imagination. His account of the last sighting appeared in the *Times* on 10 July and what he wrote has fascinated climbers for over seventy-five years:

At 12:50, just after I had emerged in a state of jubilation at finding the first definite fossils on Everest, there was a sudden clearing of the atmosphere, and the entire summit ridge, and the final peak of Everest became unveiled. My eyes became fixed on one tiny black spot silhouetted on a small snowcrest beneath a rock-step in the ridge, and the black spot moved. Another black spot became apparent and moved up the snow to join the other on the crest. The first then approached the great rock-step and shortly emerged at the top; the second did likewise. Then the whole fascinating vision vanished, enveloped in cloud once more. There was but one explanation. It was Mallory and his companion moving, as I could see even at that great distance, with considerable alacrity, realizing doubtless that they had none too many hours of daylight to reach the summit from their present position and return to Camp VI, at night fall. The place on the ridge mentioned is a prominent rock-step at a very short distance from the base of the final pyramid, and it was remarkable that they were so late in reaching this place.

This account was written before Odell had left Base Camp. He maintained that Sandy and Mallory had probably been benighted on the mountain and would have died of exposure. As to whether they made it to the top or not he wrote: 'in my opinion, from the position in which they were last seen, they should have reached the summit at 4 pm at latest, unless some unforeseen and particularly difficult obstacle presented itself on the final pyramid'.

He was the only member of the 1924 expedition who held fast to the belief that Sandy and Mallory had summitted successfully. Norton convinced himself and the others that it was unlikely, given the lateness of the hour, and he maintained that there had been a simple mountaineering accident in which they had both died. It was this version of events that, ultimately, became most widely accepted but the debate raged on with a few notable dissenters remaining convinced that Everest had been conquered.

Mallory and Sandy became common property and the nation swallowed it up. So great was the interest that the King's telegram to the families was published in the *Times* under the headline 'Everest Disaster. The King's Message. 'Two Gallant Explorers'. It read:

The King is greatly distressed to hear the sad news of the death of Mr. Mallory and

Mr. Irvine, who lost their lives in making a final attempt to reach the summit of Mount Everest. His Majesty asks whether you [Younghusband] will be good enough to convey to the families of these two gallant explorers, as well as to the Mount Everest Committee, an expression of his sincere sympathy. They will ever be remembered as fine examples of mountaineers, ready to risk their lives for their companions and to face dangers on behalf of science and discovery.

Another announcement appeared in the *Times* a day or so later: 'The dance at the Speaker's House on July 11, for which Mrs. Whitley had sent out invitations, is cancelled, owing to the death on Mount Everest of Mr. A. C. Irvine, who was a close personal friend of a large number of the guests invited.'

Memorial services for Sandy and Mallory were held all over the country, at their old schools and universities and in their home town of Birkenhead.

In the meantime Willie and Evelyn were busy fielding the hundreds of letters and cards of condolence which came flooding in from everyone who had known or claimed to have known Sandy. So great was the volume of correspondence that Evelyn called Aunt Ankie to come over to Birkenhead to help out with the task. Every letter was read, listed and replied to by one of the three of them. The list runs to over 500 and contained amongst it a beautiful letter from Ruth Mallory, a moving tribute from General Bruce's wife, letters from Unna, Longstaff, Noel, from his school masters and university tutors and a simple but extraordinary letter from Peter Lunn, Sandy's runner-up in the Strang-Watkins Challenge Cup in Mürren in January 1924. Peter was nine and his father, Arnold, told Lilian that the letter was written entirely without input from himself or his wife.

Dear Mrs Irvine,

I am so sorry that Mr Irvine was killed on Mt Everest. I think that it is much worse for you than for Mr Irvine. For it is quite likely he died a painless death and now he is quite happy in heaven with Mr Mallory and other great explorers like himself. Besides, perhaps he has the honour in Heaven of having climbed Mt. Everest. He was constantly admired at Mürren, especially by me.

I admired and loved him for that great gift, which many who are as great as he cannot control, that gift of modesty.

At Mürren in the skiing he was always so cheery. He took bad luck and mis-fortunes in the skiing line so quietly. He kept away from all praise if he could and he would not let anybody get into any skiing book the fact he was going on Everest.

At the Palace he and I were next door, so he explained to me all about compasses, barometers, oxygen etc. without showing any sign of getting bored of my questions. I especially loved that side of his modesty that enabled him to speak to me as though I were a grown up.

I am very sorry for you at having lost your son, for having a mother, I know what it would be like.

Your affectionate Peter Northcote Lunn

This letter, more than any of the other seventy-odd which Willie chose to keep, catches me out every time I read it. I found it in May 2000 and sought Peter's permission to publish it. He had no recollection of writing the letter but his memories of Sandy are still very strong and he feels sure that it accurately reflects the admiration and sadness he felt when he learned of Sandy's death. It seems to say everything about Sandy and to say it so bluntly and honestly that I feel there is nothing in any of the other letters, some of which are deeply compassionate and moving, that can add to Peter's sentiments.

The first memorial service for Sandy was held in Merton College Chapel on 26 June 1924. The immediate family was represented by Sandy's younger brother Kenneth, who was already in Oxford. He wrote to his mother the following day: 'People at Oxford were very nice to me indeed. I stayed up for the service but it was too much for me – I don't think I can face the Shrewsbury Service next Sunday evening after it.' He listed all the people who were at the Merton Service including several Irvine aunts and uncles and a whole host of Sandy's friends including Milling, Ian Bruce, George Binney and A. T. Wilder. Kenneth concluded: 'If there is anything that I can do to help in any way, and in any fraction to strive to fill the gap, do let me know.'

Willie and Lilian were not at the Merton service as they had chosen to go with Evelyn to a local one, one which for them was probably the most deeply moving of any of the services dedicated to the memory of Sandy and Mallory. It was held in St John's Church, Birkenhead on the same day. It opened with the hymn 'For Ever with Thee Lord!' and the lesson was taken from Revelation 7, verses 9 to the end, which concludes, 'For the Lamb which is in the midst of the throne shall feed them, and shall lead them unto living fountains of waters; and God shall wipe away all tears from their eyes.' Mallory's father, the Revd Herbert Leigh-Mallory, took the service. 'How much braver can you be,' Evelyn once asked my father with her back turned in typical Irvine fashion, 'than to take the memorial service for your own son?'

When Odell returned from Everest on 13 September 1924 he spent two days in London with Mona and his son Alasdair before leaving for Birkenhead to see Willie and Lilian. His visit was a great comfort to them and he was able to answer many of the questions they had about Sandy. He spoke to them about his final view of them climbing towards the summit and about his own search during the following days. Odell was deeply impressed by Willie and Lilian's calm acceptance of the facts. They held no grudge and were unwilling to attribute responsibility for his death to anyone. If Odell had been at all worried on that count, for it was indeed he who had encouraged Sandy to go to Everest, he was reassured on that occasion. His loyalty to the Irvines and to Sandy's memory has been something which the whole family has felt deeply humbled by. I cannot be sure but I would hazard a guess that Odell was the only person that Willie would ever discuss Sandy with. If anyone else attempted to draw him on the subject he would politely divert the conversation, but Odell visited him regularly until the end of Willie's life and was always a very welcome guest in Birkenhead and later Bryn Llwyn. But his friendship did not stop there. Over the years he visited Kenneth, Alec, Evelyn, and many of my older cousins and uncles have memories of meeting Odell at one or another of the Irvine houses. The last time my father met him was at his parents' house in the late 1950s when he joined them for dinner. Odell wrote to Bill Summers in 1986 after a letter Bill had written to the *Times* had caught his attention. He was by then in his ninety-sixth year.

Norton had offered to meet Willie on his return to England to answer any questions he might have about the expedition. The rendezvous took place in Coniston in October 1924, just before the meeting of the Alpine Club and Royal Geographical Society in London at which papers on the expedition were published. No record of this meeting exists other than the brief entry in Willie's diary, but Norton was held in very high esteem by the whole family so I can only suppose that they had found much in common on that occasion.

Lilian had been out of the picture as the news of Sandy's death was announced, taken up as she was with caring for and comforting the younger children. Life had to carry on for them and in August she and Willie took them on holiday to Whitby, where Willie taught Alec to row. At the beginning of October Hugh announced his engagement to Kit Paterson which provided for Lilian a very welcome diversion. She wrote a letter of congratulations in which she expressed her hope that God who had been her guide and friend all her life would protect her children. She added that when Sandy had asked for permission to go up Everest she and Willie had prayed earnestly and that thus 'I have never had any regrets or questioning about the right or wrong of letting Sandy go up Everest – it does not stop the hole in our hearts however.' The fact that Lilian kept out of the public eye over Sandy's death has led people to conclude that she was unable to accept it. Great though her sadness must have been, she sought and found great strength in her belief and the main focus of her life were the other children who needed protecting and reassuring at what was a very difficult time.

On 17 October a memorial service for both men was held in St Paul's Cathedral. The families were seated in the choir, sheltered from the view of the body of the congregation. The address given by the Bishop of Chester spoke of their courage and their achievement and of Odell's last sighting of them so close to the top. 'That is the last you see of them, and the question as to their reaching the summit is still unanswered; it will be solved some day. The merciless mountain gives no reply! But that last ascent, with the beautiful mystery of its great enigma, stands for more than an heroic effort to climb a mountain, even though it be the highest in the world.' The service was attended by representatives of the King, the Prince of Wales, the Duke of York, the Duke of Connaught and Prince Arthur of Connaught in addition to the members of the expedition, the entire Mount Everest Committee, members of the Irvine and Mallory families and a great number of friends of both men. No other climbers had ever been so honoured. Willie, who was no lover of big occasions, attended the service out of duty and respect for his son, but it was for him and also for Lilian nothing like as personal an occasion as the service taken by Mallory's father in Birkenhead in June.

After the service there was a joint meeting of the Royal Geographical Society and the Alpine Club at the Royal Albert Hall where reports from the expedition were presented by General Bruce, Norton, Geoffrey Bruce and Odell. The talks were illustrated with slides from the expedition and it was here, for the first time, that Willie and Lilian saw photographs of Sandy in Tibet. This was a great moment for them all when they really had a chance to understand what life had been like for him over the last few months before his death. Lilian was particularly impressed by the photograph of the rope ladder taken by Somervell and asked Willie to arrange for a copy to be given to the family.

One person from the Mount Everest world who turned out to be extraordinarily kind and sympathetic, rather against expectation from what else I have ever read of him, was Arthur Hinks. He was in constant touch with Willie from June onwards and made every attempt to communicate any new information received as quickly as possible. He also ensured that copies of all the official letters and telegrams were forwarded to Birkenhead and as soon as Sandy's personal effects arrived in England he arranged for them to be sent straight to the family. Hinks was instrumental in getting for the family as many photographs of Sandy as were known to exist and it was he who fulfilled Lilian's request for a picture of the rope ladder Sandy had made. Hinks saw that copies were sent to her and an enlargement of it hung in the study at Bryn Llwyn until Willie's death. He was also concerned to retrieve the disassembled 1922 oxygen apparatus that Sandy had taken from the RGS in November 1923. In a rather amusing exchange of letters he and Willie discussed whether the bits and pieces that were returned actually constituted a whole apparatus, so completely had Sandy dismantled it. In the summer of 1925 Hinks wrote again to Willie enclosing a copy of the photograph taken by Odell of Sandy and Mallory leaving Camp IV that had only then come to light.

Over the next months and years memorials to the two men sprang up all over the country. Sandy was commemorated at Merton College by a sculpture of an eternal flame on a plinth with the lettering carved by the artist Eric Gill and at Shrewsbury by a relief plaque on the chapel wall. Birkenhead named two new streets after their famous sons and a joint memorial window was unveiled in early 1925 in the cloisters of

Chester Cathedral. It depicts St Bernard with his dog standing in front of a huge mountain with the inscription below: 'To remember two valiant men of Cheshire. George Leigh-Mallory and Andrew Comyn Irvine who among the snows of Mount Everest adventured their lives even unto death. "Ascensiones incorde suo disposuit" Ps LXXXIV'. It was the family's local memorial and on every anniversary of Sandy and Mallory's death Willie would drive to Chester, often with Lilian, to place flowers beneath the window. Lilian once told Hugh that they were very conscientious and would return a few days later to remove the flowers.

After the memorial service and meeting in London the family returned to Birkenhead, the only outstanding arrangement being the sorting through of Sandy's possessions and his will. Hugh took responsibility for the legal matters, as Sandy's executor, and settled all the accounts which were still to be paid. He and Willie went through the suitcases that Odell had packed at Base Camp and sorted what should be kept. Sandy's spare ice axe turned up in the post a few weeks after the suitcases had arrived. It simply bore the label 'Irvine: Birkenhead' in Odell's neat handwriting. This axe was the one Bill Summers saw hanging in the gun room at Bryn Llwyn twenty-five years later. The label was preserved in an envelope along with all the other papers that had come back from Everest. I suspect Willie threw nothing away.

The first years after Sandy's death were busy ones for the family. Willie retired from business in 1926, shortly before his father died aged 91, and he and Lilian moved from Birkenhead to Bryn Llwyn in 1927. Evelyn married Dick Summers in 1925 and Hugh married Kit Paterson in 1926. Then followed grandchildren which kept Lilian both happy and fulfilled. All the five children led full and active lives. Hugh became senior partner in the law firm, Slater Heelis in Manchester; Kenneth qualified as a GP and lived and worked all his life in Henley. He became a member of the Alpine Club and was always a keen climber and regular visitor to the Pen-y-Gwryd hotel in Snowdonia. Alec spent a part of his working life in India and moved to Bryn Llwyn in the 1970s. He continued to keep in touch with Odell and was the member of the family who was most keen to pass on his memories of Sandy to his children. Tur lived at Bryn Llwyn until he married. Like the others he studied at Magdalen College after which he went into the Church, becoming the Dean of St Andrew's,

Dunkeld and Dunblane in 1959, an office he held until he retired in 1983.

In 1931 Evelyn received a small package from India. It came from George Wood-Johnson, a prominent member of the International Kangchenjunga expedition, and had been given to him by Lobsang, one of Sandy's porters in 1924. In the package was a small piece of material bearing Sandy's name in English and Nepali which had wrapped in it twenty tiny Himalayan garnets. Willie wrote to Odell about the package who replied, 'I was interested to hear about the garnets, but cannot understand how they were "recovered" on Kangchenjunga by Lobsang! I think myself it must be that Lobsang made a little collection of these stones in the Kangchenjunga neighbourhood as a present & a recollection of Sandy.' Evelyn kept the garnets safely tied up in the piece of material and when she died my father found them amongst her most personal possessions.

In 1925 the official expedition book appeared entitled *The Fight For Everest: 1924*. It is a wonderful and vivid account of the whole expedition from the outset to the trek back to Darjeeling. All the expedition members contributed to the book and in Norton's piece, which considers the characters of the two climbers who died, he wrote of Sandy:

Young Irvine was almost a boy in years; but mentally and physically he was a man full grown and able to hold his own with all modesty on terms with the other members of our party, who averaged twelve years older than he. One more invaluable characteristic was his turn for things mechanical, for in this respect he was nothing short of a genius, and he became our stand-by in dealing with the troubles and difficulties we encountered over this year's oxygen apparatus, and, for the matter of that, in every department – from a lampshade to a rope ladder.

He shares with Odell the credit of having shown us all how to 'play for the side', stifling all selfish considerations, for nothing in the record of 1924 was finer than the work these two put in as 'supporters' at Camp IV.

Sandy Irvine's cheerful camaraderie, his unselfishness and high courage made him loved, not only by all of us, but also by the porters, not a word of whose language could he speak. After the tragedy I remember discussing his character with Geoffrey Bruce with a view to writing some appreciation of it to The *Times*; at the end Bruce said: 'It was worth dying on the mountain to leave a reputation like that.' Men have had worse epitaphs.

Epilogue

Sandy and Mallory became legendary figures. Their final hours were minutely scrutinized by the press and public alike, and whenever anything to do with climbing Everest was written, their names appeared and accounts of their climb were published.

Great debate raged over the 'last sighting' by Odell who, over the course of the following years, changed his story in the light of so much interest and informed opinion. His initial diary entry stated that he saw the two men 'at the foot of the final pyramid'. This was altered by the time he arrived at Base Camp and in his dispatch to the *Times* he wrote the now renowned paragraph in which he described the tiny black spots silhouetted against the snowcrest beneath a rock-step in the ridge. A few months later he had changed his story again. Scrutiny of his sighting and subsequent analysis convinced him, it would appear, to rethink. In his account in *The Fight for Everest: 1924* he wrote, 'I noticed far way on a snow slope leading up to what seemed to me to be the last step but one from the final pyramid, a tiny object moving and approaching the rock step. A second object followed, and then the first climbed to the top of the step. As I stood intently watching this dramatic appearance, the scene became enveloped in cloud once more, and I could not actually be certain that I saw the second figure join the first.'

People immediately latched on to Odell's change of mind. They pointed out that the 'last but one' rock step was what is now known as the Second Step, a fifteen-foot vertical slab of rock, not in itself insurmountable, but a technical pitch at an altitude when the human brain is functioning at a mere fraction of its normal capacity and where a climber's strength is almost completely played out. It was inconceivable, in the minds of experienced mountaineers of the day, that this obstacle could have been overcome. Even if Mallory had been technically able to climb the rock step, what of Sandy? Surely his inexperience would have held them back, they argued. Now there is a ladder up the Second Step, put there by the Chinese in the 1970s which greatly eases a climber's passage on this route to the summit. When an American climber called Conrad Anker 'free climbed' the Second Step in 1999, that is to say without using the ladder, his initial reaction was that he felt sure Mallory could have done it too and radioed this message down to his expedition leader, Eric Simonson, at Advance Base Camp. Not only did Anker, a very experienced rock climber, succeed in climbing the step, but he did so with considerable speed. Anker later changed his mind, however, and in his written account of the adventure concluded that it was unlikely that Mallory and Sandy could have made it up the step. It seems to me that the one thing that is certain about opinions people form high up on Everest is that they are never certain.

Some proposed that Odell had seen nothing at all – black rocks in the snow, perhaps a chough (a hardy bird which flies happily at that altitude) – and others suggested he had been hallucinating. All these claims Odell countered fiercely. He had for the whole of his life superb eyesight and, as a geologist, knew the difference between a rock and a human body, nevertheless the more that people queried his original sighting, the more unsure he became. When he wrote to Willie Irvine in 1934 he was still convinced – or at least prepared to tell Willie – that Sandy and Mallory had made it to the summit, but by the time he met my father twenty years later he thought it unlikely.

A few years after Sandy's death a bizarre letter arrived out of the blue from a man named Sir Oliver Lodge who claimed, via a medium, to have been in touch with Sandy 'from the other side'. Lodge had written a book about the subject of messages from the dead and sent Willie a proof of the book for his information. In his measured reply Willie dismissed Lodge's theories completely saying that the tone of the message did not at all accord with his and others' memory of Sandy: 'the complete absence of any reference to Mallory who was his leader is very difficult to understand. If there was one outstanding feature in his character it was his natural modesty. Another marked characteristic was his horror of the dramatic & one feels sure that any account he might give of the disaster would be plain to the point of baldness.' That was his last written word on the subject of his son to anyone but Odell for thirty years.

In 1933, however, a further, far more substantial, piece of evidence came to light after another British expedition attempted to reach the summit of Mount Everest. It was an unsuccessful bid but a small stir was caused by the climber Percy Wyn Harris who came down from the upper mountain with an ice axe he had found lying on some flat slabs at about 27,500 feet. It could only have been left by either Mallory or Sandy in 1924 and Wyn Harris believed it marked the site of a fall. Once again the story was revived and opinions aired in the press. Initially it was believed to have been Mallory's axe but later it was identified by Odell as Sandy's owing to the three horizontal markings on the handle just below the head.

The finding of the axe disturbed Willie's memories and he wrote to Odell in 1934 asking for his opinion on the find. Odell's reply was another of the letters found in May 2000. Although it does not say anything new as far as the experts are concerned, it is nevertheless interesting that Odell believed that Sandy had shared his idea for identifying his kit with the horizontal markings with Geoffrey Summers. It therefore confirmed beyond doubt, in Odell's and the family's minds, that the ice axe was indeed Sandy's. What no one could agree upon, however, was the significance of the axe in the position it was found. Odell told Willie, 'I am prepared to believe that they may have overcome the 2nd step, and actually reached the summit, as previously argued, and that the axe was dropped accidentally, at the spot where found, during their descent in the dark.' Odell visited Willie on his way up to Harlech in March of that year to discuss the find in more detail but there was very little Odell or anyone else could say to shed light on the final outcome of events ten years previously.

Willie seemed to be content to let the matter rest thereafter and took no further part in any communication about Sandy's role in the 1924 Everest expedition. He was well into his sixties and working hard in retirement on his historical papers. However, he kept an Everest file in amongst his other papers and when he was approached in 1957 by an American journalist who wanted to write a biography of Sandy he replied politely that having consulted members of his family, 'they all agree that this should be left to me to do as I have all the material, besides the personal memory. I have collected a good deal of information and am still gathering small additional material.' By now he was eighty-eight and the book was never written.

In 1953 the summit of Everest was finally reached from the south side in a triumphant and magnificent ascent by Edmund Hillary and Tenzing Norgay. For several years their achievement naturally outshone anything else in connection with Everest for they had proven that the mountain could be climbed. Further ascents followed and the mountain has now been climbed over 700 times. The North Col route was climbed in 1960 by the Chinese but it was not until 1980 that a European ascended Everest from the north. This time it was Reinhold Messner, the South Tyrolean climber, who ascended the route alone and without oxygen. It was hailed as one of the most extraordinary climbs of all times. In a delightful twist of fate Messner happened to be sitting in Dehli airport at five o'clock in the morning, on his way back to Germany, at the same time as Bill Norton, son of E. F. Norton. Bill was with a party of trekkers who were returning from the Himalaya and one of his group recognized Messner. Bill's brother, Dick, had already written in 1978 to congratulate him and Peter Habeler on their first oxygenless ascent of the mountain so Bill felt able to go over on this occasion to talk to him. Messner was initially sceptical, suspecting he might be from the press, but soon realized who he was and in the ensuing conversation Bill was able to congratulate him on having beaten his father's height record, from the north side, without oxygen.

It seems that every new generation revives the interest in the 'Mallory and Irvine' legend and forty years after the ice axe was found a Chinese climber came across an 'English Dead' about ten minutes from his own Camp VI. He described to a Japanese climber, Ryoten Yashimoro Hasegawa, in 1979 a body with a hole in its cheek, lying on its side 'asleep' at 27,000 feet, wearing old-fashioned clothing which disintegrated when he touched it. The Chinese climber, Wang Hong Bao, was tragically killed in an avalanche the following day so no further questions could be asked. When Hasegawa related the story it hit the headlines all over the world. This was the first piece of new evidence since the ice axe was found. The experts concluded it could only possibly be the body of either Mallory or Sandy as Tibet had closed its borders to all Western climbers before the Second World War and there were no other British fatalities at that height.

An American businessman and part-time climbing historian, Tom Holzel, had become so fascinated by the story that he decided to put together an expedition to the north side of Everest in 1986 in an attempt to locate the body which, based on his research, he concluded must be that of Sandy Irvine. By this time Willie Irvine was dead, as were Hugh and Evelyn so it fell to Alec to field the enquiries, which he did with his usual dry wit. Alec had already contributed to the only book on Sandy, a brief history of his life with excerpts from his diaries both on Spitsbergen and Everest, entitled *The Irvine Diaries*, published in 1979. At that time he was without doubt the person with more knowledge of Sandy than anyone else alive, although he had been but thirteen in 1924.

Holzel had enlisted the help of the highly respected historian Audrey Salkeld to research the history of the 1920s climbs and she visited Alec to obtain from him as much information as she could about Sandy. The resulting book, *The Mystery of Mallory and Irvine* became, for several years, the last word on the subject. Holzel and Salkeld's search took place on Everest in the autumn of 1986. They took with them to Tibet the climber and high altitude cameraman David Breashears in the hope that any find could be documented and a film made for television. It was a high-minded undertaking and had, at its heart, the memory of the two climbers. The search was hampered by the snows that lay on the mountain after the monsoon and they were unable to conduct a proper investigation. Nothing was found that year and interest waned a little. Then, in 1999, an Anglo-American search expedition was mounted, inspired in part by BBC Graham Hoyland's quest to find the camera which he believed his great-uncle Howard Somervell had lent Mallory. Using research undertaken by a German student, Jochen Hemmleb, they made the astonishing discovery of Mallory's body on the upper slopes of the mountain. Like others before them they had expected to find Sandy not Mallory, but in mountaineering terms the find was all the more significant for it being the body of the more famous of the two men.

The news broke on 4 May 1999 and the press pored over the details as they came out of Tibet. Opinions were aired loudly on the television and radio, in the newspapers and, for the first time, on the Internet. Netbrowsers could zoom in on the desiccated remains of the legendary George Leigh Mallory. Once again he had become common property. It was a deeply distressing time for the Mallory family and pretty worrying for the Irvines too, as the expedition planned to go back up to the site where Mallory lay to continue their search for Sandy. The expedition had been hoping to find Somervell's Kodak Vestpocket camera which he had lent to Mallory for the final assault, Mallory having lost his own at some stage earlier on the expedition. Kodak had indicated to Holzel in 1986 that if a film had been exposed and then kept at the subzero temperatures, which are the norm above 27,000 feet, it might still be possible, with careful handling of the camera, to develop any photographs that had been taken. The camera was not found on the body but other items were, and these gave rise to great excitement amongst the mountaineering community. The snow goggles found in his pocket *might* have meant the men were descending in the dark, the notes made on the back of an envelope recording oxygen pressures in the numbered cylinders *might* indicate that they went up on three and not two cylinders, as previously supposed. These and other finds, however, raised more questions than they answered and the mountaineers were no nearer knowing what happened on 8 June 1924 than they had been before. The find spawned several books on the subject, almost all with conflicting conclusions and there is still deeply divided opinion on whether or not Mallory and Sandy had made it to the summit before they died.

Whilst some experts argued that the body Wang Hong Bao found was in fact that of Mallory, others were more sceptical as the description given by the Chinese did not at all match with what was found in May 1999. For one thing, the body was lying in a completely different position from that in Wang's description and for another, Mallory had, apparently, no hole in his cheek. Therefore, many – but not all – concluded Sandy must still be up there.

In spring 2000 a further search for his body was launched, again by Graham Hoyland who this time joined the New Zealander Russell Brice's expedition. Appalling snow and storm-force winds during the whole of May and part of June prevented a high-altitude search and the question of whether or not Mallory and Sandy were the first to stand on the top of the world remains unanswered. I can only assume that there will be further searches, for it would seem that the mystery as to whether they reached the summit twenty-nine years before Hillary and Tenzing continues to fascinate people.

I'm frequently asked if I want them to find Sandy's body and it is not a question I find easy to respond to. Frankly the memory of his life is of far more significance and interest to me than how he died, although my interest does extend as far as the camera or other concrete evidence, that might be found on his body. Only by confirmation of the details of their final climb via photographic or written evidence would I be prepared to believe that they had reached the summit. The one piece of consolation I have, as Graham Hoyland pointed out, is that we might one day know whether Sandy and Mallory stood on top of the world, but no one will ever be able to prove conclusively that they did not.

Appendix 1

Rowing Crews

Shrewsbury First VIII – 1919

   W. F. Smith, bow
2 E. C. Garton
3 T. F. Bingham
4 A. C. Irvine
5 W. B. Fletcher
6 G. S. Nason
7 W. F. Godden
   M. H. Ellis, stroke

   W. O. S. Scott, cox

Shrewsbury First VIII – 1920

   D. C. Bennett, bow
2 E. C. Garton
3 S. F. L. Dahne
4 J. E. Pedder
5 T. F. Bingham
6 A. C. Irvine
7 W. F. Godden
   W. F. Smith, stroke

   I. Robertson, cox

Shrewsbury First VIII – 1921

   I. R. Bruce, bow
2 J. N. Rofe
3 T. R. A. Bevan
4 J. E. Pedder
5 E. R. J. Walmsley
6 A. R. Armitage
7 A. C. Irvine
   W. F. Smith, stroke

   I. Robertson, cox

UNIVERSITY BOAT RACE

LXXIV **Saturday, 1 April 1922, at 4.40 p.m.**

OXFORD (SURREY)	*Weight*	
P. C. Mallam, Qu. Bow	11 st	6 lbs
2 A. C. Irvine, Mert.	12 st	8 lbs
3 S. Earl, Magd.	12 st	6 ½ lbs
4 J. E. Pedder, Worc.	12 st	9 lbs
5 G. O. Nickalls, Magd.	12 st	8 lbs
6 D. T. Raikes, Mert.	13 st	6 ½ lbs
7 G. Milling, Mert.	11 st	10 lbs
A. V. Campbell, Ch.Ch. Str	11 st	5 ½ lbs
W. H. Porritt, Magd., Cox	8 st	10 lbs
Average 12 st 4 lbs		

CAMBRIDGE (MIDDLESEX)	*Weight*	
T. D. A. Collet, Pem., Bow	12 st	3 lbs
2 A. J. Hodgkin, 1 Trin.	12 st	6 ½ lbs
3 K. N. Craig, Pemb.	12 st	8 ½ lbs
4 A. D. Pearson, 1 Trin.	13 st	10 ½ lbs
5 H. B. Playford, Jesus.	13 st	10 ½ lbs
6 B. G. Ivory, Pemb.	13 st	8 lbs
7 Hon J. W. H. Fremantle, 3 Trin.	12 st	6 ½ lbs
P. H. G. H-S. Hartley, LMBC, Str	11 st	6 lbs
L. E. Stephens, Trin H., Cox	9 st	4 lbs
Average 12 st 11 lbs		

Cambridge won by 4 ½ lengths in 19 min. 27 sec.

LXXV **Saturday, 24 March 1923, at 5.10 p.m.**

OXFORD (SURREY)	*Weight*	
P. C. Mallam, Qu., Bow	11 st	12 lbs
2 P. R. Wace, BNC	12 st	6 ½ lbs
3 A. C. Irvine, Mert.	12 st	10 ½ lbs
4 R. K. Kane, Ball.	13 st	9 ½ lbs
5 G. J. Mower-White, BNC	13 st	11 ½ lbs
6 J. E. Pedder, Worc.	13 st	3 ½ lbs
7 G. O. Nickalls, Magd.	12 st	12 lbs
W. P. Mellen, BNC., Str	10 st	12 lbs
G. D. Clapperton, Magd., Cox	7 st	11 lbs
Average 12 st 8 ½ lbs		

CAMBRIDGE (MIDDLESEX)	*Weight*	
W. F. Smith, 1 Trin., Bow	11 st	7 ½ lbs
2 F. W. Law, LMBC	12 st	12 lbs
3 K. N. Craig, Pemb.	13 st	0 lbs
4 S. H. Heap, Jesus	13 st	7 ½ lbs
5 B. G. Ivory, Pemb.	13 st	10 lbs
6 T. D. A. Collet, Pemb.	12 st	7 lbs
7 R. E. Morrison, 3 Trin.	12 st	1 lbs
T. R. B. Sanders, 3 Trin., Str	11 st	12 lbs
R. A. L. Balfour, 3 Trin., Cox	8 st	8 lbs
Average 12 st 8⅞ lbs		

Oxford won by ¾ length in 20 min. 54 sec.

Appendix 2

Everest Team Members

1921

Lt.-Col. Charles K. Howard-Bury *(Leader)*
Harold Raeburn *(Climbing Leader)*
George H. Leigh Mallory *(Acting Climbing Leader)*
Guy H. Bullock
Dr Alexander M. Kellas
Dr A. M. Heron
Maj. Henry T. Morshead
Maj. Edward O. Wheeler
Dr Alexander F. R. Wollaston *(Medical Officer/Naturalist)*
Gyalzen Kazi *(Interpreter)*
Chettan Wangdi *(Interpreter)*

1922

General Charles G. Bruce *(Leader)*
Lt. Col. Edward Lisle Strutt *(Deputy Leader)*
Capt. C. Geoffrey Bruce
Colin G. Crawford
C. John Morris
George Ingle Finch
Dr Tom G. Longstaff *(Medical Officer/Naturalist)*
George H. Leigh Mallory
Maj. Henry T. Morshead
Maj. Edward F. Norton

Capt. John B. L. Noel *(Photographer/Film-maker)*
Dr T. Howard Somervell
Dr Arthur W. Wakefield *(Medical Officer)*
Karma Paul *(Interpreter)*
Gyaljen (Gyalzen Kazi) *(Sirdar or Head Sherpa)*

1924

General Charles G. Bruce *(Leader)*
Lt. Col. Edward F. Norton *(Leader)*
George H. Leigh Mallory *(Climbing Leader)*
Bentley Beetham
Capt. C. Geoffrey Bruce
John de Vere Hazard
Maj. Richard W. G. Hingston *(Medical Officer)*
Andrew C. 'Sandy' Irvine
Capt. John B. L. Noel *(Photographer/Film-maker)*
Noel E. Odell
Edward. O. Shebbeare
Dr T. Howard Somervell
Karma Paul *(Interpreter)*
Gyalzen Kazi *(Sirdar)*

Appendix 3

Climbing Programme
from Base Camp Diary, Everest 1924

DATE	MALLORY & IRVINE	ODELL	HAZARD	NORTON & SOMERVELL	BRUCE
5 May	To III & stay	To III & stay	To III & stay		
6	Rest	Rest	Rest		
7	Reconnaisance	Establish Camp IV	Establish Camp IV		
8	Rest	Rest	Go Down	To III	
9	Rest	Rest		Rest	To III
10	1st escort to IV & stay	Rest		Rest	Rest
11	To III	2nd escort to IV & stay		Rest	2nd escort to IV & stay
12	Rest	Establish Camp V		3rd escort to IV & stay	Establish camp V
13	4th escort to IV & stay	Go down		Rest IV	Go down
14	Rest IV			Rest IV	
15	Rest IV		To III (?)	To V	
16	To VI			To VII	
17	To summit			To summit	To III

BEETHAM	NOEL	PORTERS [A, B = camp porters; V, W, X = high altitude porters]	LOADS
		Party **A** (20 men) to III & stay	20 to III
		Party **A** & make camp. Party **B** (20 men) to III & return to II	20 to III
		Party **A** to II & back. Party **B** rest at II	20 to III
		A rest. **B** to III. Porters re-shuffled into 3 groups: **V** (12 men) **W** & **X** (14 men each). **V** stay III. **W** & **X** to II	20 to III
		W to III & stay, **X** to III & return II, **V** rest III, nb all tents available	28 to III
		V to IV & stay, **W** rest III, **X** rest II, 4 porters tents go up, 10 remain	12 to IV
To III		**V** rest IV, **W** to IV & return, **X** to III and stay, ½ loads	14 to IV 3 to VII
Rest		**V** to V, **W** rest III, **X** to IV & return	12 to V, 14 to IV
Rest		**V** to II & exit, **W** to IV & stay, **X** rest III	14 to IV
5th escort to IV & stay	5th escort to IV & stay	**W** rest IV, **X** to IV & stay	Remaining loads to IV
In support	In support	**W** to **V** & stay, **X** return to IV or III	Was 12, now 8 to 7
In support	In support	**W** to VII (8 men) & return, **X** 4 men to V & return III, 10 men to VI & return IV	6 to VII, 8 to VI 4 to V
In support	In support		

Appendix 4

Sandy Irvine's climbing diary on Mount Everest

3 May	to camp I with Mallory, Hazard and Odell
4	camp I to camp II with Mallory, Hazard and Odell, meet Noel
5	camp II to camp III with Mallory, Hazard and Odell
6	remains in camp III; *Mallory down to Camp II*
7	− 21°F remains in camp III sorting porters' loads
8	remains in camp III; rearranges camp and gets stoves working; *Somervell arrives from II*
9	remains in camp III trying to fix roarer cooker; *Hazard down to II, Mallory, Noel and G. Bruce up to III*
10	down to camp II with Mallory, suffering from dehydration
11	down to base camp after Norton calls first retreat
12	base camp resting
13	base camp working on Noel's camera; *Shamsher (NCO) died ½ mile from base camp*
14	base camp repairing Noel's camera and teaching porters to operate roarer cooker
15	visit to Head Lama at Rongbuk Monastery
16	base camp repairing carrying frames and instructing porters with the stoves
17	base camp (the day they were scheduled to reach the summit); *Norton, Somervell, Mallory, Shebbeare and Odell left base for camp I*
18	up to camp I with Hazard and Noel; suffering from diarrhoea for three days
19	up to camp II; feeling better
20	up to camp III with Hazard; spends day mending tent poles and cookers

21	sets out for North Col carrying porters loads up ice chimney; returns to camp II for the night
22	camp II preparing six oxygen apparatus until midnight for following day
23	−24°F up to camp III
24	down to camp II as Norton calls second retreat; *rescue of porters from IV*
25	down to camp I; *Manbahadur dies of frostbite*
26	camp I; suffering from severe sunburn to face
27	camp I; *revised climbing plan leaves Sandy out of the summit teams*
28	up camp II; begins work on rope ladder
29	camp II; spends all day working on rope ladder with Odell and Shebbeare
30	up to camp III with Mallory; makes a rucksack out of carrying frames which he gives to G. Bruce; *G. Bruce, Norton, Somervell, Odell and Beetham arrive later*
31	up to camp IV at North Col; fixes rope ladder into ice chimney
1 June	camp IV in support; *Mallory and G. Bruce head up to camp V*
2	camp IV in support; down to camp III in evening; writes of sunburn and badly cracked lips; *Norton and Somervell leave for camp V; Mallory and Bruce retreat*
3	camp III suffering from severe sunburn; works all day on oxygen apparatus after Mallory informs him they will make an attempt with oxygen after all
4	camp III prepares with Mallory for oxygen attempt; up to camp IV in afternoon breathing oxygen; *Norton and Somervell return having set altitude record of 28,126 feet without oxygen*
5	camp IV preparing oxygen apparatus for assault on summit. Sunburn gives him trouble; the handwritten diary breaks off at this point
6	sets off for camp V with Mallory
7	leaves camp V for camp VI with Mallory
8	leaves camp VI for summit attempt with Mallory. Never seen alive again

Acknowledgements

Sandy Irvine's life, brief though it was, had impact from school to the river, from the ice fields of the Arctic to the mountains of Tibet, from Birkenhead to Bombay. When I started to research the book I began to understand just how many people had in one way or another been affected by his life and death.

The Sandy Irvine Trust was set up in 1999 to preserve memorabilia relating to Sandy's life and to benefit mountaineering charities by monies accrued through publication permissions and donations. Its three trustees are all nephews or nieces of Sandy and they act on behalf of the now very large family, dealing with all matters that arise in connection with his memory. John Irvine, in his role of Chairman of the Sandy Irvine Trust, has been extremely encouraging, for which I would like to thank him.

My family, both Irvine and Summers, have been marvellous in their support and enthusiasm. They have shared personal memories and stories, made available material and photographs, most of which have never been published before, and I am very grateful to them all but reassure them that the conclusions I have drawn in the book are entirely my own. My particular thanks go to Julia Irvine who has stood by me throughout and been a true friend. It was she who made the great find of the Everest letters and I truly appreciate the way in which she made them available to me so quickly. Also to my uncle, Bill Summers, who shared with great generosity his own material on Sandy and his memories of Willie, Lilian and Evelyn. We spent a happy evening down memory lane over a bottle of wine and many of the stories about cars come from this meeting.

I had the great privilege to meet two people who knew Sandy in the 1920s: my cousin Ann Lake, daughter of Geoffrey Summers, who had a number of lovely memories she shared with me, and Peter Lunn who was nine when he met Sandy in Switzerland in 1923. Peter has kindly given permission for me to quote in full the letter he sent to Lilian after Sandy's death which turned up in the trunk of material we found in May 2000.

I owe a deep debt of gratitude to Audrey Salkeld for her immense patience with me. She has been unfailing in her support and wonderfully generous in her advice. It was she who encouraged me to put pen to paper in the first place. She put me in touch with many key people concerned with the Everest story including Peter Odell, grandson of N. E. Odell, who has been so kind in giving me information relating to his grandfather and recalling anecdotes about Sandy told to him by his own father. Through Audrey I also came into contact with Sandra Noel, daughter of the expedition photographer, Capt. John Noel who was most generous in lending me photographs for the book, and Dick and Bill Norton, sons of Colonel Edward Felix Norton. They very kindly gave me permission to read their father's 1922 and 1924 diaries, which provided a fascinating background to the picture of Tibet. I feel very fortunate to have been able to meet such exceptional people and am extremely grateful for their support.

Peter Gillman, biographer, with his wife Leni, of George Leigh Mallory, has been wonderfully helpful and I am very grateful to him for all his advice given at a time when he was completely occupied with their own book. He has stood by me and supported me when I had doubts and concerns; shared my pleasure over the May 2000 find and made many helpful suggestions.

When I came to write about Sandy's rowing career it became obvious that I needed a great deal of guidance. Richard Owen, a rower and mountaineer, claims he was inspired at Shrewsbury by the example of Sandy. He spent a whole day coaching me in the art of writing about rowing and another day rowing me up and down the course at Henley in the middle of the 2000 Regatta. I am deeply indebted to him.

When I began to uncover material on Sandy's life it all needed documenting and photographing. David Piper has been marvellous in taking many of the photographs of the original material for inclusion here. I gave him horrendous deadlines and he always seemed to meet them. I owe him many thanks and wish him well in his retirement which I hope wasn't precipitated by my onerous requests. Another key person was Flora Nell who worked tirelessly with me on this project from November 1999 and I have appreciated her support enormously, both from the point of view of research, her criticism during the formation of my ideas, and her efficient and methodical help in presenting the text. It was a race at the end to see whether the book would be finished before her baby son was born. Thomas won by nine days.

I could never have written this book without the help and support of my immediate family and closest friends. My husband Chris and my three sons, Simon, Richard and Sandy have been endlessly patient and I love them very much. Janice Haine and her daughter Daisy have been wonderful in keeping my three boys entertained, fed and the house in order while I have been hiding away upstairs writing. I will miss Jan's friendship when we move to Oxford. To Deborah Kearns and Maggie Syversen I say a very big thank-you for keeping me sane and giving me support whenever I needed it. I was advised to write the book 'to' someone and it was to these two friends that I turned my thoughts and pen. Carolyn Butler and Nicola James have also helped me more than they could have imagined.

My editor, Ion Trewin, made a great leap of faith when he agreed to take responsibility for publishing this book. I feel very honoured to have had the chance to work with him. His patience and kindness with me have been greatly appreciated. His editorial team at Weidenfeld & Nicolson includes Alison Provan and Alice Chasey: I thank them for their input as well, and Jenny Page at Orion. Simon Adams copy-edited the book and did a marvellous job for which I am most grateful.

There are many other people who have helped me with the research. I worked in 1999 on an exhibition at Shrewsbury School in honour of Sandy's memory and learnt a great deal from Stephen Holroyd, housemaster of Severn Hill and I thank him for all the information he made available to me. At Merton College Library I met and worked with Sarah Bendall and Fiona Wilkes, who were extremely generous with their time and advice. Roger Barrington braved the PRO and British Library archives on my behalf and unearthed some important material for me, for which I owe him a big thanks. At Magdalene College, Cambridge librarians Dr Richard Luckett and Aude Fitzsimmons were very kind in allowing me to read Mallory's letters from the 1920s. At the Alpine Club I had the help and assistance of Margaret Ecclestone and Bob Lawford; and at the Royal Geographical Society of Huw Thomas and Joanna Scadden.

Graham Hoyland at the BBC offered great encouragement when I said I was going to write the book and has been hugely generous in sharing his own Everest experiences with me. When the 2000 search was taking place on the mountain he made a very great effort to keep in touch about the goings-on in Tibet and I am profoundly grateful for his respect for Sandy's memory.

In North Wales my father and I learned a great deal from meetings with Andrew Hinchliffe in Llanfairfechan and Peter Wilson in Llandyrnog and I am most grateful for their time and information.

Other people have played a more personal role in this book, sharing memories and material, reading drafts and I thank them all very much indeed, in particular Harry Abrahams, Dave Bimson, Russell Brice, Anne Cooksey, Gill Drake, John Gleave, Elizabeth Irvine, Jenny Irvine, Marjorie Irvine, Mike James, Christopher Milling, Salena Moffat, Fiona Morrison, Sheila Pearson, Vera Steele, Rebecca Stephens, Gillian Summers, Mark Summers, Patrick Toosey and Owen Whittaker.

Finally, much of this book is the result of a very happy and productive partnership between myself and my father, Peter. His unstinting support and absolute faith in my abilities is hugely appreciated. He chased librarians, churchwardens, archivists and family members on my behalf. More than anything else, however, we have had such fun working together and I could not have teased out half the stories I have about Sandy without his participation, patience, humour and brilliant mind.

The following organisations and individuals have very kindly given permission for material in their collections to be used:

The Trustees of the Sandy Irvine Trust: letters from A. C. Irvine to: L. Irvine, W. F. Irvine, E. V. Irvine 1909–1924, A. Davies-Colley 22–9–20; K. N. Irvine to L. Irvine 26–6–24; L. Irvine to H. C. Irvine 2–12–14, 24–2–15, 2–10–24; W. F. Irvine to Sir Oliver Lodge (draft) 2–4–28; W. F. Irvine to Marvin Stevens 30–9–57; I. R. Bruce to A. C. Irvine 22–2–23; E. F. Norton to W. F. Irvine 13–6–24; N. E. Odell to W. F. Irvine 22–6–24, 8–2–34; diaries from 1912, notes on oxygen apparatus 23–11–23.

The Warden and Fellows of Merton College, Oxford: A. C. Irvine's diaries, Spitsbergen and Everest, A. C. Irvine to G. Mure 14–4–24, N. E. Odell Spitsbergen account, Spitsbergen Prospectus by G. Binney, the minutes of the Myrmidon Club.

Royal Geographical Society, RGS/IBG Archives, London: A. R. Hinks to P. Farrar 26–4–22; P. Farrar to A. R. Hinks 27–4–22; Gen. C. Bruce to A. R. Hinks 4–4–22, 7–5–22; G. Abraham to C. E. Meade 10–10–23 (RGS/IBG 28/1/1); C. E. Meade to A. R. Hinks 12–10–23 (RGS/IBG 28/1); climbing schedule from Everest Base Camp Diary (RGS/IBG box 41a).

The Master and Fellows of Magdalene College, Cambridge: George Leigh Mallory to Ruth Mallory, Geoffrey Young and Sir Francis Younghusband.

The Alpine Club: diary of E. O. Shebbeare (1–4–24; 2–4–24; 6–4–24; 7–4–24; 15–5–24).

David Breashears and Audrey Salkeld: *Last Climb*, pp. 37, 104.

Peter and Leni Gillman, *The Wildest Dream*, pp. 251–252.

John Kitchin, letter from W. Bridgeman to A. E. Kitchin 28–10–19.

C. D. Milling: G. Milling Spitsbergen diary 1923; letter from A. C. Irvine to G. Milling 28–3–24.

Reinhold Messner, *The Crystal Horizon*, p. 126.

Dick and Bill Norton: E. F. Norton's Everest diaries (11–4–22 & 7–4–24).

Peter Odell: letter from A. C. Irvine to N. E. Odell 27–1–24.

Audrey Salkeld: *The Mystery of Mallory and Irvine*, pp. 179, 180.

Bibliography

ABRAHAM, GEORGE & ASHLEY ABRAHAM *Rock Climbing in North Wales*, G. P. Abraham 1906

ASHCROFT, ROBIN *The Long Routes: Mountaineering rock climbs in Snowdonia and the Lake District*, Mainstream Publishing Company, Edinburgh 1999

BEERBOHM, MAX *Zuleika Dobson*, Penguin Books

BOUKREEV, ANATOLI & G. WESTON DEWALT *The Climb*, St Martin's Press, New York 1997

BREASHEARS, DAVID & AUDREY SALKELD, *Last Climb*, National Geographic, Washington D.C. October 23, 1999

BURNELL, R. D. *The Oxford and Cambridge Boat Race 1829–1953*, Oxford University Press 1954

CARR, HERBERT *The Irvine Diaries*, Gastons-West Col Publications, Britain 1979

CLARKE, PETER *Hope and Glory: Britain 1900–1990*, Allen Lane, The Penguin Press, London 1996

COBURN, BROUGHTON *Everest*, National Geographic Society

COWBURN, PHILIP *A Salopian Anthology: Some impressions of Shrewsbury School during four centuries*, MacMillan, London 1964

DAVIS, ROBERT H. *Breathing in Irrespirable Atmospheres and, in some cases, also Under Water*, The Saint Catherine Press, London

DAWSON, H. N. *Shrewsbury School Register*, Volume II 1908–1958, Wilding & Son, Shrewsbury 1964

ERIKSEN, STEIN *Come Ski with Me*, Martin Luray (ed.), Frederick Muller, London 1966

FIRSTBROOK, PETER *Lost on Everest: The Search for Mallory & Irvine*, BBC Worldwide 1999

GILLMAN, PETER & LENI *The Wildest Dream*, Headline, London 2000

HARRER, HEINRICH *Seven Years in Tibet*, Flamingo, London 1994

HEMMLEB, JOCHEN, LARRY A. JOHNSON & ERIC A. SIMONSON *Ghosts of Everest*, The Mountaineers Books, Seattle 1999

HOLZEL, TOM & AUDREY SALKELD *The Mystery of Mallory & Irvine*, Pimlico, rev. ed. 1996

IRVINE, LYN *So much Love, So little Money*, Faber, London 1956

KRAKAUER, JON *Into Thin Air*, Macmillan Publishers, London 1997

LUNN, ARNOLD *The Bernese Oberland*, Allen & Unwin, London 1973

LUNN, ARNOLD *The British Ski Year Book 1924*, The Federal Council of British Ski Clubs, London 1924

LUNN, ARNOLD *Mountains of Memory*, Hollis and Carter, London 1948

LYTTON, THE EARL OF, *Antony (Viscount Knebworth) A Record of Youth*, Peter Davies, London 1935

MACNEICE, LOUIS *The Strings are False*, Faber, London 1965

MALLABY, GEORGE *From My Level*, Hutchinson, London 1965

MANTOVANI, ROBERTO ET AL. *Everest: The History of the Himalayan Giant*, Mountaineers Books, USA 1997

MESSNER, REINHOLD *The Crystal Horizon*, The Crowood Press, Great Britain 1989, translated by Jill Neate and Audrey Salkeld

NOORDEN, S. B. VAN & PATRICK MONKHOUSE (ed.) *Oxford and Cambridge Mountaineering 1924*, The Holywell Press, Oxford

NORTON, E. F. ET AL. *The Fight for Everest: 1924*, Edward Arnold, London 1925

PENDLEBURY, W. J. & J. M. WEST *Shrewsbury School: Recent Years*, Wilding & Son, Shrewsbury 1934

PEVSNER, NIKOLAUS & EDWARD HUBBARD *The Buildings of England: Cheshire*, Penguin, London 1971

PEVSNER, NIKOLAUS & JENNIFER SHERWOOD *The Buildings of England: Oxfordshire*, Penguin, London 1974

PYE, DAVID *George Leigh Mallory*, Oxford University Press, London 1927

REDHEAD, BRIAN & SHEILA GOODDIE, *The Summers of Shotton*, Hodder & Stoughton, London 1987

ROSS, GORDON *The Boat Race: The story of the first hundred races between Oxford and Cambridge*, Hodder & Stoughton, London 1954

SIMPSON, JOE *Touching the Void*, Vintage, London 1997

SMITH, L. C. *Annals of Public School Rowing*, Blackwell, Oxford 1920

SOMERVELL, H. *After Everest*, Hodder & Stoughton, London 1936

STRUTT, E. L. *The Alpine Journal*, vol. XLVI no. 249, November 1934

YOUNGHUSBAND, SIR FRANCIS *The Epic of Mount Everest*, Edward Arnold, London 1926

From journals and specialist publications I have used the following articles:

The Geographical Journal
December 1924
Bruce, Brig.-Gen. C. G. 'The Organisation and Start of the Expedition' pp. 434–36
Bruce, Cap. J. G. 'The Journey through Tibet and the Establishment of the High Camps' pp. 443–50

Norton, Col. E. F. 'The Personnel of the Expedition' pp. 436–43
Ibid. 'The Climb with Mr Somervell to 28,000 Feet' pp. 451–55
Odell, N. E. 'The Last Climb of Mallory and Irvine' pp. 455–61
Vol. 90, 1937
Warren, Dr C. B. 'The Medical and Physiological Aspects of the Mount Everest Expeditions' pp. 126–147

Alpine Journal
Vol. 35, 1923
Longstaff, Dr T. G. 'Some Aspects of the Everest Problem' pp. 57–68
Finch, George Ingle. 'Equipment for High Altitude Mountaineering, with Special Reference to Climbing Mount Everest' pp. 68–74
Vol. 37, 1925
Norton, E .F. 'The Problem of Mount Everest' pp. 1–19
Vol. 44, 1934
Smythe, F. S. 'Everest: The Final Problem' (correspondence) pp. 442–446
Odell, N. E. 'The Ice Axe Found on Everest' (correspondence) pp. 447–449
Vol. 51, 1939
Finch, George Ingle. 'Oxygen and Mount Everest' pp. 89–90

Oxford & Cambridge Mountaineering 1924
Obituary Notices. Irvine, pp. 33–37, Mallory, pp. 38–41

The British Ski Year Book
Vol. 2, 1924
Lunn, Sir Arnold. 'In Memoriam' pp. 368–372

Postscript 2001

'A glorious, very remarkable, very disheartening end to a beautiful young man, who probably ... Let's leave him with the likelihood that he got there and did it. Leave him in peace.'

Harry Abraham, 5 May 2001

Since the publication of the first edition of this book in November 2000 the feedback from all quarters has been as remarkable as it has been unexpected. It would seem that Sandy Irvine's life touched more people than even I had anticipated. People wrote to me saying that memories, dormant for fifty or sixty years, had come flooding back. Some were reminded of specific events, such as the lantern slide lectures given by Noel Odell in the late 1920s, others had memories of various members of the Irvine family. Then there were people who had strong recollections of things pertaining directly to Sandy himself.

John Kemp, helping out at in the cellars of Hertfordshire County Library during the Second World War as a boy, told me of 'packing what I remembered as junk into large wooden boxes brought down from London for safety from air raids. It belonged to the Alpine Club Library. I clearly remember an ice axe and have vague memories of notebooks, goggles and clothing. Whatever it was it must have been of some value to store it. This incident remained hidden in my memory for over sixty years and reading your book revived the memory and the rather morbid feeling I had at the time.' For a long while the ice axe was one of the only articles belonging to Sandy Irvine known to be in existence and I well remember seeing it for the first time. It was difficult to believe that I was holding something that had been found so high on Everest nine years after his death. It looked and felt so ordinary and that made the tragedy all the more poignant.

Other items of memorabilia began to emerge, particularly relating to Sandy's rowing career. Mark Chapman, a printer from Abingdon, offered the Irvine family a 1919 Peace Regatta programme from Wednesday 3 July when Shrewsbury had rowed against Pembroke College, Cambridge. I also found two Henley flags, from 1919 and 1920, rolled up in a suitcase belonging to Willie Irvine. Then Richard Owen sent me an original *Times* press cutting of the account of the race between Shrewsbury and Bedford in the final of the Elsenham Cup. However, the most significant find amongst the rowing items was of Sandy's Blue's blazers, both the winter and summer ones. Each blazer has the tailor's label, dated Feb '22. They had been given to his brother Kenneth for safe keeping but he felt it was better that they should be used and enjoyed by another Oxford Blue. Like the rest of the family Kenneth was a keen oarsman. He had rowed for Shrewsbury and for Magdalen College, Oxford, and had won an Oxford Trials cap but had not rowed for the university. In later years, even when a busy general practitioner in Henley, he found time to coach the post-war Magdalen crews with some success. He was well liked by these crews and he knew some of them well. John Gleave had rowed for Magdalen 1945–49, for Oxford 1946–48 and for Leander 1948–49. When Kenneth thought it time to pass the blazers on John was the Oxford Blue whom he knew best. He gladly accepted the blazers and promised to look after them whilst they were in his care. There is no doubt in my mind that Sandy would have been delighted to know his blazers were with such a distinguished oarsman.

John Gleave contacted me in March 2001 to tell me that he had had the blazers since the mid-1950s. He had been wondering what to do with them and after the appearance of the book decided to offer them back to the family for further safe keeping. He had worn them on special occasions and apart from replacing the silk bindings on the summer blazer and letting out its shoulders a little, the blazers are unaltered.

Further searches in the attics at Bryn Llwyn did not reveal any more material directly relating to Sandy. I had hoped his photograph album from Spitsbergen might have come to light, or perhaps photographs from the early part of the voyage to Darjeeling. There were, instead, boxes and boxes of correspondence relating to the family, meticulously bound and labelled by Willie. Apart from over two hundred letters from

Hugh to his parents written during the First World War there was one surprise discovery. It was a travel diary from the early nineteenth century by a John Irvine who had journeyed around Switzerland on foot, crossing several passes including the Simplon and the St Gotthard over a period of two years, often in the company of a German guide. He made a trip to Wengen in July of 1827, climbing up on to the Aletsch glacier and spending a night in a hut in the shadow of the Jungfrau. The letter was written in tiny but clear handwriting with a sketched map showing all the places he stopped and the heights to which he ascended. It would seem that Sandy was not the first Irvine to set foot or ski on the Aletsch glacier. Perhaps Willie had shown this letter to Sandy before he went out to Mürren in 1923.

There was more to come: in February 2001 I was approached by two independent film makers who asked me if I should be interested in helping them to put together a documentary about the life of Sandy Irvine. They were interested in finding out as much as they could about his life prior to the Mount Everest expedition. It was great fun to find others who were as enthusiastic as I about Sandy's early life and Dave Bimson and Mike James had knowledge that I had not about where to look for old films. They found, to my delight, footage of the 1922 and 1923 Oxford and Cambridge Boat Races. This was the first time I had ever seen film footage of Sandy and it was very touching to watch him striding down to the river carrying his oar, smiling broadly at the camera.

These two also succeeded in tracking down another individual who remembered meeting Sandy, namely Harry Abraham. Now nearly ninety-two, he was the son of Ashley Abraham, one of the so-called Abraham or Keswick brothers who had been leading lights in promoting rock climbing in the early part of the twentieth century, writing books on climbs in the Lake District and North Wales as well as putting up many first routes in the Alps. It was George Abraham who had written a letter of recommendation to the Mount Everest committee suggesting they consider including Sandy.

Harry Abraham gave the most lucid and moving interview, speaking for over two hours about his recollection of meeting Sandy Irvine at the Screes, the Abraham family home in Keswick, in the summer of 1923.

He was fourteen and a half at the time but his memories were as clear as if it had happened only yesterday. He recalled the afternoon when George Abraham phoned Ashley from the photography shop they owned in Keswick to say that Sandy would be dropping in to talk about photographic equipment for the Mount Everest expedition for which he hoped to be selected. 'My father told us that we'd be holding back supper because we'd got a chap coming to see us who was trying his damnedest to be a member of the next expedition to climb Mount Everest,' he remembered. 'He's getting himself fit, he's been climbing in the Lake District and he's been to see Uncle George,' Ashley had told Harry and his mother.

Sandy arrived at the house a little before 6 p.m. and after being greeted formally in the hall was led into the dining room. Harry took up his accustomed place at the right-hand side of the dining table and his father sat down beside him with Sandy opposite. 'As I remember him,' Harry recalled, 'he had knickerbockers on and a reefer jacket, which rather appealed to me at the time. He was extremely fit and he looked a tough cookie. I had the impression from the way he spoke with my father that he was a young chap fighting very, very hard to win support for a nomination by Odell, who had suggested him for the 1924 expedition. He was a "getting into action" chap.' Harry was struck, too, by Sandy's physique. 'He was strong and well built with tremendously strong hands. As he ate his meal he reached out for the salt and pepper and seemed to do it with his left hand rather than his right.' Although Sandy wrote with his right hand I have often found myself wondering whether in fact he was actually left-handed. This might explain his poor handwriting and spelling rather better than the other theory put forward that he was mildly dyslexic.

Over a dinner of poached salmon and new potatoes they talked all the while about what would happen if Sandy were picked for the Mount Everest expedition. One of the matters occupying him was what would be the best kind of camera to take to Tibet. Ashley Abraham was able to advise him that of the two best cameras available at the time the Rolleiflex $2\frac{1}{2} \times 2\frac{1}{2}$ would be the most suitable for the job, seeing that it was light, reliable and capable of producing an image of such quality that it could be enlarged to a foot or more square. Sandy seemed obsessed with a need to reduce weight to the minimum and Harry remembered him worrying about the very last detail on his climbing boots, quizzing his father about the weight and suitability of different sorts of nails whilst acknowledging that avoidance of frostbite was a very real concern. He was obviously determined to leave no stone unturned and to prepare himself in every possible way. They talked too about the oxygen apparatus and Sandy confessed that he was going to have to learn all about the system before he went on the expedition. He seemed to realise even then that it would be up to him of all the team members to ensure a functioning, preferably light-weight apparatus would be carried to the high camps for the final assault.

'He visualised always the last ascent would be made with oxygen and the success or failure would depend on his analysis of what could be achieved with it and what couldn't,' Harry said. 'He seemed to be looking forward to a phase when it was going to take every bit of guts he had to put one foot in front of another and nothing was too much trouble. He was determined this was the target, to climb Mount Everest. He was prepared to give it everything he'd got; without any doubt at all. It's the outstanding impression I have. I was just a schoolboy but obviously very interested and it seemed to catch his attention, the fact that I listened to every word he said.'

I couldn't help thinking how similar Harry's response was to that of Peter Lunn in Mürren four months later. Both of them felt the same ease in Sandy's presence and fondly remembered the patience he showed in giving them his full attention for as long as they wanted it. He had a rare talent for getting the best out of young people and giving them confidence to talk to him although he was an adult, as Geoffrey Summers' daughter Ann has confirmed.

According to Harry, Sandy had been staying up in the Lake District for a week walking and climbing on his own. He had been over to Wasdale Head and had climbed Scafell Pinnacle, telling them that he had found Scafell very tough indeed. He had also climbed on Great End, at the other end of the Scafell range, which has some steep crags and interesting climbing. This was news to me as I was not aware that Sandy had done any climbing following his return to England after the Spitsbergen expedition but Harry Abraham's recollections filled in a gap. The introduction to the Abraham family came from Geoffrey Summers, not just from Odell as I had previously supposed. Geoffrey was a close friend of George Abraham and had often stayed with him in Keswick and climbed with him. Harry was always amused by the fact that Geoffrey would arrive in the newest model of Rolls-Royce and once he was taken for a spin, which he described as the 'worst example of a drive in a Rolls-Royce' he could ever imagine. George and Geoffrey shared not only an interest in climbing but also in photography and it is not difficult to see why he recommended Sandy to head for Keswick after returning from Spitsbergen to visit the Abrahams.

Sandy left the Screes, the Abraham home, after supper and Harry never saw him again. But the visit made a great impact on him and he recalled the scene in the hall when they took leave of him. 'I can see him now. He put his hands on my shoulders and looked up at my father and said, "If we get to within about a couple of hundred yards, however hard work, if we get that near and we can see the highest point clearly, we shall go for it. And if it's a one-way traffic, so be it." He turned round and I was too excited to wish him luck.'

Sandy went out and walked down the garden steps to catch the bus back to the King's Head in Thirlspot where he was staying. Ashley Abraham had been quite as impressed by Sandy as had been his son and as they came back into the house he turned to Harry and said, 'You heard what he said? He's a very, very strong young man.' 'My father was a very good judge of character, of people,' Harry added, 'and he looked at Sandy Irvine as if he'd have been proud to have him for a son. He was tremendously taken with him.' 'That's the sort of chap you want to grow up into', Ashley had said to him as he closed the door.

Ashley Abraham took Harry up to the Isle of Skye in 1928 where they met Benthley Beetham. Four years after Sandy and Mallory had died on Mount Everest Harry remembers his father and Beetham talking very calmly and seriously about Sandy. 'My father and Benthley Beetham were in no doubt at all. It was simply their nous, they reckoned the two of them got up. Sandy would have gone on on his own, that's the impression left with Ashley Abraham and Benthley Beetham and this was in the calm talk of 1928, four years after I met Sandy Irvine.'

This interview was one of the least expected developments and gave

a most vivid picture of Sandy. It reminded me – as if I needed reminding – what a lasting impact he made on the people whose paths he
crossed. Harry's recollection enabled me to see Sandy from yet another
perspective and brought home to me his iron determination to be
selected for the expedition.

But without doubt the most exciting find of all was once again linked
to Mount Everest. In March 2001 my cousin John Irvine was having a
clear out when he chanced upon an envelope at the very back of a drawer
and underneath a pile of papers. It had A.C.I. written on it in pencil.
He rang me to tell me he had found this package and he thought I might
be interested in some negatives which had, amongst other things, a
photograph of Sandy on his motorbike on Foel Grach above Llanfairfechan. There was also a faded typewritten note in a frame, which
had come from Sandy's workshop at Park Road South. It read:

Police Notice

Any person entering this abode is liable to
a fine of 2/- (unless special permission is
obtained from the caretaker).

Any person found borrowing <u>anything</u> & not replacing it exactly as it was found is liable
to a fine of not less than 1/6 & costs.

By order
Caretaker Lilian Irvine
Owner A. C. Irvine

After Sandy's death the notice had hung in Kenneth's workshop and
then, finally, in John's. Sandy was protective of his own property but it
seemed to run in the family, as Hugh had complained bitterly in a letter
to his mother from Shrewsbury: 'Sandy has probably pinched all my
scarves and shoes ...' Only Mrs Killen, the housekeeper, and Lilian had
keys to the workshop.

A letter from Sandy to Lilian written on 24 June 1923 from Oxford
carried the surprising news that Sandy had performed well in 'Schools',
the end of year examinations at Oxford. 'I don't think my own tutor
ever expected it,' Sandy wrote to Lilian cheerfully, 'he always said that

he thought I could pass Chemistry but was very doubtful about the Physics; as it was he tells me the examiner who corrected my Chemistry was much impressed with the way I answered the big questions which were more "finals" standard than "prelim" standard and which they do not expect to be attempted by most people. Personally I found them the easiest because I could deduce or invent what I didn't know while the usual prelim questions are all hard facts which one knows or doesn't know!' He had gained 87 per cent and was within two marks of the top candidate, with which he declared himself delighted but added wryly 'the only draw back is that now they will expect much more from me than if I had only just scraped through!'

The envelope also contained a handful of climbing photographs amongst the negatives, taken, it would appear, by Sandy on an expedition in North Wales. The brothers had no form of climbing protection other than two belts buckled together with which Hugh was photographed hauling Kenneth up onto Adam and Eve on Tryfan's summit.

I asked if there was anything else, and John told me that there were two typewritten letters from Everest Base Camp, dated 30 April and 18 May 1924 which began, 'My dear Peter ...' I almost jumped out of my skin. In May 2000 I had found an exchange of letters between Willie Irvine and Arnold Lunn, who taught Sandy to ski Mürren. In one of them Arnold thanked Willie for returning the letters Sandy had written to his son Peter from Base Camp. The original letters that Arnold had sent to Willie were later destroyed in the Second World War and when I first met Peter in 1999 he told me of his great regret that they had ever been taken from him. I had therefore just wondered in May 2000 whether Willie might have had the letters copied and that I would find them. In the event they did not come to light and I had to tell Peter so. I had no proof that a transcript had ever existed but what had given me hope were the copies of George Mallory's letters home to Ruth from Tibet. Willie was such a meticulous historian and he valued source material so highly that I was certain that he would have had the contents recorded before returning the letters to Arnold Lunn. He had. And they had reappeared. They had been saved for posterity by Kenneth. It was a moment to savour.

All of a sudden I was catapulted back to 1924 Everest Base Camp where Sandy sat scribbling away in order to catch the post which was due to leave the following day. 'My dear Peter,' he wrote, 'Just a line to tell you how the expedition is getting on. You will have heard the disaster about General Bruce having to go back.

We arrived here yesterday in miserable weather but today has been perfectly wonderful and everyone working like niggers sorting out stores for the high camps.

My particular job has been to improvise the oxygen apparatus, as out of the eleven supplied not a single one was fit to use when taken out of their cases and after several days work I've only got four safe to use, so I have had to redesign the whole thing and throw most of the instruments or the apparatus away. It has been a long and rather heart-breaking job with the few tools I happened to bring of my own, but it's nearly finished now. I hope to be able to report 6 new design and four old fit for use.

Peter had been fascinated by all the mechanical aspects of the Everest expedition and had questioned Sandy closely when they sat together at dinner in Mürren in January 1924. Sandy knew that Peter would be interested in what he had been doing. This description of the work he had done during the trek is less angry than his outbursts in his diary but is nevertheless a heart-felt expression of his feelings towards what he had sometimes described as the 'infernal apparatus'.

He went on to give Peter exact details of the climbing plan:

Norton and Somervell are making the first non-oxygen attempt on May 17th from Camp 7 at 27,300 feet. Mallory and I are to make the first Oxygen attempt on the same day from Camp 6 at 26,800 feet. The idea is for them to leave the North Col the day before Mallory and I and spend one night at Camp 5. 25,000 ft. and another at 27,700 while we spend only one night at 26,800. The mountain looks wonderfully easy from here in the evening light.

Mallory and I leave on May 3rd to go up to Camp 3 to acclimatise and climb a bit of the way up the North Peak to try and spot camp sites. After 3 or 4 days there we come down to Camp 1 to rest and then go up for our attempt. Weather permitting.

We are all sitting in the Mess tent writing letters for tomorrow's Dak[1] or eating bulls eyes to help digest the Yak meat we had for dinner tonight. It's great fun this expedition, you would love it if you were a bit older!

This tiny vignette of life at Base Camp rather caught me by surprise. I could just imagine the scene with Sandy sitting along side Mallory, Norton and Odell, all hunched over the table in the mess tent in the failing light, together but isolated in their private worlds as they committed their thoughts and feelings to letters and diaries.

Throughout this letter one can sense Sandy's excitement at being part of the climbing team chosen to make an assault on the summit despite his frustration with the oxygen.

You will probably hear the result of the 1st attempt before you get this letter I hope it will be to say that at any rate the Oxygen party reached the top. I really hate the thought of it. I'd give anything to make a non-oxygen attempt. I think I'd sooner get to the foot of the final pyramid without oxygen than to the top with it. Still as I'm oxygen mechanic I've got to go with the beastly stuff to look after it. After all I've got nothing to complain about being in the first party.

Did he really think that it was 'unsporting' to climb with oxygen, or was he just aware of the fact that the apparatus was likely to fail and that that may scupper the whole attempt? I suspect a bit of both. Interestingly, Odell used this exact quote in his obituary in November 1924 and I do wonder whether Odell too had seen these two letters which Arnold Lunn had sent to Willie.

He signed off the first letter in high spirits: 'I'll write sometime and tell you what the climb was like if the altitude doesn't do me down before I get to the North Col!! Cheerio Peter. Did you pass the Q1 before the season was over? Ad montem! Sandy Irvine.' The Q1 was a skiing examination which Peter would be taking and it touched him deeply at the time that Sandy had remembered to ask him about it.

In the second letter, written nearly three weeks later on 18 May, Sandy described the appalling conditions the party had encountered below the

1 Postal service.

North Col and detailed the injuries sustained by the team:

My dear Peter,

This must be a very short letter as I am due to start up the glacier in a few minutes.

You will probably have seen all about our bad luck in *The Times*. I spent five days up at Camp III in most terrible conditions, a gale blowing night and day with night temperatures as low as minus 21½ F. For about three nights we had a blizzard varying between 45 and 54 degrees of frost. The driven snow was so fine that it came through everything. Each morning our tents were inches deep in snow. All our porters were sick and had to be sent down. Odell and Hazard failed to read the North Col, and after another day of it we got orders from Norton that all camps were to be evacuated.

I came down to II with George Mallory and got rather a nasty touch of the sun on the glacier as we came down a long trough sheltered from the wind with a leaden sun beating down on us. Nevertheless, I had to forget all my troubles next morning as a report came in to the camp of an accident on the glacier. We had to turn out and bring back a porter with a broken leg, while I had to go up towards Camp III to meet the rest of the party evacuating and hurry the doctor (Somervell) down to the sick man.

The same day half the Sahibs went right through to the Base Camp and all the rest to Camp I. One porter had both feet and legs very badly frost-bitten. We did not expect to save much below his knees but fortunately today the Doctor reports that he may be saved as far as his heels.

One of our N.C.O.s suddenly got paralysis at Camp II probably due to a clot on the brain from frost bitten fingers. The poor fellow died within ½ a mile of the Base Camp being brought down on a stretcher.

Despite the nature of the news he was telling Peter Lunn, Sandy appeared to be in good spirits and his account of the meeting with the High Lama, although brief, has a typical humorous twist.

Two days later we went down to the Rongbuk Monastery (porters, cooks and all) to be blessed by the chief Lama. It was a very impressive ceremony. The old Lama was very sensible and told the porters to work hard – obey their Sahibs and look after themselves. He then prayed for fine weather as he thought it was a devil on the mountains making this quite exceptionally bad weather. By a curious coincidence the very next day was perfect and so we decided to start right away on the following day.

I like this tongue-in-cheek account of the visit to the monastery and particularly the implication that the mountain goddess had been touched by the Lama's words into calling for better weather. He went on,

Norton, Somervell, Mallory, Odell, Shebbeare and two lots of porters started up yesterday, while Hazard, Noel and I go in a few minutes, and Geoffrey Bruce (and Beetham (if he's well enough) follow tomorrow and Hingston stays at Base as Doctor.

I go right through to the North Col in 4 days if Mallory has been able to break a track from III to IV the day I arrive at III. Then I come down and rest at III with George and go up again to the North Col for a couple of days and VI for one day and reach the summit on Ascension Day we hope! In haste, Sandy Irvine

Arnold Lunn wrote in his obituary notice to Sandy in 1924: 'Few young men would have had enough imagination to realise the joy which such letters would cause, or enough unselfishness to make the real effort to write them among all the excitements of that great adventure.' Reading the letters for the first time in March 2001 I was able to understand just how Peter's father must have felt. The letters are fresh, optimistic and exude a liveliness which some of the accounts in his diary and his letters to Lilian do not. Peter Lunn was, after all, only nine years old and Sandy wrote in a straightforward and direct way, telling not only the disasters but also the joys of the expedition and the letters sum up his whole approach to life. Finding and reading them has closed the chapter for me on Sandy's Everest experiences.

After John Irvine had sent the letters to me I rang Peter Lunn, who was in his winter quarters in Mürren. I spoke to him while he was down at dinner and, unable to contain my excitement, I burst out that we had found the letters. Peter's reaction was one of quiet but unmistakable delight. 'Well, that's magnificent,' he said. I sent him copies of the letters the next day and he wrote by return: 'You can imagine my excitement opening the envelope containing the letters from Sandy. I was deeply touched by the two personal comments to me in the 30 April letter. Sandy was one of the most modest and unassuming of men. This is indeed proving a "magical story".

I believe that Sandy recognised in Peter Lunn something of himself at that age. Serious, considered, slightly shy but with an inquisitive mind that yearned to find answers to the myriad of questions racing around in his head. As a child Sandy had longed to be heard but in his early youth he had always been treated as the 'one to keep an eye on'. If ever there was a prank or a bit of trouble it was assumed that Sandy had been involved and was more than likely at the bottom of it too. I think he felt kept down by his family and in particular by his elder brother Hugh. So he was able to pay Peter Lunn the compliment he was probably himself never paid, at least until he got to Shrewsbury: to be listened to. In this he showed not only great humanity and humility, but also a rare understanding of young people.

If at the planning stage for this book I was struck by how much Sandy managed to crowd into his twenty-two years, I am not one bit less so now. I am left with the overwhelming image of a man of great character and modesty, of humour and strength, but above all of somebody who felt compelled to give his all in whatever he did. Peter Lunn wrote to me in November 2000 and had the following to say:

Child monarchs get into the history books; successful Olympic competitors hit the headlines but are quickly forgotten. Sandy must be the youngest person ever to achieve by his own efforts a truly enduring fame. In the long history of human endeavour there are hardly any enigmas more intriguing than what Sandy and Mallory did when they vanished upwards so close to the loftiest spot on earth. Perhaps we shall one day have the proof that they did stand on the summit 29 years before anybody else.

I feel that Peter had it right when he used the word 'magical' to describe the story which developed around Sandy Irvine's life. I could hardly have hoped for Sandy's rowing blazers to re-emerge, nor to see captured on film the recollections of a ninety-two-year-old man, nor especially to find the letters to Peter Lunn. Yet they all materialised in the space of six months. Is that it, now, I wonder?

Julie Summers
Oxford, August 2001

INDEX